"In *Pattern Focused Therapy*, Dr. Sperry offers another remarkably timely, practical, easy-to-read contribution for both students and professionals in health and mental health care professions. In our current healthcare marketplace clinicians must provide brief, evidence-based, practical, and efficacious treatments for their clients and this new book will help them to do so. It represents the new third wave of cognitive behavioral therapy that addresses six compelling trends in the field just perfectly. Clearly, this book should be in the hands of all practitioners today and is likely to become a classic."
— **Thomas G. Plante, Ph.D.**, Santa Clara University and Stanford University School of Medicine

"*Pattern Focused Therapy* is one of the most practical texts available on how to do brief CBT evidence-based practice therapy. This book provides all the necessary tools for assessment, case conceptualization, technique selection, and outcomes monitoring in clear step-by-step procedures and therapy session examples. Beginners and experts alike will benefit from a special chapter dealing with practical strategies for preventing premature termination. If you want to learn how to do effective therapy in 4–6 sessions, this book will show you how."
— **Brian A. Gerrard, Ph.D.**, Western Institute for Social Research, Berkeley, and University of San Francisco

"Dr. Sperry's book is a valuable addition to third wave cognitive-behavioral therapy. *Pattern Focused Therapy* is a clear and accessible presentation of Sperry's brief, relationally focused, and evidence-based approach to progressive cognitive-behavioral therapy. It is an essential resource for therapists-in-training, therapy educators, and seasoned clinicians."
— **Richard E. Watts, Ph.D.**, distinguished professor, Sam Houston State University

# Pattern Focused Therapy

*Pattern Focused Therapy* incorporates brief cognitive behavioral therapy (CBT) interventions for symptom reduction and a step-by-step therapeutic strategy for effectively changing clients' maladaptive patterns and increasing their well-being.

Integrating research, clinical expertise, and client needs and values, Pattern Focused Therapy is a highly effective third-wave CBT approach that can be applied to a wide range of clients. This text guides therapists through the pattern focused approach, facilitating learning through session-by-session transcriptions and commentaries from the first to the final session. Interventions for optimizing treatment and indicators of successful therapy are included along with a chapter on Pattern Focused Therapy in integrated care settings.

Seasoned and beginner therapists alike will benefit from this invaluable method for learning and mastering this evidence-based approach.

**Len Sperry, M.D., Ph.D.,** is a Professor at Florida Atlantic University. He has practiced, taught, and written about CBT for four decades. Among his 1000+ professional publications are six other CBT books.

# Pattern Focused Therapy

## Highly Effective CBT Practice in Mental Health and Integrated Care Settings

Len Sperry

NEW YORK AND LONDON

First published 2021
by Routledge
52 Vanderbilt Avenue, New York, NY 10017

and by Routledge
2 Park Square, Milton Park, Abingdon, Oxon OX14 4RN

*Routledge is an imprint of the Taylor & Francis Group, an informa business*

© 2021 Taylor & Francis

The right of Len Sperry to be identified as author of this work has been asserted by him in accordance with sections 77 and 78 of the Copyright, Designs and Patents Act 1988.

All rights reserved. No part of this book may be reprinted or reproduced or utilised in any form or by any electronic, mechanical, or other means, now known or hereafter invented, including photocopying and recording, or in any information storage or retrieval system, without permission in writing from the publishers.

*Trademark notice*: Product or corporate names may be trademarks or registered trademarks, and are used only for identification and explanation without intent to infringe.

*Library of Congress Cataloging-in-Publication Data*
Names: Sperry, Len, author.
Title: Pattern-focused therapy : highly effective CBT practice in mental health and integrated care settings / Len Sperry.
Description: New York : Routledge, [2020] | Includes bibliographical references and index. | Identifiers: LCCN 2020007191 (print) | LCCN 2020007192 (ebook) |
ISBN 9780367429300 (hardback) | ISBN 9780367429317 (paperback) | ISBN 9780367429331 (ebook)
Subjects: LCSH: Cognitive therapy.
Classification: LCC RC489.C6 S64 2020 (print) | LCC RC489.C6 (ebook) | DDC 616.89/1425—dc23
LC record available at https://lccn.loc.gov/2020007191
LC ebook record available at https://lccn.loc.gov/2020007192

ISBN: 978-0-367-42930-0 (hbk)
ISBN: 978-0-367-42931-7 (pbk)
ISBN: 978-0-367-42933-1 (ebk)

Typeset in Perpetua
by Taylor & Francis Books

# Contents

| | | |
|---|---|---|
| *Acknowledgments* | | viii |
| *Introduction* | | ix |
| 1 | Pattern Focused Therapy and Psychotherapy Practice: Today and Tomorrow | 1 |
| 2 | Pattern: Assessment and Case Conceptualization | 16 |
| 3 | Practicing Pattern Focused Therapy | 44 |
| 4 | Ultra-Brief Therapeutic Interventions | 63 |
| 5 | Outcomes Assessment and Indicators of Successful Treatment | 80 |
| 6 | The First Session | 98 |
| 7 | The Middle Sessions | 120 |
| 8 | The Final Sessions | 141 |
| 9 | Interventions for Optimizing Treatment | 156 |
| 10 | Pattern Focused Therapy in Integrated Care Settings | 184 |
| *Index* | | 204 |

# Acknowledgements

I am deeply grateful to those who have mentored me over the years in the fine points of psychotherapy practice. Of particular note are Rudolf Dreikurs, M.D., Kenneth I. Howard, Ph.D., Richard Cox, Ph.D., and Barry Blackwell, M.D. Special thanks to the editorial staff of Routledge, particularly my editor Nina Guttapalle, for their valuable input. Finally, I want to acknowledge two of my former doctoral students. Vassilia Binenstzok, Ph.D. who collaborated with me on some related projects, and Gerardo Casteleiro, Ph.D. for editorial assistance with this project.

# Introduction

There is little doubt that psychotherapy practice today is changing and changing rather dramatically. It is much different than it was 10 years ago, and it is expected to change even more in the near future. Several factors account for this change, but three stand out.

The first is reimbursement. Reimbursement of psychotherapy and related mental health services increasingly requires that therapists document the use of evidence-based approaches and interventions. Currently, all clinical psychology graduate programs require their students to master at least one evidence-based treatment approach. Unfortunately, very few other graduate therapy training programs emphasize evidence-based approaches or require the teaching and learning of evidence-based practice and interventions.

The second is that treatment is getting shorter. Not only is the duration or length of therapy getting shorter, but therapy sessions are getting shorter. Instead of the usual 12-20 sessions as the norm, the typical course of treatment will more likely to be 4-8 therapeutic encounters. Instead of 50 minutes sessions, the length of the therapeutic encounter will last as little as 15-30 minutes.

The third is that is that where it takes place, the treatment context, is beginning to change. It is predicted that much of psychotherapy practice will shift from dedicated mental health settings to integrated primary care medical settings. Here, the therapist will function as part of a health care team which includes physician, nurse, medical assistant, and a therapist in the role of behavioral health consultant. While at first this may seem alien to many therapists, it may actually be a welcome change. For starters, integrated primary care is more compatible with psychotherapy's focus on strengths and prevention in addition to pathology. For another, there is little or no need to seek authorization for treatment or provide extensive documentation for counseling services in a medical setting. Finally, working as a salaried member of a team beats competing with other mental health professionals for HMO panels and insurance reimbursement.

These three anticipated changes are very real and will require significant changes in how therapists are trained and practice. There is little doubt that therapists will be expected and required to practice new or greatly revised treatment approaches that are evidence-based. What is needed is a learning resources to help both trainees and practicing therapists to learn and begin to master evidence-based approach and interventions that will ensure they meet the demands for accountable care and be reimbursed for counseling/therapy services rendered.

*Pattern Focused Therapy: Highly Effective CBT Practice in Mental Health and Integrated Care Settings* is an invaluable resource for learning a very brief, evidence-based therapy approach. It was developed, researched, and used successfully to train graduate students in cutting-edge psychotherapy approaches and interventions at Florida Atlantic University since 2012. It provides an in-depth description of Pattern-Focused Therapy, and how it is practiced effectively in both mental health and primary care settings.

Pattern Focused Therapy is a third wave Cognitive Behavior Therapy (CBT) approach which include Acceptance and Commitment Therapy, Cognitive Behavior Analysis System of Psychotherapy, Dialectical Behavior Therapy, and Mindfulness-based Cognitive Therapy. Like other third wave approaches, Pattern Focused Therapy emphasizes the therapeutic relationship, effecting deep change, but unlike other approaches.it is applicable to nearly every clinical presentation, and is designed to be practiced in both mental health and integrated care settings.

Pattern Focused Therapy incorporates brief CBT interventions for symptom reduction and a step-by-step therapeutic strategy, called the Query Sequence, for quickly and effectively changing personality and pattern. In my experience, Pattern Focused Therapy is relatively easy to learn, master, and apply to a very wide range of clients. Practicing this approach is illustrated in two completed and successful clinical cases. The first is a six-session therapy, 45-minute sessions, with transcriptions and extensive commentary. The second case illustrates how Pattern Focused Therapy is practiced in an integrated care setting in four sessions of 30-minute duration. In short, the book is an accessible and practical resource for learning and mastering an evidence-based therapy approach that is brief, effective, reimbursable, and applicable to mental health and integrated care settings.

This book will be of clinical value to psychotherapists and other clinicians in both mental health and integrated care settings. It will also serve as a main or companion text for graduate and undergraduate psychotherapy and counseling techniques courses, advanced therapy intervention courses, and introduction to counseling/psychotherapy courses in professional counseling, human services, and psychology programs; as well as for psychotherapy and counseling practicum and internship courses.

## Overview of the book

The first chapter discusses the six professional trends that are increasingly impacting the practice of psychotherapy and related clinical services. It then shows the timeliness of Pattern Focused Therapy and how it dovetails with these trends.

Chapter 2 begins by defining pattern and its centrality in Pattern Focused Therapy and then describes the assessment process and the place of case conceptualization in this therapy approach. Chapter 3 details the origins, components, and clinical aspects of this approach including the Query Sequence which is its core therapeutic strategy for achieving deep therapeutic change. Chapter 4 describes 12 ultra-brief CBT interventions for reducing symptoms and stabilizing the client. Pattern Focused Therapy combines both of them in tandem to effect therapeutic change: ultra-brief interventions for first order change, i.e., symptom reduction and stabilization, and the Query Sequence for second order change, i.e., pattern or personality change. Chapter 5 details how brief measures, including screening instruments, are utilized to assess and monitor progress throughout the therapy process. Next, Chapters 6, 7, and 8 describe the treatment process of Pattern Focused Therapy with a completed and successful six session therapy that illustrates its application with extended transcriptions and commentaries. Two final chapters round out the book. Chapter 9 provides some advanced therapeutic interventions for dealing with complicating situations that can derail the therapeutic process. These include transference-countertransference enactment and common therapy interfering behaviors. Finally, Chapter 10 addresses and illustrates the application of Pattern Focused Therapy to health and mental health issues in integrated care settings. A completed and successful four session therapy illustrates its application with extended transcriptions and commentaries.

My hope is that by encountering the content of this book readers will come to appreciate the value of this third-wave CBT approach, particularly how it is practiced from an insider's perspective—through transcriptions and commentaries —and how Pattern Focused Therapy can quickly and easily effect change in a wide range of clients.

# Chapter 1

# Pattern Focused Therapy and Psychotherapy Practice
## Today and Tomorrow

The Introduction to *Pattern Focused Therapy: Highly Effective CBT Practice in Mental Health and Integrated Care Settings* highlighted three significant changes already occurring in psychotherapy practice: (1) increasing expectations and demands for reimbursement of psychotherapy services rendered; (2) shorter durations of treatment length and session length; and (3) changes in where therapy will be provided. Yet, these are just the tip of the iceberg. Other major changes are also impacting practice today and will inevitably impact it tomorrow. This chapter will highlight six predicted trends that are influencing and will continue to influence psychotherapy practice. Each of these trends will be described. Then, Pattern Focused Therapy is suggested to be one of the few contemporary therapeutic approaches that dovetails with or meets the demands of all six of these trends. Before all this, a word on these prediction sources.

## Professional Prognostication and Psychotherapy Research

Two extraordinarily accurate sources of the status of psychotherapy practice are worth reviewing. The first involves prognostications by well-regarded professionals in the field, and the second is the implications of recent psychotherapy research. Both portrayals are briefly introduced before turning to the predicted trends.

### Professional Prognostication

The recent Delphi study results reported by Norcross, Pfund, and Prochaska (2013) are discussed first, followed by some additional prognostications. For the past three decades, at intervals of 10 years, Norcross, Pfund, and Prochaska (2013) have conducted Delphi polls on the future trends in psychotherapy practice. Their predictions can be characterized as specific and uncannily accurate. Some 70 psychotherapy experts were empaneled in 2012 to forecast trends for the next decade. The five areas of focus were: theoretical orientations, therapeutic interventions, psychotherapist background, therapy formats, and forecast scenarios (Norcross et al., 2013).

The Delphi study predicted that cognitive-behavioral, integrative, mindfulness, and multicultural theoretical orientations would increase the most. On the other hand, Jungian therapy, classical psychoanalysis, and transactional analysis were expected to decline. The prediction regarding transactional analysis has already been realized in the United States. Regarding therapeutic interventions, technological, skill-building, self-change, and relationship-fostering interventions were predicted to be most utilized. As far as psychotherapist background, master's degree practitioners were predicted to be the dominant group of providers of mental health services. Therapy formats such as teletherapy, comprised of either web-based or telephone-based programs, were predicted to increase dramatically. It was concluded that the four driving themes for these trends are: (1) the economy of technology; (2) evidence-based treatment; (3) innovative ideas; and (4) practices (Norcross et al., 2013).

They summarized their predictions as:

> In 2022, we expect briefer episodes of individual, group, and couple treatments increasingly conducted by master's-level professionals involving evidence-based methods and relationships; theoretical formulations and clinical methods more associated with the cognitive, integrative, multicultural, and mindfulness orientations; and progressively more on the Internet, smart phones, and social networking.(Norcross et al., 2013, p. 369)

Similarly, Silverman (2013) predicted four trends in the future of psychotherapy. The first trend identified four levels of sophistication in technology for both providers and clients, rather than by ethnicity, race, or sexual orientation. The second trend indicated addressed the expansion of technology such as social media (e.g., Twitter, Facebook, etc.) and other online service platforms (e.g., Skype, Slack, etc.). Third, the development of new forms of healthcare would surface, rewarding successful efforts in evidence-based practice, prevention, and disease treatment, requiring documentation of clinical outcomes, and a focus on the discovery of successful new treatments. The fourth trend addressed emerging markets for individuals seeking increased quality of life and enhancement of performance (Silverman, 2013).

Just prior to Silverman's prognostications, Thomason (2010) made several predictions about evidence-based practice. He predicted a chasm between evidence-based and non-evidence-based practices. Essentially, reimbursement would be contingent on evidence-based practice, while non-evidence-based practices would not qualify. Finally, Thomason (2010) predicted that psychotherapy would become briefer, as well as integrated with, primary care practice.

The common themes among all three professional prognostications are that treatment will become much shorter, be evidence-based, and have increased levels of accountability for health issues in both mental health and integrated care.

## *Psychotherapy Research*

Research on developments in the practice of psychotherapy has steadily increased in the past decade. Much of it has been summarized in a recent text (Wampold & Imel, 2015). Six of these research findings are reported here.

For the past seven decades psychotherapy has focused on two questions: is psychotherapy effective?; and how does it work? Research has verified that psychotherapy is not only effective but is very effective. In fact, the effects of psychotherapy are greater than the effects of many medical practices. Psychotherapy has been found to be as effective as medication for most mental disorders, without the side effects. Furthermore, psychotherapy is longer-lasting than medications and is less resistant to additional courses of treatment (Wampold & Imel, 2015). This finding is incredibly important since its effectiveness was seriously questioned by Eysenck's (1952) influential study. The second question of how it works initially focused on specific factors—interventions—or on common factors, and now on what some consider an even more important independent variable: therapist expertise (Castonquay & Hill, 2017). Instead of moving the psychotherapy profession forward, this question fragmented the field, leaving outcomes unchanged for many decades. The result of this fragmentation is that the field has not created new generations of highly effective therapists. The "way out" of this dilemma is for research and clinical practice to focus on the therapist's contribution to treatment outcome and the acquisition of therapist expertise and a commitment to using client feedback to inform therapy and to deliberate practice. In short, highly effective therapists are able to tailor treatment to their clients (Castonquay & Hill, 2017).

Therapists vary in their expertise and effectiveness: Some therapists consistently achieve better outcomes with their clients than do other therapists, in both clinical trials and in everyday practice (Wampold & Imel, 2015). Approximately 15–20% of therapists are highly effective, 15–20% are relatively ineffective, and the remainder are average (Barkham, Lutz, Lambert, & Saxon, 2017).

Therapists do not get better with time or experience. On average, over the course of their professional careers, it appears that therapists do not improve, in terms of achieving better outcomes. The exception are those therapists who engage in deliberate practice and utilize client feedback to inform the ongoing therapeutic process (Rousmaniere, 2019).

Specific therapeutic factors are clearly related to successful treatment outcomes. These include the therapeutic alliance, empathy, realistic expectations, psychoeducation about the disorder, and other "common factors." Of particular importance is that therapists who can effectively form an effective therapeutic alliance with a range of clients, who have a sophisticated set of facilitative interpersonal skills, who work to maintain their effectiveness, and who engage in deliberate practice, these are the therapists who achieve better outcomes (Wampold & Imel, 2015).

Providing information about client progress improves the quality of psychotherapy, primarily by reducing the likelihood of treatment failures for clients not making the expected progress. Monitoring client progress to improve the quality of services, which is often called practice-based evidence, is becoming more widely used (Rousmaniere, 2019).

It appears that "treatments" with no structure are less effective than treatments that are structured and focused on the client's problems. Therapists delivering non-structured treatments are not able to share with the client an explanation in the form of a case conceptualization for two aspects of therapy that seem to be important for producing benefits. First, to explain why they became distressed, and, second, how their engagement in the therapeutic process will help them with their problems (Wampold & Imel, 2015).

In short, psychotherapy research finds that psychotherapy is very effective, and highly effective therapists tend to monitor outcomes, utilize client feedback to tailor treatment and align the therapeutic alliance to engage the client in the treatment process, apply focused interventions, and achieve positive therapeutic outcomes.

## Predicted Trends of Psychotherapy Practice

### 1. Short-Term Therapy Practice

This prediction is that the practice of psychotherapy will be for more short-term therapy practice. It was also predicted that the duration of therapy and session length would be considerably shortened.

In January 1, 2013, the Current Procedural Terminology (CPT) codes for billing insurers for mental health services, which includes Medicare and Medicaid, took effect. Prior to that date, the 50-minute hour was billed, using the code 90807. Currently, there is no code that can be used to bill a 50-minute session. The Centers for Medicare and Medicaid Services implemented a CPT code of 90834 to bill for a 45-minute session, reportedly to represent more accurately the way clinicians provide services. Presumably, shortening of a session by 5 minutes was expected to lower session fees. Furthermore, clinicians worried that shortening session length would be detrimental to both treatment effectiveness and reimbursement (Miller, 2012). To date, researchers have not confirmed a loss of treatment effectiveness. Not surprisingly, the expectation that reimbursement rates would be reduced was met.

Other considerations, besides the previous CPT code changes, have contributed to the shortening of psychotherapy sessions and the push for the integration of physical and psychological services. A new model of mental health practice is emerging as a result. Some indications of the new model involve a treatment duration of 4–6 treatment sessions, instead of the previous 12–20 norm. The length of new therapeutic encounters will span 15–30 minutes, greatly differing from the prior 50-minute standard. Cummings and O'Donohue (2008) predicted these changes. Cummings and others have advocated for the last 30 years that, just like physicians, psychotherapists should be able to assess, diagnose, and begin treatment with clients within 15 minutes. In my experience ultra-brief interventions can be delivered in as little as 10–20 minutes.

The projected durations are similar to the Delphi polling results. Experts polled reached a consensus that, by 2022, treatment duration would not be unlimited, and would likely not exceed 20 sessions. Instead, it was expected that there would be an increase in short-term therapy (5–12 sessions) and very short-term therapy (1–4 sessions), with long-term therapy (longer than 20 sessions) resulting in a significant decline (Norcross et al., 2013, p. 367). Table 1.1 provides a summary of these projections.

## 2. Health Issues and Integrated Care Practice

The prediction is that the practice of psychotherapy will increasingly incorporate health issues and that integrated care settings will become the main setting for the practice of psychotherapy.

The most significant change predicted for mental health practice is that increasingly more of it will be provided in integrated care settings. In such settings, the mental health provider will assume the role of behavioral health consultant as part of a team, including a physician and a nurse, at minimum. While it may be an alien concept for most mental health clinicians, many advantages can be predicted, such as focusing on prevention as opposed to pathology, requiring less

*Table 1.1* Treatment duration and session duration

| Treatment duration | |
|---|---|
| Long-term therapy | 12–20 sessions |
| Short-term therapy | 5–12 sessions |
| Very short-term therapy | 1–4 sessions |
| Session duration | |
| Conventional therapy session | 45 (previously 50) minutes |
| Brief therapy or consultation session | 15–30 minutes |

extensive documentation to be provided, and working as a salaried member of a team. This would be a welcome change to ongoing competition with other professionals for Health Maintenance Organization (HMO) panels and extensive documentation requirements for insurance reimbursement. Therapists practicing in integrated care settings, as opposed to mental health settings, can expect less stress, less paperwork, as well as increased variety and knowledge about medical and other health conditions (Noonan, 2018).

Called the triple aim, three primary goals for providing mental health services in primary care settings have been established: (1) increase the quality and satisfaction of the patient's healthcare experience; (2) increase prevention and therefore the overall health of the population; and (3) reduce healthcare costs (Berwick, Nolan, & Whittington, 2008). Reduced emergency room and hospital admissions are the factors that reduce cost of services, if mental health services are provided in integrated health settings. Additionally, patients are more likely to receive appropriate and necessary services due to the identification of undiagnosed conditions and concerns.

The Delphi survey found that psychotherapy practice in integrated primary care settings would steadily increase. This was predicted not only to provide higher quality care but also to control costs. It was also predicted that, in addition to providing psychological services in integrated care settings, psychotherapists in mental health settings would also routinely treat the behavioral components of health problems and chronic illnesses (Norcross et al., 2013).

## 3. Evidence-Based Approaches

This prediction is that evidence-based approaches will survive the major changes occurring in healthcare. It will replace non-evidence-based approaches, and it will be the only one that will be reimbursable.

While graduate mental health training programs intend that their trainees will inform their clinical decisions with research evidence, few programs can claim this achievement. Most programs require one or more research courses, but trainees are seldom taught how to use research clinically. Statistics and research methods courses are necessary to inform clinical practice, but insufficient for establishing this competency. Specific training in critical thinking is needed to utilize research as a basis for clinical practice. That is, the capacity to apply research to inform clinical decisions. In the past two decades, evidence-based practice has surfaced to address such transactional issues. This section focuses on the core features of evidence-based practice and the implications for psychotherapy practice.

Evidence-based practice is defined as the integration of three elements for interventions: (1) a high degree of evidence, such as research support, has been identified; (2) the results are individualized to clients' needs, values, and expectations; and (3) the outcomes are expertly planned and implemented by trained clinicians. The underlying premise is that evidence will be the basis for informing clinical decision-making and clinical practice once these three elements are present (Williams, Patterson, & Edwards, 2014).

Sackett et al. (1996) originated the concept of evidence-based practice. It was formally defined by the Institute of Medicine in 2001 and subsequently adopted by the American Psychological Association in 2006. Providing the best individualized treatment that is both effective and accountable, i.e., measurable and reportable, is the basic intent of evidence-based practice. "Evidence-based treatments" and "empirically supported treatments" are terms that are commonly confused with evidence-based practice. While both have varying levels of research support, they are not expertly applied by clinicians, nor are they individualized to a specific client.

Historically, clinicians commonly made treatment decisions based on their theoretical orientation. That began to change in the 1990s with the emergence of evidence-based practice (Margolin, Shapiro, & Miller, 2015). Evidence-based practice was originally described as a process of inquiry for the purpose of helping therapists and their clients make important treatment decisions. Throughout the process, a clinician selects interventions after considering research evidence, their experience and expertise, ethics, situational circumstances, the availability of resources, as well as the client's preferences and values (Gambrill, 2011). This differs greatly from decision-making derived from espoused orientations, which give secondary importance to what can be considered safe, effective, and appropriate.

Some clinicians have mistakenly assumed that the "evidence" in evidence-based practice "requires" the use of empirically supported treatments. In part, this may be due to Division 12 of the American Psychological Association promoting a list of empirically supported treatments. However, this was not the intention of the originators of evidence-based practice (Sackett et al., 1996). They indicated that two kinds of evidence exist: internal and external. External evidence is quality empirical research. On the other hand, internal evidence involves gathering information about the client and applying external evidence with expert accuracy and specificity. Therefore, empirically supported treatments may be chosen, but it is "the ethical responsibility of all clinicians regardless of orientation to be guided by current empirical research as well as their own specific areas of competence, experience, and limitations when making treatment recommendations" (Sookman, 2015, p. 1295).

Unfortunately, some practicing clinicians maintain an anti-empirical research bias and antipathy toward evidence-based practice, despite increasing expectation among third party payers (Lilienfeld, Ritschel, Lynn, Cautin, & Latzman, 2013). However, a new generation of therapy trainees is emerging and is eager for scientifically informed treatment interventions. Trainees are asking "'What does the research say about that treatment approach or intervention approach in addressing problem X?' Their assumption is that there should be research to support what we do" (Williams et al., 2014, p. 206). Additionally, they are "most motivated to learn evidence-based practice when the evidence-based practice skills help them with their own clients" (Williams et al., 2014, p. 236). Regardless of experience, clinicians who succeed in integrated or specialized mental health settings will be those who adopt ultra-brief interventions and evidence-based practices.

Therapists may question if there are ethical implications in evidence-based practice. However, there is an inseparable link between professional ethics and evidence-based practice. Many believe that the realm of ethical practice is confined to issues with confidentiality, informed consent, and conflicts of interest. However, these considerations—while important—are secondary to beneficence and non-maleficence, which are essential to ethical decision-making. The real test of whether clinical decisions and practice are ethical is whether they meet three criteria: the treatment is safe, effective, and appropriate for a given client and his or her needs and concerns (Sperry, 2018b).

Few current therapeutic approaches report empirical support. The risk is that approaches that do not demonstrate empirical support will lose eligibility for third party reimbursement. This is a result of increasing demand for evidence-based interventions. On the other hand, a few approaches do provide sufficient empirical evidence to inform clinical decision-making and they are the most likely to receive third party reimbursement.

The Delphi study predicts that evidence-based practices will be incorporated in at least two ways. The first is that evidence-based practices will be required by healthcare systems, and, second, that practice guidelines will become a standard part of everyday psychotherapy practice. They also predicted that psychotherapy research will provide prescriptive treatments of choice and emphasize the importance of fostering meaningful therapeutic alliances, expressing warmth, and providing interpersonal support (Norcross et al., 2013).

They also forecast that therapy approaches with the most controlled research will increase in stature and use, while those with the least controlled research are expected to be less widely practiced. Furthermore, they predicted that approaches and interventions with the highest impacts will be those that are data-driven, both in terms of using data gathered to tailor interventions to clients but also to report outcomes data that demonstrate that clinical change was effected (Norcross et al., 2013).

## 4. Clinical Outcomes Monitoring

The prediction is that clinical outcomes monitoring with feedback incorporated into treatment process will become the norm for psychotherapy practice. An essential component of current clinical practice is incorporating clinical outcome measures (Meier, 2015).

The collecting and monitoring of clinical outcomes data are receiving considerable attention today. Without an objective means of evaluating their clinical outcomes and their effectiveness as therapists, how are clinicians able to evaluate their work and their effectiveness? Research shows that clinicians tend to hold overly optimistic views of their effectiveness and treatment progress made by their client in relation to actual measured change (Walfish, McAlister, O'Donnell, & Lambert, 2012). Clinicians typically overlook negative changes and have difficulty accurately gauging the benefit that clients have received during treatment, particularly for clients who are failing to improve (Hannan et al., 2005). Clinical outcomes of more than 6,000 clients treated in everyday practice settings showed that only one-third improved (Hansen, Lambert, & Forman, 2002).

In an attempt to reduce negative outcomes, some therapists have begun to use routine and continuous outcome monitoring. This involves regularly measuring and monitoring client progress with standardized self-report scales over the course of treatment with routine feedback provided by therapists before and after each session (Lambert, Hansen, & Finch, 2001; Newham, Hooke, & Page, 2010). Such feedback provides information to the therapist that goes beyond what therapists observe and understand about client progress without such information. This helps therapists recognize problematic treatment response and provides problem-solving tools that improve collaborative efforts in cases where positive response to therapy is in doubt. Because certain monitoring methods have been shown to enhance client outcome, the American Psychological Association has recommended routine outcome monitoring to be a part of effective treatment (APA, 2006).

In short, therapists will increasingly be challenged not only to utilize clinical outcome measures, but also to incorporate feedback and modify treatment accordingly. Reporting and documenting such clinical outcomes will be an additional challenge. Reporting and documenting are crucial because, without measurable outcomes, psychotherapy can devolve into friendly conversations between clinicians and clients, resulting in treatment that is costly, inappropriate, ineffective, and likely unethical.

## 5. Core Therapeutic Strategy

The prediction is that therapeutic approaches with effective core therapeutic strategies that are applicable to a higher percentage of clients and presentations will be favored over those that do not. Presumably this means that such approaches are more likely to be reimbursable.

While some 400 different therapeutic approaches have been developed, there are only seven different core therapeutic strategies which inform those various approaches (Sperry, 2018a). Core therapeutic strategy is the action plan for focusing and implementing specific interventions to achieve specified treatment goals. The seven different core therapeutic strategies that underlie evidence-based treatments are: (1) modification of behavior; (2) skills training; (3) cognitive disputation; (4) cognitive restructuring; (5) interpretation; (6) distancing; and (7) replacement. Predictably, each one of these therapeutic strategies is associated with a given therapeutic approach. Each is described below (Sperry, 2018). Table 1.2 lists these strategies and the corresponding therapeutic approaches.

- *Cognitive disputation.* Cognitive disputation is a core therapeutic strategy for changing troubling thoughts or beliefs. It involves directly questioning the validity of clients' thoughts and beliefs that underlie and maintain their anxiety, so they become more adaptive and psychologically healthier. This strategy is the hallmark of Rational Emotive Behavior Therapy.
- *Cognitive restructuring.* Cognitive restructuring is another core therapeutic strategy for changing troubling thoughts or beliefs. Various tactics or techniques are utilized in restructuring troubling thoughts or beliefs. These include guided discovery, Socratic questioning, and examining the evidence. This strategy is the hallmark of Cognitive Therapy and cognitively-oriented CBT.
- *Interpretation.* Interpretation is a hypothesis or guess about the connection between an individual's thoughts, behaviors, or emotions and his or her unconscious emotions or thoughts. Interpretation remains the core strategy

*Table 1.2* Core therapeutic strategies and representative therapeutic approaches

| Core therapeutic strategy | Therapeutic approaches |
| --- | --- |
| Cognitive disputation | Rational Emotive Behavior Therapy |
| Cognitive restructuring | Cognitive Therapy<br>Cognitive Behavior Therapy |
| Interpretation | Psychoanalytic Therapies |
| Modification of behavior | Behavior Therapy, i.e., Exposure Therapy |
| Skills training | Dialectical Behavior Therapy |
| Distancing | Acceptance and Commitment Therapy |
| Replacement | Pattern Focused Therapy<br>Cognitive Behavioral Analysis System of Psychotherapy<br>Reality Therapy<br>Narrative Therapy |

in the various psychoanalytic therapies, starting with classical psychoanalysis and extending to the brief psychodynamics therapies.
- *Modification of behavior.* Modification of behavior is the basic therapeutic strategy in Behavior Therapy. Currently, exposure is one of the key interventions for modifying behavior. It involves intentional and prolonged contact with a feared object combined with actively blocking undesirable avoidance behaviors. Even though the client will experience increased anxiety in the short term, in the long term, after repeated and incremental exposure to that feared stimulus, the anxiety and the avoidance response are extinguished.
- *Skills training.* Skills training is a broad therapeutic strategy of educating and training individuals experiencing psychological disturbance to increase their knowledge, coping capacity, and skills required to solve their presenting problems. Skills training is an intentional way to increase specific skill sets, such as assertive communications training, emotion regulation training, and distress tolerance training. Skills training is a central intervention strategy in some Behavior Therapy and CBT approaches but is central in Dialectic Behavior Therapy practice.
- *Distancing.* Distancing from a particular thought is the core strategy for dealing with distressful habitual thinking. Rather than engaging in the more challenging and lengthier process of interpreting, disputing, or restructuring, the client can be quickly guided to step back from a particular thought with relative ease. Also known as cognitive defusion, it is a major core therapeutic strategy of Acceptance and Commitment Therapy.
- *Replacement.* Replacement is a core therapeutic strategy for intentionally replacing hurtful behaviors and thoughts with healthier ones. Therapists assist clients to find alternative thoughts and behaviors. This process is much quicker than interpreting, disputing, restructuring thoughts or beliefs, and modifying behaviors. Replacement is the core therapeutic strategy in the Cognitive Behavioral Analysis System of Psychotherapy (CBASP), Reality Therapy, and Narrative Therapy. In the latter, re-storying or re-authoring replaces a less healthy story or narrative with a more healthy one. In addition, therapists who espouse other therapeutic approaches will also use replacement as an adjunctive strategy when there may not be sufficient time in the session to process a compelling issue with an interpretation, disputation, or cognitive disputation.

The first five core therapeutic strategies have been on the therapy scene the longest, while the last two are more recent. Optimal outcomes of some of these therapeutic strategies require a certain degree of client capacities and are not as effective for those with lesser degrees. For example, the core therapeutic strategies of cognitive disputation, cognitive restructuring, and interpretation are better employed with clients who can relatively easily engage in rational thinking, i.e., formal operations and post-formal thinking, but are not as effective with clients who typically engage in emotional thinking, i.e., pre-operations. Techniques consistent with the modification of behavior core therapeutic strategy may require considerable distress tolerance and emotion regulation to face feared objects or situations as in the context of exposure therapy. In contrast, skills training, distancing, and replacement require less cognitive development and emotion regulation coping skills. In fact, one of the hallmarks of third-wave CBT approaches is that these were developed for use with a wide range of therapeutic indications. Pattern Focused Therapy, which incorporates a key component of CBASP, has only two contraindications: acute psychosis and cognitive blunting, as in moderate dementia, delirium or acute substance intoxication or withdrawal.

While not specifically mentioning core therapeutic strategies, the Delphi survey identifies a number of therapeutic approaches that reflect the core therapeutic strategies that are most likely to be employed in clinical in the future. These included Acceptance and Commitment Therapy, Exposure Therapy, Dialectical Behavior Therapy, and other third-wave CBT approaches. In contrast, the Psychoanalytic Therapies were predicted to have limited usage (Norcross et al., 2013).

### 6. More Targeted, Briefer, and Effective Interventions

The prediction is that approaches that incorporate more targeted, briefer, and effective interventions will be favored over those that do not. The Delphi survey identified 45 interventions in current usage and predicted that 19 would increase in use while the remaining 26 would decrease. Those predicted to increase were largely targeted, briefer, and research-supported interventions. They include relapse prevention, homework, assertive communication, meditation, and self-therapy—as in third-order change efforts. They also forecast that aversive conditioning, free association, and dream interpretation would diminish the most (Norcross et al., 2013).

## Pattern Focused Therapy in Psychotherapy Today and Tomorrow

The chapter began with a set of prognostications and psychotherapy research findings followed by six trends. Pattern Focused Therapy seems to be well suited to the temper of the times. In the section on professional prognostication, three common themes emerged: (1) treatment will become much shorter; (2) treatment will be evidence-based; and (3) treatment will have increased levels of accountability for health issues in both mental health and integrated care. From a review of recent psychotherapy research, these following themes stand out: psychotherapy is very effective; highly effective therapists tend to monitor outcomes; they utilize client feedback to tailor

*Table 1.3* Predicted Trends and Pattern Focused Therapy

| Predicted trends | Pattern Focused Therapy |
| --- | --- |
| More short-term therapy practice | Well suited for short-term therapy practice |
| Account for health issues and/or practice in integrated care settings | Well suited for health issues and practice in integrated care settings |
| Evidence-based approaches will be reimbursable | Evidence-based |
| Outcomes monitoring with feedback incorporated into treatment process | Emphasizes outcomes monitoring and incorporating feedback |
| Core therapeutic strategy is applicable for a greater percentage of clients and presentations | Core therapeutic strategy has broadest applicability for clients and presentations |
| More targeted, briefer, and effective interventions | Emphasizes ultra-brief interventions |

treatment and align the therapeutic alliance to engage the client in the treatment process; and they apply focused interventions and achieve positive therapeutic outcomes.

In terms of the six trends, Pattern Focused Therapy seems to be one of the few current therapeutic approaches that dovetails with or meets the demands of all six trends (Table 1.3). It is a short-term therapy can be practiced in both mental health settings and integrated care settings. In either setting it is well suited to effectively deal with the psychological or behavioral aspects of the most common health conditions. It is also an evidence-based approach incorporating key components from CBASP and motivational interviewing. It emphasizes outcomes monitoring and the incorporation of client feedback to better inform and tailor treatment. Its core therapeutic strategy has perhaps the broadest applicability among other contemporary approaches for clients and presentations. Finally, it easily incorporates ultra-brief interventions.

## Conclusion

These are exciting times to start or continue practicing psychotherapy. With the excitement is also a sense of the unknown and with it a measure of fear. Nevertheless, recent research findings and Delphi predictions about what therapy practice will be like in 2022 offer a measure of hope. This chapter introduced Pattern Focused Therapy in the context of expert predictions about the future practice of psychotherapy as well as recent research in psychotherapy practice. Chapter 2 further discusses Pattern Focused Therapy and the centrality of pattern in it.

## References

APA (American Psychological Association). (2006). Evidence-based practice in psychology: APA Presidential Task Force on evidence-based practice. *American Psychologist*, 61(4), 271–285.

Barkham, M., Lutz, W., Lambert, M. J., & Saxon, D. (2017). Therapist effects, effective therapists, and the law of variability. In L. G. Castonguay & C. E. Hill (Eds.), *How and why are some therapists better than others?: Understanding therapist effects*. Washington, DC: American Psychological Association.

Berwick, M., Nolan, A., & Whittington, J. (2008). The triple aim: Care, health and cost. *Health Affairs*, 27, 759–769.

Castonquay, L. G. & Hill, C. (Eds.). (2017). *How and why are some therapists better than others?: Understanding therapist effects*. Washington, DC: American Psychological Association.

Cummings, N. A. & O'Donohue, W. T. (2008). *Eleven blunders that cripple psychotherapy in. America*. New York, NY: Routledge.

Eysenck, H. J. (1952). The effects of psychotherapy: An evaluation. *Journal of Consulting Psychology*, 16, 319–324.

Gambrill, E. (2011). Evidence-based practice and the ethics of discretion. *Journal of Social Work*, 11(1), 26–48.

Hannan, C., Lambert, M. J., Harmon, C., Nielsen, S. L., Smart, D. W., Shimokawa, K., & Sutton, S. W. (2005). A lab test and algorithms for identifying clients at risk for treatment failure. *Journal of Clinical Psychology*, 61, 155–163.

Hansen, N. B., Lambert, M. J., & Forman, E. (2002). The psychotherapy dose-response effect and its implications for treatment delivery services. *Clinical Psychology: Science and Practice*, 9, 329–343.

Lambert, M. J., Hansen, N. B., & Finch, A. E. (2001). Patient-focused research: Using patient outcome data to enhance treatment effects. *Journal of Consulting and Clinical Psychology*, 69, 159–172.

Lilienfeld, S. O., Ritschel, L. A., Lynn, S. J., Cautin, R. L., & Latzman, R. D. (2013). Why many clinical psychologists are resistant to evidence-based practice: Root causes and constructive remedies. *Clinical Psychology Review*, 33, 883–900.

Margolin, G., Shapiro, L. S., & Miller, K. (2015). Ethics in couple and family psychotherapy. In J. Sadler, B. Fulford, & C. Van Staden (Eds.), *Oxford handbook of psychiatric ethics*, vol. 2 (pp. 1306–1314). New York, NY: Oxford University Press.

Meier, S. (2015). *Incorporating progress monitoring and outcome measures into counseling and psychotherapy: A primer*. New York, NY: Oxford University Press.

Miller, D. (2012). The end of the 50 minute hour?: Will the new CPT codes change mental health practices? *Psychology Today*. December 2, 2012. Retrieved from www.psychologytoday.com/us/blog/shrink-rap-today/201212/the-end-of-the-50-minute-hour.

Miller, S. D., Hubble, M. A., Chow, D. L., & Seidel, J. A. (2013). The outcome of psychotherapy: Yesterday, today, and tomorrow. *Psychotherapy*, 50(1), 88–97.

Newham, E., Hooke, G. R., & Page, A. C. (2010). Progress monitoring and feedback in psychiatric care reduces depressive symptoms. *Journal of Affective Disorders*, 117, 139–146.

Noonan, D. (2018). Integrated care: Perspectives from a behavioral health consultant. *Psychiatric News*, 53(15). https://doi.org/101176/appi.pn.2018.8b11.

Norcross, J. C., Pfund, R. A., & Prochaska, J. O. (2013). Psychotherapy in 2022: A Delphi poll on its future. *Professional Psychology: Research and Practice*, 44(5), 363–370.

Rousmaniere, T. (2019). *Mastering the Inner skills of psychotherapy: A deliberate practice manual*. Seattle, WA: Gold Lantern Books.

Sackett, D., Richardson, W., Rosenberg, W., & Haynes, R., & Brian, S. (1996). Evidence based medicine: What it is and what it isn't. *British Medical Journal*, 312, 71–72.

Silverman, W. H. (2013). The future of psychotherapy: One editor's perspective. *Psychotherapy*, 50(4), 484–489.

Sookman, D. (2015). Ethical practice of cognitive behavior therapy. In J. Sadler, B. Fulford, & C. Van Staden (Eds.), *Oxford handbook of psychiatric ethics*, vol. 2 (pp. 1293–1305). New York, NY: Oxford University Press.

Sperry, L. (2018a). Achieving evidence-based status for Adlerian therapy: Why it is needed and how to accomplish it. *Journal of Individual Psychology*, 74(3), 247–264.

Sperry, L. (2018b). Mindfulness, soulfulness, and spiritual development in spiritually oriented psychotherapy. *Spirituality in Clinical Practice*, 5(4), 225–230.

Thomason, T. C. (2010). The trend toward evidence-based practice and the future of psychotherapy. *American Journal of Psychotherapy*, 64(1), 29–38.

Walfish, S., McAlister, B., O'Donnell, P., & Lambert, M. J. (2012). An investigation of self-assessment bias in mental health providers. *Psychological Reports*, 110, 639–644.

Wampold, B., & Imel, Z. (2015). *The great psychotherapy debate*, 2nd ed. New York, NY: Routledge.

Williams, L., Patterson, J., & Edwards, T. M. (2014). *Clinician's guide to research methods in family therapy: Foundations of evidence-based practice*. New York, NY: Guilford Press.

# Chapter 2

# Pattern
## Assessment and Case Conceptualization

This chapter introduces pattern and its relationship to assessment and case conceptualization. It presumes that case conceptualization is a "cognitive map" of the client's maladaptive pattern of perceiving and responding that can be therapeutically "shifted" to an alternate pattern that is more adaptive (Sperry, 2010a). It also presumes the pattern is the "heart" of case conceptualization and that "the primary focus of clinical assessment is pattern recognition" (Sperry & Sperry, 2012, p. 33). The chapter begins with a description of pattern and its central role in Pattern Focused Therapy. Then, it describes the components of assessment in Pattern Focused Therapy. Finally, it describes the role of case conceptualization in Pattern Focused Therapy. The recurring theme of this chapter is that pattern is the central concept in Pattern Focused Therapy.

## The Centrality of Pattern in Pattern Focused Therapy

In everyday language, pattern is understood as a recurrent way of thinking and behaving in a given situation. Patterns are quite powerful in that they can set expectations, make connections, and impact one's relationships and overall well-being They also engender a sense of predictability and continuity. Recognizing patterns is like looking through a telescope for the first time and viewing reality in a new way. In the past, pattern recognition helped our ancestors stay alive by identifying edible plants and predatory animals and interpreting weather and sea conditions. Today, pattern recognition is useful in diagnosing health conditions and identifying ineffective and harmful personal and relational behaviors.

In short, most people are quite comfortable with the notion of patterns and with some practice most can learn to recognize and even change their own patterns. Germane to the practice of psychotherapy, Livesley (2003) notes:

> Most patients readily accept the idea that there a "pattern" underlying their behavior. The word is reassuring, for it suggest that there is order and meaning

to behavior and experience. Educating patients about these patterns helps them to distance themselves from events and promotes self-observation. At the same time, pattern recognition promotes integration connecting events, behaviors, and experience that were previously assumed to be unconnected.

(p. 274)

In the technical language of Pattern Focused Therapy, a pattern is defined as a succinct description of a client's characteristic way of perceiving, thinking, and responding (Sperry, 2010a). It is the predicable, consistent, and self-perpetuating style and manner in which individuals think, feel, act, cope, and defend themselves (Sperry, Brill, Howard, & Grissom, 1996; Sperry, 2006).

Pattern is what links client presentation with the precipitant and makes sense of the situation. Patterns are "driven" by the client's predispositions and reflect the client's personality dynamics or style (Sperry, 1989). Patterns can be adaptive or maladaptive. An adaptive pattern tends to be flexible, appropriate, and effective, and is reflective of personal and interpersonal competence. In contrast, a maladaptive pattern tends to be inflexible, ineffective, and inappropriate, and causes symptoms, impairment in personal and relational functioning, and chronic dissatisfaction. If the maladaptive pattern is sufficiently distressing or impairing, it can be diagnosed as a personality disorder (Sperry, 2010a).

Is it possible to change from a maladaptive to an adaptive pattern? Yes, it is possible and typically requires a course of focused psychotherapy. It is a change process that involves three steps. First, identify the maladaptive pattern. Second, relinquish the maladaptive pattern and replace it with a more adaptive pattern. Third, maintain the adaptive pattern (Beitman & Yue, 1999).

In Pattern Focused Therapy, this second step is called pattern shifting, which is the therapeutic process for relinquishing the maladaptive pattern and replacing it with a more adaptive pattern. The successful shift to a more adaptive pattern indicates that second-order change has been achieved (Sperry & Binensztok, 2019b).

Patterns may be situation-specific or longitudinal. Situation-specific maladaptive patterns provide an explanation that is unique to the current situation. In contrast, longitudinal patterns provide an explanation that is common to the current as well as to previous situations. In short, a longitudinal pattern reflects a lifelong pattern that provides a reasonable explanation or set of reasons for the client's situation (Sperry, Blackwell, Gudeman, & Faulkner, 1992; Sperry, 2005; 2010a).

Furthermore, the client's pattern reflects and is reflected in all elements of a Pattern Focused Therapy informed case conceptualization, particularly in precipitant, presentation, perpetuants, and predispositions or predisposing factors. These factors are common to most case conceptualization models (Kendjelic & Eells, 2007). Pattern analysis is the process of examining the interrelationship among five factors: (1) precipitating factors; (2) predisposing factors; (3) perpetuating factors; (4) presentation factors, including relational response factors; and (5) pattern (Sperry et al., 1992).

While it may appear that predisposing factors, such as traumatic events, maladaptive beliefs or schemas, defenses, personality style, or systems factors primarily "drive" one's thoughts, feelings, and actions, both individual and systemic dynamics are a function of all four factors, and so are included in a pattern analysis. Including both individual and systemic dynamics, pattern analysis provides a systematic and comprehensive basis for developing and articulating a clinically useful case conceptualization (Sperry, 2010). Table 2.1 provides a capsule summary of the key terms related to pattern.

## Assessment in Pattern Focused Therapy

Therapists use assessments in order to select interventions that are useful in the least amount of time. Thorough assessments inform the therapist of mental health disorders, seek out the pattern or personality style of the client, determine the client's level of functioning and how the presenting problem affects it, and evaluate risk to self or others. Such an assessment is essential to Pattern Focused Therapy. This section describes the key components of a Pattern Focused Assessment: (1) pattern identification; (2) diagnostic assessment; (3) functional assessment; (4) risk and protective factors; (5) assessment of goals; (6) use of screening instruments; and (7) outcomes assessment.

## Pattern Identification

The client's pattern is a crucial component in guiding treatment and determining interventions. Pattern is defined as the style and manner in which individuals think, feel, behave, manage their lives, and protect themselves in ways that are predictable, consistent, and self-perpetuating (Sperry, Brill, Howard, & Grissom, 1996; Sperry, 2006). Patterns are adjudged to be adaptive or maladaptive. Maladaptive patterns

*Table 2.1* Key concepts

| Key concept | Definition |
| --- | --- |
| Presentation | The individual's presenting problem, i.e., symptom or conflict. Typically, it is a response to a precipitant that is congruent with the client's pattern. |
| Precipitant | Triggers that activate the client's pattern, leading to the presenting problem |
| Predisposition | Factors that foster and lead to either maladaptive or adaptive patterns |
| Pattern | The predictable, consistent, and self-perpetuating style and way individuals think, feel, act, cope, and defend themselves |
| Perpetuants | Factors that maintain the presenting problem and pattern |

are characterized as ineffective and inflexible. These patterns, if left unaddressed, can lead to the presenting problems reappearing or the emergence of a related problem once the client's pattern is triggered in the future.

Pattern identification is a process involving clues from both formal assessment and informal observation. Gathering clues to the pattern begins with the first contact with the client. Observed informal data includes the client's unique demeanor, language usage, and posture, as well as data from the diagnostic and functional assessment, as well as formal questioning. Pattern is derived from these various data sources and clues throughout the assessment process. This includes a focus on the client presentation, precipitating factors, predisposing factors, risk and protective factors, as well as perpetuants. The pattern can be identified after eliciting the presentation, precipitants, perpetuants, and predispositions.

It is critical to note that maladaptive pattern and adaptive pattern rather consistently reflect an individual's core personality dynamics. Accordingly, it can be helpful for therapists to identify an individual's basic personality style or personality disorder. Then, the therapists can develop hypotheses about corresponding maladaptive patterns. It is important to specify a corresponding adaptive pattern since this will be reflected in the second-order treatment goal. These hypotheses can be checked against the common patterns associated with specific personality styles and disorders.

Formal questioning begins by eliciting the client's self-description as well as how others describe the client. At times, clients present with more than a single pattern, one of them being more prominent or defined than the other. The presence of a personality disorder will inevitably be reflected in an impairing maladaptive pattern which predictably complicates the treatment process. Accordingly, it is essential that a DSM-5 personality disorder is formally ruled in or out.

In Pattern Focused Therapy, the process of pattern identification is facilitated by connecting the client's movement and activity, personality style/disorder, and purpose with prototypic or likely maladaptive and adaptive patterns. Table 2.2 provides a summary of movement—activity, purpose, personality style, as well as prototypic or likely patterns, both adaptive and maladaptive. With formal instruction and appropriate supervision, it is a reasonable expectation for trainees to develop the competency of identifying an accurate maladies pattern within 30 minutes of the initial session.

## Examples of Pattern Recognition

One example of pattern recognition is shown in the case of Geri (Sperry, 2010b). Geri presented with depression and an avoidant personality style. Her pattern was identified as: avoid or disconnect when feeling unsafe. This is a common theme among those with an avoidant personality or an Avoidant Personality Disorder,

*Table 2.2* Pattern identification in Pattern Focused Therapy

| Movement/activity level | Personality style/disorder | Purpose | Likely adaptive [A] or maladaptive [M] pattern |
|---|---|---|---|
| Toward/active | Histrionic | Get attention | [A] gets attention AND feels worthwhile [M] gets attention, BUT pays a high price and/or becomes compromised |
| Toward/passive | Dependent | Enlist others' help/be pleasing | [A] pleases others by meeting their needs AND one's own needs [M] pleases others by meeting their needs BUT not meet one's own |
| Against/passive | Narcissistic | Get special treatment | [A] is self-confident AND respectful of others [M] elevates self BUT uses or belittles others |
| Against/active | Paranoid | Anticipate harm and retaliate | [A] sizes up AND careful in relating to others [M] sizes up BUT expects to be harmed by others |
| Against/active | Antisocial | Harm others/protect self | [A] lives by own internal code AND is law-abiding [M] lives by own internal code BUT is not law-abiding |
| Away/active | Avoidant | Avoid harm | [A] feels safe AND safely connects with others [M] feels safe BUT avoids/isolates/disconnects |
| Away/passive | Schizoid | Avoid involvement | [A] limited need for companionship AND more comfortable alone [M] limited need for companionship BUT actively avoids others |
| Away/passive | Schizotypal | Act differently/distance others | [A] indifferent to social convention AND relates with familiar people [M] indifferent to social convention BUT wary of unfamiliar people |
| Ambivalent/active | Obsessive-compulsive | Be perfect/do things right/conscientious | [A] reasonably conscientious AND somewhat emotionally close [M] overly conscientious/perfectionistic BUT emotionally distant |
| Ambivalent/passive | Passive-aggressive | Resist demands | [A] agrees to do what is expected of them AND will do that only [M] agrees to do what is expected of them BUT will not do it |
| Variable | Borderline | Pattern reflects the decompensated version of the underlying personality (dependent, histrionic, or passive-aggressive) | |

but because of individual differences the wording of the pattern may differ slightly. A pattern focused case conceptualization was developed, and her maladaptive pattern informed how treatment was subsequently focused. Geri presented with social isolation and depressive symptoms, and by replacing her maladaptive pattern with a more adaptive one, these issues were resolved (Sperry, 2010b).

Another example involves a client who presented with a dual pattern, a situation that can both confuse the therapist and complicate the treatment process. While a single maladaptive pattern is the most common presentation, occasionally clients present with a secondary pattern. Recognizing this secondary pattern is necessary in reducing confusion and effecting therapeutic change. The case of Aimee is an example of this dual pattern. Aimee's primary maladaptive pattern was identified as: meet the needs of others but not meet her own needs. Her secondary pattern was identified as over-conscientiousness. Taken together, her dual pattern was identified as being over-conscientious in taking care of and pleasing others. Through a brief course of effective psychotherapy, Aimee was able to replace this dual maladaptive pattern with more adaptive one, while also resolving her presenting concerns (Sperry & Carlson, 2014).

## Diagnostic Assessment

Clients referred for clinical mental health conditions, such as anxiety and depression, among others, require a diagnostic evaluation. Similar to traditional mental health assessments, this evaluation targets the presenting problem or another area that is warranted. Clients who are referred for medical concerns or noncompliance may also experience mental health symptoms, concurrently or as a result. Diagnostic evaluations are thus indicated to rule out potential mental health disorders. Presumably therapists will use *Diagnostic and Statistical Manual* DSM-5 (American Psychiatric Association, 2013) criteria to rule out possible symptom diagnoses and personality disorder diagnoses. They may also use screening instruments to ascertain the direction of diagnostic evaluations and determine if risk assessment is warranted.

Table 2.3 provides a set of general and specific screening questions that trainees have found clinically useful in structuring a diagnostic assessment. These questions are keyed to nine diagnostic categories in DSM-5 (Frances, 2013), plus additional screening questions for harm to self or others. The ability to follow up with more specific questions to rule in and rule out specific diagnoses depends on experience, clinical sensitivity, and careful listening. Typically, in their practicum and internship experiences, trainees can complete a diagnostic evaluation guided by these screening questions.

*Table 2.3* Diagnostic screening questions: General and Specific

| Reason for treatment | Screening question |
| --- | --- |
| ANXIETY DISORDERS | |
| General/Specific Screening Q's | Would you say you're a nervous person? |
| Panic Disorder | Have you experienced fear so intense that you thought you might die, have a heart attack, or couldn't catch your breath? |
| Agoraphobia | Are there any things you're afraid to do and many places you're afraid to go? |
| SAD | Are there activities that you're afraid to do in public, like giving a presentation? |
| Specific Phobia | Do you have particular fears that cause you special trouble, like flying, heights, the sight of blood, or getting an injection? |
| GAD | Are you a worry wart, unnecessarily anxious all the time about a lot of different things? |
| OCD | Do you have recurring thoughts that bad things will happen or repetitive behaviors that you feel driven to perform? |
| PTSD | Have you experienced a traumatic event that keeps haunting you with terrible memories, flashbacks, or nightmares? |
| Anxiety Disorder—Medical Condition | Have you had symptoms of anxiety associated with a medical condition like an overactive thyroid? |
| DEPRESSIVE AND BIPOLAR DISORDERS | |
| General/Specific Screening Q's | How would you describe your mood? |
| Major Depressive Episode | Do you ever get so depressed that you can't function? |
| Persistent Depressive Disorder | Are you almost always depressed? |
| Bipolar Disorder I | Do you have mood swings—sometimes way up, other times way down? |
| Bipolar Disorder II | Do you have mood swings—sometimes going up, other times going down? |
| Cyclothymic Disorder | Do you have constant mood swings, alternating from high to low? |
| Substance-Induced Depressive Dx | Might your depression be related to your use of alcohol (drugs, or medications)? |
| PSYCHOTIC DISORDERS | |
| General/Specific Screening Q's | Have you ever had unusual or strange experiences? |
| Schizophrenia | Do you ever hear voices, believe that people mean to harm you, or lose touch with reality? |
| Schizoaffective Disorder | Do you ever hear voices, believe that people mean to harm you, or lose touch with reality? Do you have mood swings? |
| Delusional Disorder | Do people say you have really strange ideas? |
| Substance-Induced Psychotic Dx | Do you have strange experiences when you are under the influence of drugs or alcohol? |

## Table 2.3 (Cont.)

| Reason for treatment | Screening question |
|---|---|
| **DISSOCIATIVE DISORDERS** | |
| General/Specific Screening Q's | Does your mind ever play tricks on you? |
| Dissociative Amnesia | Are there parts of your life that you can't remember? |
| Depersonalization Disorder | Do you ever get the weird detached feeling that you are watching yourself go through the motions of life? |
| **EATING DISORDERS** | |
| General/Specific Screening Q's | Is food or eating a problem for you? Do others think or say it is a problem for you? |
| Anorexia Nervosa | Do you feel fat even when others think that you're much too thin? |
| Bulimia Nervosa | Do you often lose control and find yourself taking in a really large amount of food in a very short time? |
| **ADJUSTMENT DISORDERS** | |
| General Screening Q | Are you having problems dealing with stresses in your life? |
| **MEMORY: DEMENTIA & NEUROCOGNITIVE DISORDERS** | |
| General Screening Q | Have you had a big decline in memory? |
| **SUBSTANCE-RELATED & ADDICTIVE DISORDERS** | |
| General/Specific Screening Q's | Tell me about your use of alcohol and drugs |
| Alcohol-Related Disorders | Have you gotten in trouble because of alcohol? |
| Substance-Related Disorders | Have you gotten in trouble because drugs? |
| **PERSONALITY DISORDERS** | |
| General Screening Q | Do you have a way of doing things and relating to others that gets you into the same kind of mess over and over again? |
| **HARM TO SELF OR OTHERS** | |
| General/Specific Screening Q's | Have you had thoughts of harming yourself? |
| | Have you had thoughts of harming others? |

## Functional Assessment

A functional assessment should be completed on each client, regardless of whether a diagnostic evaluation is indicated. Through functional assessments, therapists gather information about ongoing problems and how they are affecting the client's life (Sperry, 2014). Presenting problems can become obstacles in client's vocational and/or educational functioning, ability to maintain intimate relationships, social functioning, and capacity for maintaining self-care and personal responsibilities, such as household tasks. Clients may worry about their finances, how well they can maintain the care of dependents, or other stressful situations. Presenting problems also typically affect cognitive and emotional responses. For example, a client who presents with insomnia may experience increased irritability, self-criticism, and difficulty with focusing on certain tasks. The functional assessment ascertains the manner in which the presenting problem effects on the client's daily life (Sperry & Binensztok, 2019a). This also allows the therapist to make more accurate decisions on whether a diagnostic evaluation is needed.

It is important to determine how clients adjust to their presenting problems, as individuals react variously to problems, contingent on their personality, environment, and other factors. For instance, two people struggling with chronic pain may respond extremely differently to their circumstances. One may choose to adapt their lifestyle to include healthy nutrition and exercise while the other resorts to substance use to cope with the agony. The client who resorts to medication or substance dependence will likely experience a compounding effect of problems. The client who copes by adopting a healthier and more active lifestyle is unlikely to experience these unwanted outcomes. Understanding the client's responses to their problems uncovers information about their strengths and need for improvement or further inquiry.

## Structure of the Assessment

Prior to beginning an assessment, the therapist must clarify the reason for the referral in order to assess the reason for seeking psychotherapy. This also facilitates an assessment of the client's understanding of the problem and a collaborative introduction of the context of psychotherapy. Some clients may disagree with the reasons why they were referred and may experience some resistance to treatment. The therapist must assess the duration, triggers, and frequency of the presenting problem as well as intensity. A client struggling with chronic pain may not be experiencing pain during that meeting. Therefore, the therapist must assess for the presentation of the problem during that specific session and how it fluctuates through time (Sperry & Binensztok, 2019a).

Subsequently, the therapist must assess how the problem affects the client in other settings or while the client engages in other activities. Common areas of exploration are: social relationships, household duties, and performance at work, hobbies, exercise, or other enjoyable activities. Other symptoms resulting from the presenting problem, such as decreases in appetite, sleep, or energy, should also be assessed, particularly in clients presenting with low mood. They should also be assessed for suicidal and homicidal ideation, two risk factors covered in more detail in the section on risk assessment.

As part of the health history, the therapist can assess for over-the-counter medications, supplements, alcohol, tobacco, or the use of caffeine. For example, Monica is a 43-year-old mother of two. She presents with low mood, difficulty sleeping, and decreased energy throughout the day. She states that she is stressed and finds it difficult to fall asleep almost every night. On average, she sleeps for about four hours until her children wake her up. When the therapist asks her about her caffeine use, she reports that due to her irritability, sleepiness during the daytime, and difficulty concentrating on tasks, she has been coping by drinking 4–6 cups of coffee daily. She has been drinking coffee until 6 or 7 p.m. some days in order to complete all of her tasks. As a result of this information, and later when appropriate, the therapist can explains that the caffeine may be a significant contributing factor in her insomnia and further exacerbate her depressive symptoms (Sperry & Binensztok, 2019a).

## Risk and Protective Factors Assessment

Risk factors are factors associated with the increased likelihood of experiencing or developing a medical or clinical condition (Masten & Garmezy, 1985). Self-harm is a key risk factor in therapy. Clients should be assessed for self-harm and suicide risk whenever they present with symptoms resulting from trauma, anxiety, or fluctuations in mood. Furthermore, because clients with chronic pain are three times as likely to report suicidal thoughts than the normal population (Tang & Crane, 2006), they must be assessed for risk. Given client reports of suicidal ideation, past suicide attempts, or history of self-harm, a more thorough assessment of risk is necessary. Client ideation may be characterized as passive or active. Passive suicidal ideation is indicated when the individual states that they would not mind if life ended but they are not keen on ending it and their ideation does not include a plan. On the other hand, active suicidal ideation includes thoughts of doing self-harm and intentionally ending one's life. Suicide assessment must include evaluating any potential plan for self-harm, the means to carry out such a plan, and history of prior attempts. Suicidal thoughts must be assessed for frequency, duration, and intensity.

In contrast to risk factors, protective factors are factors associated with decreased likelihood of experiencing or developing a medical or clinical condition (Rutter, 1987). Common protective factors are a secure attachment style, coping skills, religiosity, a social support network, and the experience of leaving and never returning to an abusive relationship.

Protective factors are related to strengths which are "psychological processes that consistently enable a person to think and act so as to yield benefits to himself or herself and society" (Rutter, 1987, p. 3). Examples of strengths include resilience, self-confidence, and self-control. Pattern Focused Therapy is a strength-based approach and emphasizes identification and incorporation of protective factors in the case conceptualization and treatment plan.

## Assessment of Goals

Assessing goals directs the treatment focus for the course of treatment. Goals are variable and contingent on presenting problems and the client's resources or motivation. However, they all share common elements. Goals must be specific. Specificity helps clients stay on track and they are more likely to attain goals that are measurable and concrete. There are three types of treatment goals: first-order change, second-order change, and third-order change. The first-order and second-order goals are set in the first session.

Goal-setting that is collaborative is the norm. Clients are more likely to attain their goals when they are actively involved in setting them. Attaining small goals results in an increase in self-efficacy, which helps to compound and work toward larger ones (Bodenheimer & Handley, 2009). Ultimately, clients respond more positively to goals that are directly applicable to their daily lives than those that are not. Clients are more likely to follow through with goals related to social relationships, daily functioning, and the regulation of their emotions (Lenzen, van Dongen, Daniels, van Bokhoven, van der Weijden, & Beurskens, 2016).

## Use of Screening Instruments

Screening instruments are used to assess the client and gain useful insight into clients' presenting concerns. These can be easily administered and scored. They can also help with determining a diagnosis. Clients are prompted to rate their symptoms by intensity and severity. The validity and reliability of screening instruments are of the utmost importance. Instruments must demonstrate that they consistently measure what is intended, and instruments must be appropriate and relevant to the presenting concern. Typically, they are administered prior to each session to aid in ongoing monitoring and tracking the client's progress. For example, the Patient Health Questionnaire-9 (PHQ-9) would be appropriate for monitoring a client presenting with depression. This instrument would provide useful details about the effectiveness of the treatment. Chapter 5 provides specific information on the PHQ-9 and other screening instruments.

## Outcomes Assessment and Progress Monitoring

Increasingly, therapists are being held accountable for the effectiveness of their treatments, progress monitoring has become increasingly predominant in the field of counseling (Meier, 2015). Persons and Mikami (2002) have estimated that treatment fails in up to 50% of cases. Therapists must remain vigilant of client progress, especially with the added challenge of effecting change in short-term therapy. Monitoring and tracking the client's progress can guide the treatment and indicate when different interventions are needed. Therapists can utilize standardized instruments prior to each session in order to assess outcomes and monitor progress. Client logs, the Mood Scale, the Subjective Units of Distress Scale (SUDS), and various screening instruments can be helpful throughout this process. Client logs can provide information, such as activity, nutrition habits, compliance with out-of-session tasks, and frequency of relaxation. Chapter 5 provides more information on outcomes assessment and progress monitoring.

## Conducting the Assessment

As discussed in prior sections, assessment in Pattern Focused Therapy tends to be focused and skillfully conducted in both mental health and integrated care and settings. A focused diagnostic evaluation can be conducted in approximately 10 minutes while other pertinent assessment information can be gathered in 15–20 minutes. Thus, it is possible to accomplish both and begin developing a therapeutic alliance in as short a time as 30 minutes.

## Implications for Treatment Planning

Accurate and appropriate assessment can largely influence effective treatment planning and quantifiable results in short-term therapy. A greater understanding of the consequences of the presenting problem and how they influence the client's functioning is crucial for determining ultra-brief interventions. For instance, a client with heightened anxiety or symptoms of panic can benefit from ultra-brief interventions, such as controlled breathing. On the other hand, a client struggling with depression and social isolation would necessitate interventions to increase their engagement and activity, such as behavioral activation.

A key factor that helps therapists select treatments is the identification of the client's pattern. This allows therapists to determine how to approach a client and predict potential barriers to treatment. For example, a client who presents with paranoia or has difficulty trusting others may demonstrate increased resistance to working with a therapist. This type of client requires validation and the perception of control within the context of therapy. These treatments are achievable through interventions, such as motivational interviewing and a patient, empathic, and collaborative demeanor from the therapist.

An adequate assessment may at times indicate that further evaluation is necessary. Risk screening or exploring for medication misuse can lead to uncovering the need for a more thorough evaluation. Assessment can also help the therapist determine if culturally sensitive treatments are needed. A thorough assessment is essential to providing highly effective intervention in short-term therapy.

## Putting It All Together

Assessment is a crucial component of the effective provision of Pattern Focused Therapy. Assessments aid in gathering information about the client's presentation and its consequences on the client's functioning. It also aids in collaboration and establishing the therapeutic relationship. In order to complete this in a 30-minute session, therapists must demonstrate interest and concern toward the client while simultaneously deciding on appropriate assessments. Every client needs to be assessed for functioning, including the problem's impact on social, personal, academic, and vocational functioning. Functional assessments are structured and consist of short, closed-ended, questions. In the case that the presentation includes one or more mental health symptoms, a diagnostic evaluation is necessary. Therapists must determine if diagnostic evaluations are necessary in other cases as well.

Identifying the client's pattern is of crucial importance. Understanding the client's pattern is necessary to plan treatment and anticipate obstacles. It is also helpful in focusing the session toward the disruption, shift, or change of the maladaptive patterns. This resulting focus can lead to increased likelihood of the client remaining compliant with medical treatment and the prevention of relapse back into behaviors that maintained or contributed to the presenting problem.

Clients presenting with mental health conditions, such as depression, post-traumatic stress, anxiety, or others do require risk assessment. Additionally, therapists must screen for risk with clients who are suffering with chronic pain, as they are higher risk for suicidal ideation. If ideation is reported, the therapist must follow up with a more thorough and complete risk assessment.

Another important assessment is the cultural assessment, which includes gathering information about cultural factors which may be salient for many clients. Therapists must remain cognizant that cultural factors influence symptom presentations and treatment planning. The client's family in different cultures can largely influence their treatment. They can function as supports or protective factors. On the other hand, they can become barriers and a detriment to ongoing treatment. In lieu of emotional display, clients from collectivistic cultures have a higher likelihood of demonstrating somatic symptoms. Therapists must maintain awareness that somatic symptoms may surface and indicate conditions, such as depression and anxiety.

Finally, clients must all be assessed for both long- and short-term treatment goals. Short-term goals are especially important as they are practical and achievable. Therapists must connect treatment goals to the client's goals while avoiding technical or jargon-like language. Goal setting should be a pragmatic and collaborative process. The progression of goals and symptoms can be tracked through progress monitoring. Assessment and progress monitoring can use standardized screening instruments.

Given the time constraints, a lot is compacted into the assessment sessions in short-term therapy. The use of screening instruments and questions can guide the focus of assessment and ensure timely completion. Therapists must establish a caring relationship through expressions of concern in their interactions and the role-induction of the assessment sessions, especially since so many of the questions are closed-ended and there are so few opportunities for reflection.

## Case Conceptualization in Pattern Focused Therapy

Case conceptualizations provide therapists with a coherent treatment strategy for planning and focusing treatment interventions in order to increase the likelihood of achieving treatment goals. While many therapists develop conceptualizations to guide their practice, not all therapists explicitly articulate these conceptualizations. There are a number of reasons for developing and articulating a case conceptualization, but the most cogent reason is that a conceptualization enables therapists to experience a sense of confidence in their work (Hill, 2005). Hill (2005) believes that this confidence is then communicated to the client, which strengthens the client's trust and the belief that the therapist has a credible plan, and that therapy can and will make a difference. In other words, an effective case conceptualization increases "clinician credibility" (Sue & Zane, 1987).

Case conceptualization is the clinical strategy for obtaining and organizing client information, identifying maladaptive patterns, focusing treatment, and anticipating challenges and roadblocks throughout treatment, as well as preparing for termination (Sperry, 2010a).

The case conceptualizations also provide a tool for therapists to coherently plan and focus treatment interventions to increase the likelihood of favorable outcomes (Eells, 2007; 2010). Case conceptualization is undoubtedly the most important competency in psychotherapy. In my graduate courses and workshops, I have used a nautical metaphor that really drives home the importance and clinical value of case conceptualization for trainees and therapists and makes sense of case conceptualization: "A therapist without a case conceptualization is like a ship's captain without radar or rudder and thus aimlessly floats about with little or no direction."

Case conceptualization is fundamental to effecting therapeutic change (Sperry, 2010a). On average, therapists are able to conceptualize cases or formulate conceptualizations after initial evaluations are finalized and the therapist has evaluated diagnostic and other pertinent information. Following the interview, these therapists review the available information and begin to consider goals and interventions for treatment. For therapist trainees, this process can be more arduous, lengthy, and may require supervisor involvement and input. However, my experience with trainees is that with formal training and effective supervision this time can be reduced to 30 minutes or less.

Interpersonal, intrapersonal, and contextual factors are key components in the process of effecting change. A case conceptualization has four components:

diagnostic, clinical, cultural, and treatment formulations. The ability to specify these components with accuracy is essential to the process of identifying and modifying an existing pattern or implementing a new adaptive pattern. This is the core of effecting therapeutic change. This section provides an overview of the four components.

## Diagnostic Formulation

The diagnostic formulation is an evaluation of the client's presentation, pattern, and precipitants (Sperry, 2010a). This component answers the question: "What happened?" The therapist describes the lived experience of the client's presenting concerns, as well as assesses cross-sectionally the client's unique pattern and circumstances.

## Presentation

The presentation is comprised of the client's response to the precipitant(s). At times referred to as the presenting problem, the presentation also describes the category and severity of the client's symptoms, level of impairment or functioning, and its history. This component also includes DSM diagnostic information and medical history.

## Precipitant

The client's precipitant conveys the triggers or stressors that resulted in the client's presenting problem or presentation. Another way of thinking about the precipitant is "the spark that ignites the fire." This component can also refer to antecedent conditions present and coinciding with the onset of the presentation. Key features of the precipitant focus on context: where did it happen?, when did it happen?, who was around?, and what was done about it?

## Pattern

As previously noted, pattern is the heart or central element of a case conceptualization. The client's pattern is a concise depiction of the client's manner of thinking, perceiving, and responding. The client's pattern is the link between the presentation and precipitant, and normally explains the situation. Adaptive patterns are characteristic of flexibility, effectiveness, and appropriateness. On the other hand, maladaptive patterns are typically rigid, inappropriate, and interpersonally ineffective. Maladaptive patterns routinely result in mental health symptoms and disorders, low levels of interpersonal functioning, and chronic discontent (Sperry & Sperry, 2012).

A client's pattern may be long-lasting or situation-specific. A situation-specific pattern that is maladaptive explains only the current and unique situation. Conversely, longitudinal patterns explain current as well as previous difficulties or circumstances. Essentially, a lifelong pattern offers a consistent explanation for the client's personality (Sperry et al., 1992; Sperry, 2005; 2010a).

Typically, the pattern is derived from a full consideration of all the other elements of a case conceptualization. However, what is known as a very brief case conceptualization (described in more detail below) can also be quickly derived from finding the link between the presentation and precipitant. The link, of course, is the pattern and the pattern will also reflect the client's personality style. Cf. Table 2.2.

## Clinical Formulation

The clinical formulation explains the client's pattern. It essentially answers: "Why did it happen?" Through the clinical formulation, the therapist appraises the predisposition and perpetuants. An explanation is also provided for the client's presenting problem and pattern (Sperry, 2010a). This central component of the case conceptualization also provides a link between diagnostic and treatment formulations.

## Predisposition

The predisposition is also known as predisposing or etiological factors. This is a summary of all factors that inform and influence the client's pattern. The therapist must examine the developmental, social, and health history for clues about potential predisposing factors. The client's biological, psychological, and social vulnerabilities must also be reflected in the predisposition. Biological vulnerabilities are comprised of current health status, medical history, medications, substance abuse, and health behaviors (e.g., smoking). This section will also include personal and family history for suicide or suicidal behaviors and self-harm, and substance abuse. Psychological vulnerabilities include interpersonal, intrapersonal, and other personal dynamics, such as intelligence and temperament. The client's personality style, maladaptive beliefs and schemas, resilience, self-concept, self-efficacy, and character structure are explored. Additionally, behavioral deficits and excesses are listed and assessed, as well as the client's self-management, problem solving, relational, communication, and conflict resolution skills. Social vulnerabilities include family dynamics. These are made up of sibling characteristics and interaction styles, educational achievement, family secrets, religious involvement, sexual experiences, and early neglect and abuse in the forms of verbal, emotional, sexual, physical, or financial. The family's level of functioning is also considered in this component. So too are family stressors, divorce, separation, job stressors, peer associations, support system, and other environmental factors. For instance, factors such as living in poverty, associating with drinking friends, or working in a hostile work environment, as well as personal or familial vulnerabilities to depression and impulsivity, would be important to identify.

## Perpetuants

Perpetuants are also called maintaining factors. These are processes that reinforce and preserve the client's maladaptive pattern. Perpetuants serve to guard the client from experiencing conflict, symptoms, or others' demands. For instance, for introverted individuals, who are sensitive to rejection, a likely pattern is to live alone or maintain solitude in order to avoid others' rejection or interpersonal demands. Given the overlap of some of these factors, it is at times difficult to differentiate with certainty the predisposing from the perpetuating factors. Common examples of perpetuants are skills deficits, unfavorable work environments, relational difficulties with others, etc. There are other times in which a client's predisposition also functions as a maintaining factor, such as in the case of avoidant personality styles. Individuals with an avoidant style are likely to isolate socially and distance themselves from others in efforts related to safety. These individuals are therefore unlikely to develop appropriate or effective social skills, as they have little to no contact with others, demonstrating the "maintenance" nature of the cycle of the client's predisposition. This can result in self-confirmation of beliefs about being unworthy, unlovable, or defective.

## Cultural Formulation

The cultural formulation can support the clinical formulation and inform the focus of treatment as well as chosen interventions. The cultural formulation is comprised of a systematic exploration of the client's cultural dynamics and factors and answers the question: "What role does culture play in the life and problems of the client?" (Sperry, 2010a). More specifically, the formulation outlines the level of acculturation, the client's cultural explanation, and the cultural identity of the client (Sperry, 2010a). The level of acculturation is the degree to which an individual can assimilate to the dominant culture. That is, to what degree can they integrate new cultural patterns into their original cultural identity and dynamics? On the other hand, the client's cultural identity is the individual's self-identified sense of belonging to a particular culture. The cultural explanation is the client's perceived reason for the presenting problem or the client's conditions, as well as the assessment of whether the client's personality or cultural dynamics are most prevailing in explaining the presentation. The cultural formulation forms the basis for anticipating cultural elements that could potentially affect the therapeutic relationship with the client; it also helps identify if culturally sensitive treatment is warranted (GAP Committee on Cultural Psychiatry, 2002; Wu & Mak, 2012).

The cultural formulation is made up of four key elements: cultural identity, level of acculturation and acculturative stress, model of cultural explanation, and the effects of cultural versus personality dynamics. A more in-depth review of these elements is provided in the second edition of *Case Conceptualization: Mastering This Competency with Ease and Confidence* (Sperry & Sperry, 2020).

## Treatment Formulation

The treatment formulation functions as a blueprint for planning interventions. Logically, it is an extension of the clinical, diagnostic, and cultural formulations. The treatment formulation essentially answers: "What can be done to change it?" This component is comprised of treatment goals, treatment focus, treatment strategy, and precise interventions. It also takes into account treatment challenges and obstacles that the therapist may foresee in achieving the formulated goals. Master therapists take into account the following treatment formulation elements.

## Treatment Goals

Treatment goals are made up of what the client hopes to achieve within their treatment. Other common designations for treatment goals are treatment targets and therapeutic objectives. Goals are the basis for the work therapists and clients collaborate on (Sperry & Sperry, 2012). For treatment goals to be clinically useful, they must be measurable, achievable, and realistic. They must also be effective and mutually agreed upon by the client and therapist. The client must adequately understand the goals, commit to them, and believe they are attainable. Goals are generally designated as short- and long-term. Short-term goals are typically comprised of first-order change: symptom reduction, increased interpersonal functioning, and return to baseline functioning. For example, for a client who is suffering from anxiety, short-term goals may be to practice grounding or breathing techniques in order to decrease their discomfort. On the other hand, long-term goals are second-order change goals. These take the form of pattern change and replacement of specific maladaptive patterns with more adaptive ones. For example, in the aforementioned example with the client suffering from anxiety, long-term, second-order, change could take the form of uncovering and modifying patterns that exacerbate or maintain the anxiety (e.g., avoidance and procrastination). In short, treatment goals become the statements of what the treatment means to accomplish.

## Treatment Focus

The treatment focus is the central therapeutic emphasis that guides and maintains the direction in treatment. It aims to replace a maladaptive pattern with a more adaptive one. Not only does the treatment focus provide direction, it also maintains the treatment's stability and focuses on change (Sperry & Sperry, 2012). Therapists who are skilled in tracking a treatment focus have higher rates of positive outcomes. Unsurprisingly, master therapists routinely and reliably maintain a productive focus in treatment.

Conversely, trainees can easily be side-tracked into unproductive discussions with clients. For instance, in a session where a client comes in without having finished their assigned out-of-session task, a novice therapist may launch into an examination of all of the reasons why the client failed to complete the task. The therapist may ask several questions about the circumstances under which the client ended up doing something else instead. Therefore, the trainee unwittingly colludes with the client, discussing reasons and excuses, rather than taking action. Typically, once the situation has been discussed and the client has exhausted their excuses, the session can shift topic and something else is discussed. Situations such as these result in the trainee following a different track, leading to the conclusion of the session with little or no change effected.

When therapists are guided by a specific approach, or therapeutic orientation, the direction has been established through specific guidelines and protocols on how to address or process the situation therapeutically. For example, the Cognitive Behavioral approach to working with a client who has failed to do their agreed homework is to focus on troublesome situations which are triggered or exacerbated by the client's maladaptive beliefs or behaviors. Thus, the therapist may recall from their conceptualization that one of the client's intermediate beliefs purports that she is worthless if she tries and fails, therefore, she does not try (Sperry & Sperry, 2012). Accordingly, it is no surprise why the client has not accomplished the assigned task. Informed by his or her conceptualization, the therapist can process the maladaptive beliefs or behavior therapeutically. Given the chosen treatment focus, the therapist may still decide to follow the directive, or choose a different path toward reaching the therapeutic goals.

## Core Therapeutic Strategy

The core therapeutic strategy is the plan of action toward focusing precise treatment interventions. Chapter 1 described the seven commonest core strategies. It was noted that the core therapeutic strategy for Pattern Focused Therapy and a number of other third-wave CBT approaches is replacement. Chapter 3 elaborates the process of pattern change or, more accurately, pattern shifting.

## Treatment Interventions

Treatment interventions are deliberately designed actions that affect the client's issue or problem in a positive manner. There are three considerations under which treatment interventions are formulated: (1) the treatment targets; (2) the client's willingness or ability to complete the intervention; and (3) the client's need for culturally sensitive treatment. Although there are many treatment interventions, those that are effective in changing the client's pattern necessarily involve interventions that operationalize a treatment strategy. Considering a metaphor for a journey, the treatment intervention is akin to choosing the right fuel grade, tires to match the terrain, as well as sufficient money, food, and water.

## Culturally Sensitive Treatment

Culturally sensitive treatment considers the following factors in the client: culture, cultural identity, and level of acculturation. The therapist's awareness of the potential cultural variables that may affect the client's treatment is their cultural sensitivity (Sperry, 2010a). Although it is a common belief in most therapists that cultural sensitivity and culturally sensitive treatment are necessary to effect favorable treatment outcomes, few therapists actually provide culturally sensitive treatment. The most prevalent reason for this state of the field is that not very many therapists have had formal training and experience in this component. The kind of training that explicitly prepares therapists to provide culturally sensitive treatment addresses factors of cultural identity and level of acculturation, knowledge, and experience with culturally sensitive treatment, and a protocol for assessing and deciding when, and if, culturally sensitive treatment must be utilized. The three types of culturally sensitive treatments are: (1) cultural interventions; (2) culturally sensitive interventions; and (3) culturally sensitive therapies.

Culturally sensitive therapies are comprised of interventions that address the cultural characteristics of diverse clients directly. That is, their beliefs, customs, attitudes, and socioeconomic status are addressed with the client deliberately. These therapies are appropriate and particularly effective with clients who have lower levels of acculturation.

Culturally sensitive interventions are conventional interventions in psychotherapy, commonly CBT, that have been adapted to particular clients and their cultural characteristics. Given their structured and educational focus, cognitive behavioral interventions are often modified to be culturally sensitive (Hays & Iwamasa, 2006); diverse clients often seem to find these interventions acceptable. For instance, given a client with lower levels of acculturation, a culturally sensitive therapist would seldom choose an intervention such as cognitive disputation or restructuring of maladaptive beliefs. On the other hand, problem solving, skills training, or a replacement approach, i.e., Pattern Focused Therapy, would be more appropriate.

## Treatment Obstacles and Outcomes

The success of the treatment plan and the achievement of the desired outcomes can be limited, depending on a number of factors. These include the therapist's ability to anticipate obstacles and treatment challenges. Factors that may impede the therapeutic progress may originate in the client, in the practitioner, or the client-practitioner fit. Otherwise, impeding factors can be related to the therapeutic process itself. A crucial component to achieving treatment success is anticipating treatment obstacles and challenges to implementing the plan for treatment. Predicting these challenges and obstacles is the test of an effective case conceptualization. When effectively conceptualized, these can predict obstacles such as resistance, ambivalence, transference, and issues which may impede the maintenance of successful effects or treatment termination (Sperry, 2010a).

## Explanatory and Predictive Power of a Case Conceptualization

There are two criteria that evaluate the adequacy and precision of a case conceptualization. These criteria are explanatory power and predictive power. High levels of explanatory power and predictive power are the characteristics of highly effective case conceptualizations.

- *Explanatory power*: The value of a case conceptualization is contingent on the degree to which it explains, accurately and compellingly, the client's maladaptive pattern, which is referred to as its "explanatory power" (Sperry & Sperry, 2012). Case conceptualizations have variable gradations of explanatory power, ranging from low to very high. When trainees are asked at case conferences: "How compelling is this case conceptualization toward answering the 'Why?' question?" and the response is "Not very compelling," it usually suggests that predisposing factors, risk and protective factors, or contextual elements might need revision in order to raise explanatory power. In my experience as a clinical supervisor and case consultant, I've found that increasing the accuracy of the maladaptive pattern factors often boosts explanatory power.
- *Predictive power*: Treatment outcomes are likely to increase when a compelling explanation provides a focused and tailored treatment plan to inform the process of therapy for the individual client. The supreme test of an effective case conceptualization is its utility in predicting obstacles and facilitators throughout the span of the therapy, which is referred to as its "predictive

power" (Sperry & Sperry, 2012). Highly predictive case conceptualizations allow the therapist to more suitably anticipate treatment obstacles. Additionally, highly predictive case conceptualizations increase the accuracy of the client's prognosis for treatment. A prognosis is an estimation of how long the therapeutic outcomes and duration of treatment will be, which are tailored to the client and context.

## Developing Clinically Useful Case Conceptualizations

Initially, developing an effective and clinically useful case conceptualization may seem like a forbidding and drawn-out process. However, this is not necessarily the case. The following sections will present a straightforward method for identifying the key elements and structure of effective case conceptualizations. The components will seamlessly fall into place once the structure is evident.

This method of case conceptualization centers on patterns (Sperry & Sperry, 2012). As previously emphasized, the ability to identify patterns with high levels of precision is essential to the process of case conceptualization. Not surprisingly, master therapists are experts in identifying patterns effortlessly and expeditiously.

A useful way to think about the case conceptualization process is as a bridge between assessment and treatment. The process of case conceptualization begins with identifying and assessing the maladaptive pattern(s). The adaptive pattern is derivative, and typically the inverse of the maladaptive pattern. Then, from the adaptive pattern, the therapist derives the goals and focus of the treatment, which informs the tailored treatment interventions to be implemented. Consistently throughout this book, treatment goals are demarcated between first-order and second-order change goals. The final component is identifying foreseeable challenges and obstacles to implementing the desired change. That, in essence, comprises the structure of case conceptualization. In discussing or observing the work of master therapists, this structure surfaced as the implicit manner in their deliberation about client issues and conceptualization of cases.

This structure also serves as the basic outline for writing case conceptualization statements. Case conceptualizations that boast high explanatory and predictive power can be the result of answering each of eight questions. This statement can be reduced to eight sentences, one for each of the eight answers, resulting in a significantly brief process. However, it can also be considerably longer as therapists may choose to elaborate on certain features.

Throughout my experience in training programs and seminars, if therapists and therapists in training are encouraged to address and answer the following eight questions, they can immediately see progress in developing useful case conceptualizations and develop their confidence in their ability to do so. In the following section, the questions will be provided and illustrated using the case of Aimee.

1. *What is the client's presentation and what precipitates it?* This question seeks to derive the "presentation" and "precipitant" elements. The beginning of the process involves seeking information in order to satisfy both, as well as the link between the two. For example, Aimee presents with depression, fatigue, insomnia, anger at her mother, and worries about her children and ex-husband. The precipitants for this case include demands to care for others as well as the anticipatory anxiety due to her ex-husband's imminent release from prison.

2. *What is the client's basic movement and what is its purpose?* The movement describes the individual's overarching interpersonal strategy (i.e., how they relate to others). The three basic types of movement are: (a) moving toward others; (b) moving away from others; and (c) moving against others. A fourth type is a combination of simultaneous movements, referred to as ambivalent (e.g., toward *and* against, toward *and* away). For example, Aimee's movement was toward others for the purpose of meeting others' needs, which was consistent with her personality structure (dependent personality style). However, as therapy progressed, a secondary movement surfaced and became increasingly evident. Aimee also moved against others and herself to satisfy needs of perfection. Aimee followed a pattern of meeting others' needs and behaving in a pleasing manner, and it was also important to her to do her best and thereafter criticize herself if she did not achieve perfection.

3. *What is the maladaptive pattern, based on the individual's movement and purpose?* This question addresses the "pattern-maladaptive" element of the case conceptualization and it is derivative of the movement and purpose. For example, Aimee's maladaptive pattern is that she focuses on meeting others' needs while ignoring her own needs. This pattern is also supported by a secondary perfectionistic pattern.

4. *What is the origin of the maladaptive pattern?* This question seeks to answer the element "predisposition" or "predisposing factors." As previously emphasized, a thorough and complete "predisposition" element supports and expands the explanatory power of the case conceptualization. For Aimee, the value of pleasing others and meeting their needs is that she will feel meaningful and worthy. This pattern is likely rooted in her upbringing, as her parents were self-centered, critical, overly demanding, and emotionally neglectful; she also has skills deficits in assertiveness and self-care, which also inform the pattern. Additionally, Aimee has beliefs about herself as nice but deficient, and she views the world as demanding, conditional, and critical. These dynamics influenced the development of her pleasing and perfectionistic pattern.

5. *What is a clinically appropriate adaptive pattern?* The appropriate adaptive pattern is the "treatment pattern" element of the case conceptualization, which is derived from the maladaptive pattern element. The adaptive pattern is

essentially the mirror opposite of the maladaptive version. For example, the opposite of Aimee's meeting others' needs while ignoring her own, is to meet others' needs while maintaining adequate care and consideration for her own needs. In addition, the next part of her maladaptive pattern is over-conscientiousness, for which the mirror opposite is reasonable conscientiousness. A combination of the two results in a statement such as: meets others' needs and also meets her own needs in a reasonably conscientious manner.

6   *What needs to happen to shift from the maladaptive pattern to the adaptive pattern?* To adequately answer this question, structural factors need to be considered, beyond common therapeutic factors, such as empathic responding and support. The client's personality and contextual dynamics must be considered. In the case of Aimee, the structural factors that must be modified are her core beliefs and schemas, as well as addressing skill deficits. Essentially, her improvement necessitates a shift toward becoming more empowered, confident, assertive, and less perfectionistic. She must behave in ways that allow engagement of self-care without guilt.

7   *What are clinically appropriate first-order change and second-order change goals?* The "treatment goals" and "treatment focus" elements of the case conceptualization are addressed with this question. These questions expand upon the structural components defined in the preceding question. They operationalize targets, the "treatment intervention" element of case conceptualization, made up of tailored goals. For Aimee, first-order goals include decreasing symptoms, such as depression, fatigue, and insomnia. Second-order goals are to increase her self-efficacy and empowerment by shifting core beliefs as well as increasing assertiveness. Also, the decrease of her perfectionistic striving falls into her second-order goals.

8   *What obstacles and facilitators are likely to be encountered in attempting to achieve these goals?* This question addresses the "treatment obstacles and outcomes" element of the case conceptualization. As previously noted, the supreme test of a case conceptualization is whether it can accurately predict therapeutic obstacles and outcomes. In the case of Aimee, due to her highly critical and demanding patterns, the therapist must be mindful of making comments that could potentially activate transference if misinterpreted as demanding or disparaging. It also makes it increasingly possible that the client will cling and make for a difficult termination of therapy, given her dependent personality style. Table 2.4 lists likely obstacles and challenges for several personality styles (Sperry & Carlson, 2014). This is a non-exhaustive list of examples of challenges or obstacles to the therapeutic process in this case. On the other hand, given that she previously had confronted her abusive husband, the therapist may note that the client has the ability to be assertive and can confront her mother, accordingly. These denote some of the potential facilitators for this case.

*Table 2.4* Anticipated treatment challenges

| Treatment pattern | Treatment challenge |
| --- | --- |
| *Avoidant Personality* | |
| Engagement | Premature termination; "testing" behavior, e.g., canceling appointments; fear of being criticized; difficulty with self-disclosure |
| Transference | Testing; overdependence |
| Countertransference | Frustration and helplessness; unrealistic treatment expectations |
| Pattern triggers | Close relationships and public appearance |
| Maintenance | Homework avoidance |
| Termination | Anxiety and ambivalence about termination |
| *Borderline Personality* | |
| Engagement | Client's difficulty viewing therapist as helpful/collaborative |
| Transference | Dependency, merger fantasy |
| Countertransference | Anger, rescue fantasies |
| Pattern triggers | Personal goals, close relations |
| Maintenance | Focus on feeling good vs. changing |
| Termination | Abandonment fears, relapse proneness |
| *Dependent Personality* | |
| Engagement | Silent demand for therapist to make decisions and solve their problems; comply rather than collaborate |
| Transference | Clinging resistance; multiple requests; idealize therapist |
| Countertransference | Rescue fantasies; directive role; failure to confront limited progress |
| Pattern triggers | Demands for self-reliance and/or being alone |
| Maintenance | Resist increasing independence, assertiveness |
| Termination | Fear of termination/abandonment with paradoxical worsening of progress |
| *Narcissistic Personality* | |
| Engagement | Demanding mirroring; easily narcissistically wounded |
| Transference | Idealizing to devaluating; projective identification |
| Countertransference | Not recognizing one's own narcissistic needs; boredom; feeling controlled, angry, hurt, impotent |
| Pattern trigger | Evaluation of self |
| Maintenance | Difficulty relinquishing specialness, entitlement |
| Termination | Premature termination |
| *Histrionic Personality* | |
| Engagement | Quickly develops therapeutic alliance; believes therapist can understand them intuitively |
| Transference | Fantasy of being rescued; erotic or eroticized transference |

Pattern 41

*Table 2.4* (Cont.)

| Treatment pattern | Treatment challenge |
| --- | --- |
| Countertransference | Messiah/rescue role; aloofness, anxiety; exploitation |
| Pattern triggers | Opposite sex relationships |
| Maintenance | Resist being ordinary |
| Termination | Fantasies of a continuing relationship; fear of termination |
| *Obsessive Compulsive Personality* | |
| Engagement | Appears eager to comply in and between sessions |
| Transference | Obsessive rambling and lists; discounting therapist |
| Countertransference | Disengagement; isolated affect; anger; collude with client's defenses |
| Pattern triggers | Authority issues; unstructured situations; close relationships |
| Maintenance | Resists getting in touch with "soft" feelings |
| Termination | Ambivalence about termination |

## Very Brief Case Conceptualizations

Therapists can greatly benefit from formulating a very brief, albeit provisional, case conceptualization. In contrast to a full-scale case conceptualization, a very brief, pattern-based case conceptualization can emerge in the first 10 minutes of the first meeting with a client.

The necessary components of such a brief, pattern-based case conceptualization are the client's presenting problem, the precipitant for the presenting problem, the client's pattern, psychological predisposition, perpetuants, and treatment plan. For example, David presents with a depressed mood (presentation) after unfortunate events in his business that resulted in a substantial loss of capital (precipitant). Throughout his life, David has demonstrated a perfectionistic pattern, holding himself to extremely high standards and beating himself up for any shortcomings, real or perceived pattern (plan). Background information and social history revealed that David's mother suffered from depression (biological predisposition). He demonstrates an obsessive-compulsive personality style and holds the belief that he can only rely on himself (psychological predisposition). Throughout childhood, David felt that his peers did not understand him and therefore he spent most of his time alone (social predisposition). He currently has few friends and maintains extremely high standards for himself and others, reinforcing his view of others and self (perpetuants). An effective treatment plan for David would indicate behavioral activation interventions and a decrease in his perfectionistic pattern.

## Conclusion

Pattern is both a critical component of assessment and the heart of the case conceptualization, particularly in Pattern Focused Therapy. This chapter described the key components of assessment with an emphasis on pattern identification. It also detailed the elements of a case conceptualization including the very brief, pattern-based case conceptualization. Clearly, the takeaway message from this chapter is that pattern is the central concept in all of Pattern Focused Therapy.

## References

American Psychiatric Association. (2013). *Diagnostic and statistical manual of mental disorders*, 5th ed. Alexandria, VA: American Psychiatric Press.

Beitman, B., & Yue, D. (1999). *Learning psychotherapy*. New York, NY: Norton.

Bodenheimer, T., & Handley, M. A. (2009). Goal-setting for behavior change in primary care: An exploration and status report. *Patient Education and Counseling*, 76(2), 174–180.

Eells, T. (2010). The unfolding case formulation: The interplay of description and inference. *Pragmatic Case Studies in Psychotherapy*, 6(4), 225–254.

Frances, A. (2013). *Essentials of psychiatric diagnosis: Responding to the challenge of DSM-5*. New York, NY: Guilford Press.

GAP Committee on Cultural Psychiatry (2002). *Cultural assessment in clinical psychiatry*. Washington, DC: American Psychiatric Press.

Hays, P. A., & Iwamasa, G. Y. (2006). *Culturally responsive cognitive-behavioral therapy*. Washington, DC: American Psychological Association.

Hill, C. E. (2005). Therapist techniques, client involvement, and the therapeutic relationship: Inextricably intertwined in the therapy process. *Psychotherapy: Theory, Research, Practice, Training*, 42(4), 431–442.

Kendjelic, E. M., & Eells, T. D. (2007). Generic psychotherapy case formulation training improves formulation quality. *Psychotherapy: Theory, Research, Practice, Training*, 44(1), 66.

Lenzen, S. A., van Dongen, J. J., Daniels, R., van Bokhoven, M. A., van der Weijden, T., & Beurskens, A. (2016). What does it take to set goals for self-management in primary care? A qualitative study. *Family Practice*, 33(6), 698–703.

Livesley, W. J. (2003). *Practical management of personality disorder*. New York, NY: Guilford Press.

Masten, A. S., & Garmezy, N. (1985). Risk, vulnerability, and protective factors in developmental psychopathology. In B. B. Lahey & A. E. Kazdin (Eds.), *Advances in clinical child psychology* (pp. 1–52). New York, NY: Plenum Press.

McCullough, M. E., & Snyder, C. R. (2000). Classical sources of human strength: Revisiting an old home and building a new one. *Journal of Social and Clinical Psychology*, 19(1), 1–10.

Meier, S. T. (2015). *Incorporating progress monitoring and outcome assessment into counseling and psychotherapy: A primer*. New York, NY: Oxford University Press.

Persons, J. B., & Mikami, A. Y. (2002). Strategies for handling treatment failure successfully. *Psychotherapy: Theory/Research/Practice/Training*, 39, 139–151.

Rutter, M. (1987). Psychosocial resilience and protective mechanisms. *American Journal of Orthopsychiatry*, 57(3), 316–331.

Sperry, J., & Sperry, L. (2018). *Cognitive behavior therapy in professional counseling practice*. New York, NY: Routledge.

Sperry, L. (1989). Integrative case formulations: What they are and how to write them. *Individual Psychology*, *45*(4), 500–508.

Sperry, L. (2005). Case conceptualization: A strategy for incorporating individual, couple, and family dynamics in the treatment process. *American Journal of Family Therapy*, *33*, 353–364.

Sperry, L. (2006). *Cognitive behavior therapy of DSM-IV-TR personality disorders*, 2nd ed. New York, NY: Routledge.

Sperry, L. (2010a). *Highly effective therapy: Developing essential clinical competencies in counseling and psychotherapy*. New York, NY: Routledge.

Sperry, L. (2010b). *Core competencies in counseling and psychotherapy: Becoming a highly competent and effective therapist*. New York, NY: Routledge.

Sperry, L. (2014). *Behavioral health: Integrating individual and family interventions in the treatment of medical conditions*. New York, NY: Routledge.

Sperry, L., & Binensztok, V. (2019a). *Ultra-brief cognitive behavioral interventions: The cutting-edge of mental health and integrated care practice*. New York, NY: Routledge.

Sperry, L., & Binensztok, V. (2019b). *Learning and practicing Adlerian therapy*. San Diego, CA: Cognella.

Sperry, L., Blackwell, B., Gudeman, J., & Faulkner, L. (1992). *Psychiatric case formulations*. Washington, DC: American Psychiatric Press.

Sperry, L., Brill, P., Howard, K., & Grissom, G. (1996). *Treatment outcomes in psychotherapy and psychiatric interventions*. New York, NY: Brunner/Mazel.

Sperry, L., & Carlson, J. (2014). *How master therapists work: Effecting change from the first through the last session and beyond*. New York, NY: Routledge.

Sperry, L., & Sperry, J. (2012). *Case conceptualization: Mastering this competency with ease and confidence*. New York, NY: Routledge.

Sperry, L., & Sperry, J. (2020). *Case conceptualization: Mastering this competency with ease and confidence*. 2nd ed. New York, NY: Routledge.

Sue, S., & Zane, N. (1987). The role of culture and cultural techniques in psychotherapy: A critique and reformulation. *American Psychologist*, *42*(1), 37–45.

Tang, N. K., & Crane, C. (2006, May). Suicidality in chronic pain: A review of the prevalence, risk factors, and psychological links. *Psychological Medicine*, *36*(5), 575–586.

Wu, E., & Mak, W. (2012). Acculturation process and distress: Mediating roles of sociocultural adaptation and acculturative stress. *Counseling Psychologist*, *40*, 66–92.

Chapter 3

# Practicing Pattern Focused Therapy

So far, the case has been made for the clinical value of this third-wave Cognitive Behavioral Therapy (CBT) approach in Chapter 1 and the centrality of pattern. The importance of a full and integrative assessment and case conceptualization in Pattern Focused Therapy were highlighted in Chapter 2. This chapter describes the origins, premises, and components of Pattern Focused Therapy. Next, its core therapeutic strategy is discussed. This is followed by a description of the most common interventions and techniques of Pattern Focused Therapy. Then, the characteristic structure to therapeutic process as well as protocol for a typical session is described. Finally, a case example illustrates the above discussion.

## Origins and Premises of Pattern Focused Therapy

This section describes the origins, premises, and components of Pattern Focused Therapy.

### Origins

Pattern-Focused Therapy was developed by Len Sperry (Sperry, 2016). It is derived from four sources: (1) the pattern focus in Biopsychosocial Therapy; (2) the processing format of Cognitive Behavioral Analysis System of Psychotherapy (CBASP); (3) specific questions from Motivational Interviewing; and (4) outcomes research and progress monitoring. Biopsychosocial Therapy is an integrative approach that incorporates biological, psychological, and socio-cultural factors in planning and implementing psychological treatment. It was developed to assist individuals, couples, and families with mental health and health care concerns. It emphasizes pattern identification, pattern change, and pattern maintenance (Sperry, 1988; 2000; 2006),

The Cognitive Behavioral Analysis System of Psychotherapy is a psychotherapy approach that focuses on identifying and changing hurtful thoughts and behaviors into more helpful ones (McCullough, 2000; McCullough, Schramm, & Penberthy,

2014). CBASP is designated as an empirically supported treatment by the Society of Clinical Psychology of the American Psychological Association.

Motivational Interviewing (MI) is a therapeutic strategy for helping individuals discover and resolve their ambivalence to change (Miller & Rollnick, 2002). While there are a number of specific interventions to increase a client's readiness for change, the basic premise of this approach and method is to invite the client's input and involvement. The specific contribution of MI is regularly asking permission of clients to proceed in the treatment process and to identify the importance of a specific change effort in their life and the confidence they have to achieve it.

Psychotherapy outcomes research assesses and evaluates the effectiveness of therapy and the mechanisms of change associated with treatments. It also involves monitoring the treatment progress and the therapeutic over the course of therapy (Sperry, Brill, Howard, & Grissom, 1996; Sperry 2010; Meier, 2015). Outcomes research is an integral part of identifying the evidence base for an approach, and I have been engaged in outcomes research throughout my professional career.

## *Premises*

Pattern Focused Therapy is based on five premises. The first premise is that individuals unwittingly develop a self-perpetuating, maladaptive pattern of functioning and relating to others. Subsequently, this pattern underlies a client's presenting issues. The second premise is that pattern change, i.e., replacement or shifting to a more adaptive pattern, is a necessary component of evidence-based practice. The third premise is that effective treatment involves a change process in which the client and therapist collaborate to identify the maladaptive pattern, break it, and replace it with a more adaptive pattern. At least two outcomes have been observed to result from this change process: increased wellbeing as well as the resolution of the client's presenting issue (Sperry & Sperry, 2012). The fourth premise is that the process of replacing non-productive thinking and behaviors with more adaptive or productive ones can more quickly lead to effective therapeutic change. This contrasts with therapeutic approaches that attempt to directly restructure or challenge cognitions, i.e., Cognitive Therapy, or to directly modify behavior, i.e., Behavior Therapy. Finally, the fifth premise is that therapy that incorporates the clients' clinically relevant strengths and protective factors can result in both a positive therapeutic alliance and positive treatment outcomes.

## Components of Pattern Focused Therapy

Components refers to the core elements and active ingredients of a therapeutic approach that can effect change. Pattern Focused Therapy involves four such components:

1	Pattern focused case conceptualization
2	Query Sequence
3	Brief therapeutic interventions
4	Outcomes assessment, progress monitoring, and incorporation of feedback

## *1. Pattern-Focused Case Conceptualization*

Case conceptualization is the first component of Pattern Focused Therapy. As previously stated, a Pattern Focused case conceptualization is the clinical strategy for obtaining and organizing client information, identifying maladaptive patterns, focusing treatment, and anticipating challenges and roadblocks throughout treatment, as well as preparing for termination (Sperry, 2010). It is, without question, the most important competency in psychotherapy and particularly in Pattern Focused Therapy. As previously noted, identifying and then shifting or replacing a maladaptive pattern with a more adaptive one is the heart of Pattern Focused Therapy. An important element of such conceptualizations is that they are attentive to clients' strengths and protective factors.

The process for developing a Pattern Focused case conceptualization was described in Chapter 2. As already stated, pattern is the heart of such a case conceptualization. This is not simply a slogan, but a practical clinical reality, because, once identified, this pattern serves as the therapeutic focus and drives treatment decisions. While such a written case conceptualization statement may be 200–300 or more words, the few words that specify the pattern become like a mantra or touchstone for the course of therapy. For example, if a client's maladaptive pattern is stated concisely as "avoid and be safe," these four words or even two words, "avoidance pattern," guide the therapy process as both client and therapist collaborate to replace or shift from the maladaptive pattern to a more adaptive one. This point will be repeatedly made and illustrated throughout this book.

### *Pattern Identification*

Accurate identification is essential to effecting therapeutic change in Pattern Focused Therapy. It is critical to note that a maladaptive pattern and an adaptive pattern rather consistently reflect an individual's core personality dynamics (Sperry, 2010). Accordingly, it can be helpful for therapist to identify an individual's basic personality style or personality disorder. Then, the therapist can develop hypotheses about corresponding maladaptive patterns. It is important to specify a corresponding adaptive pattern since this will be reflected in the second-order treatment goal. Table 2.2 in Chapter 2 is a useful guide to pattern identification. It summarizes the most common maladaptive and adaptive patterns based on personality dynamics.

## Pattern Shifting

Pattern shifting by means of the Query Sequence is the core therapeutic strategy in Pattern Focused Therapy. Shifting from a maladaptive to a more adaptive pattern indicates that second-order change has occurred (Sperry & Binensztok, 2019). Other CBT approaches which focus primarily on symptoms are not likely to achieve pattern shifting or personality change. Instead, they can achieve symptoms resolution, or personal or relationship stabilization, which are first-order change goals (Fraser & Solovey, 2007).

## 2. Query Sequence

The Query Sequence is the second component of Pattern Focused Therapy. It reflects the core therapeutic strategy of replacement in Pattern Focused Therapy. It is the unique change intervention of Pattern Focused Therapy. This questioning sequence was adapted from the Cognitive Behavioral Analysis System of Psychotherapy. Recognized as an evidence-based or empirically supported treatment by the American Psychological Association (APA, 2018), CBASP was developed by James P. McCullough for the treatment of chronic depression (McCullough, 2000).

The core therapeutic strategy of CBASP is also replacement. As such, it focuses on identifying and replacing hurtful thoughts and behaviors with more helpful ones. It consists of two phases: the situation analysis phase with six steps, and the remediation phase with two additional steps (McCullough, Schramm, & Pemberthy, 2014). The genius of this approach is that it is relatively easy to learn and apply to a wide variety of difficult client presentations. In the process of analyzing a specific situation together with their therapist, clients can "replace" problematic and hurtful thoughts and behaviors with more helpful ones. This often occurs more quickly than if the therapeutic core strategy was to cognitively restructure problematic thoughts or to modify problematic behaviors. As the expectation and demand for therapy become shorter and time-limited, there is considerable value in replacement approaches like CBASP.

To increase its teachability and clinical utility, the CBASP therapeutic process was refashioned to a standardized nine steps of a questioning sequence which I first published in 2005 (Sperry, 2005) and became a key component of Pattern Focused Therapy. Later, in order to optimize outcomes and clinical success, a tenth step was added. The questioning sequence includes two key questions for rating and scaling therapeutic progress (Sperry, 2016; Sperry, & Binensztok, 2018). The first assesses the "importance" of a making a specific change, while the second assesses the client's degree of "importance" and "confidence" in achieving that change. Both are derived from Motivational Interviewing (Miller & Rollnick, 2013).

What makes the Query Sequence unique from CBASP is the singular focus on pattern and pattern shifting. In fact, the entire purpose of therapeutically processing any concern or issue that arises in therapy is the influence of the client's maladaptive pattern. This is designated as Query-P in which the therapist brings that maladaptive pattern into play for both client and therapist to process.

## Query Sequence in Action

Table 3.1 presents the ten-plus queries in the Query Sequence. It focuses on analyzing and processing problematic situations. Invariably these situations reflect the client's maladaptive pattern.

Since the Query Sequence is the main therapeutic strategy for shifting from a maladaptive to an adaptive pattern, it is the main intervention for achieving second-order change (Fraser & Solovey, 2007). In this therapeutic processing, clients achieve their desired or expected outcomes because they replace a hurtful thought or behavior with a more helpful one. At the same time they incrementally replace their maladaptive pattern with a more adaptive one. As therapy progresses, clients come to understand how their thoughts and behaviors reflect their maladaptive pattern and underlie their presenting problem. This is what the first premise of Pattern Focused Therapy means. The second premise is that as patterns shift to more healthy ones, the presenting problem recedes.

## 3. Brief Therapeutic Interventions

The third component of Pattern Focused Therapy is brief therapeutic interventions. While the Query Sequence is the main therapeutic strategy for achieving second-order change, the use of brief therapeutic interventions, most with CBT roots, are the primary strategy for achieving symptom reduction or first-order change (Fraser & Solovey, 2007). Chapter 4 describes 12 ultra-brief interventions that are short enough to be introduced, learned, and practiced easily within a 30-minute session and then assigned as homework to be practiced between sessions.

## 4. Outcome Assessment, Progress Monitoring, and Incorporation of Feedback

The fourth component of Pattern Focused Therapy is the use of outcomes assessment measures to continuously monitor progress and incorporate client feedback into the therapy process throughout therapy. The most common of these measures are the Patient Health Questionnaire-9 (PHQ-9), the Outcomes Questionnaire (OQ-45), the Outcome Rating Scale (ORS), and the Session Rating

*Table 3.1* Query Sequence in Pattern Focused Therapy

| | |
|---|---|
| Query P | We've been talking about your _____ pattern and the need to shift to a more adaptive one. This pattern is likely reflected in daily situations. Can we talk about one of those situations? |
| Query 1 | Please describe what happened. [elicit the situation, making sure the client's narrative of the situation has a coherent beginning, middle, and ending] |
| Query 2 | What was your interpretation [your thoughts] of the situation? |
| Query 3 | What were your behaviors? [what did you say? what did you do?] |
| Query 4 | What did you want to get out of the situation? [Desired Outcome] |
| Query 5 | What actually happened [Actual Outcome] |
| Query 6 | Did you get the outcome you wanted? |
| Query 7 | Would you like to look at this situation together with me to review what happened and how it might have turned out differently? |
| Query 8 | Did your first [second, etc.] interpretation help or hurt you in getting what you wanted? <br><br>THEN: What alternative interpretation would have helped you get what you wanted? [then follow up with] So, how will that new interpretation get what you want? |
| Query 9 | How did your first [second, etc.] behavior help or hurt you in getting what you wanted? <br><br>THEN: What alternative behavior [interpretation] would have helped you get what you wanted? [then follow up with] So, how will that new behavior get what you want? <br>AND/OR: Were your expectations [desired outcome] realistic? <br>AND/OR: How can your expectations [desired outcome] be modified to be more realistic? |
| Query 10–1 | How <u>important</u> is it for you to _____ change your maladaptive pattern)? On a scale from 0–10, where 0 is not at all important, and 10 is extremely important, where would you say you are? |
| Query 10–2 | How <u>confident</u> are you that if you decided to _____, you could do it? On that 0–10 scale (not confident to extremely confident) where would you say you are? |

Scale (SRS). Client progress is also monitored using any of these. These and other self-report measures are used in the case of Jerrod described in Chapter 6, Chapter 7, and Chapter 8. Chapter 5 provides an extended discussion of the necessity and clinical value of this form of assessment and monitoring. It also details 15 commonly used measures.

## Practicing Pattern Focused Therapy

Pattern Focused Therapy begins with establishing a collaborative relationship and educating the client in the basic premises of this approach. Central to the assessment and case conceptualization process is the identification of the maladaptive pattern, and then planning treatment that focuses on pattern shifting or change. Other key factors considered in planning treatment are severity, skill deficits, motivation and readiness for change, and strengths and protective factors. A basic therapeutic strategy in the change process is to analyze problematic situations reported by clients in terms of their maladaptive pattern. Inevitably, clients report that their thoughts and behaviors were hurtful to them and that they did not achieve their expected outcome. However, as a result of shifting to a more adaptive pattern, they can now achieve their expected outcome.

A hallmark of third-wave approaches is sensitivity to the therapeutic relationship. Pattern Focused Therapy places a high value on the development and maintenance of an effective and growing therapeutic relationship. Accordingly, near the end of each session in this approach, the client rates the therapeutic relationship on the Session Rating Scale (SRS). The results are shared, compared to previous session ratings, and counselor and client discuss how their working together might be improved (Sperry, 2016).

The therapy process and sequence can be summarized as:

1  The identification of presentation, precipitant, and predisposition, which include individual dynamics, family or system dynamics, values, strengths, and protective factors.
2  A functional assessment and pattern identification.
3  A Pattern Focused case conceptualization that emphasizes and incorporates pattern and protective factors and strengths.
4  With the Query Sequence and brief therapeutic interventions, a more adaptive pattern emerges, and symptoms are reduced and eliminated.
5  Outcomes are assessed and monitored, and feedback incorporated into the therapy process.
6  Finally, as clients continue to make and maintain treatment gains, they are encouraged to become their own therapists, i.e., third order change (Fraser & Solovey, 2007) and preparation for termination ensues.

## *A Typical Session in Pattern Focused Therapy*

Here is a four-step preview of how the Pattern Focused Therapy process typically develops and proceeds. The four steps are:

1  For every session, but particularly in the early meetings, a strong therapeutic relationship is established and maintained, utilizing various relationship-enhancing strategies common among third-wave approaches, including "seeking client permission" and related MI questions.
2  Simultaneously, each session—after the first one—begins with a brief review of progress on treatment goals since the last session with the Session Rating

Scale (SRS). Client's ratings are discussed in relation to the client's maladaptive pattern and the goal of shifting to a more adaptive pattern.

3   The Query Sequence is used to analyze the client's behaviors and interpretations in a specific problematic situation, in terms of whether they help or hurt the clients in achieving his/her desired outcome. Typically, in a 30-minute session, one problematic situation can be processed whereas two might be processed in a 45-minute session. Brief therapeutic interventions are incorporated that target symptoms for reduction.

4   Near the end of the session, mutually agreed upon between-session activities (homework) are set. Then, the MI "importance" and "confidence" questions and answers are processed. The effectiveness of the therapeutic relationship in that session is assessed with the Session Rating Scale (SRS), and processed for how the counselor could be more responsive.

## Evidence-Based Practices and Pattern Focused Therapy

Evidence-based practice and evidence-based approaches are increasingly impacting psychotherapy practice. Not so long ago, it was common for therapists to make treatment decisions based on the therapeutic orientation they espoused and their experience. Less often, their decisions were based on scientific evidence that the treatment they provided would be safe, effective, and ethical. Today, because of the increasing requirement for accountability, there has been a shift to the concept of evidence-based practice. As described, evidence-based practice is a process of inquiry to help therapists and their clients make key decisions about treatment. It is a strategy for deciding which interventions to provide, based on the following factors: research evidence, clinician experience and expertise, client preferences and values, plus professional ethics, situational circumstances, and the availability of resources (Sackett, et al., 1996).

Evidence-based practice differs from an evidence-based approach or intervention, which is also known as "empirically supported treatment" (APA Presidential Task Force on Evidence-Based Practice, 2006; American Psychological Association, 2018). That means that one can provide an empirically supported treatment without considering the factors of client values and clinician expertise. Another way of saying this is that engaging in evidence-based practice is more encompassing and demanding than simply employing an evidence-based approach or intervention. More specifically, it means that a therapist may engage in evidence-based practice with or without employing an evidence-based approach or intervention.

Pattern Focused Therapy is not yet listed by Division 12 of the American Psychological Association (2018) as one of its 80 empirically supported treatments. However, a key component of Pattern Focused Therapy, CBASP, is recognized as an empirically supported treatment by the American Psychological Association. Accordingly, Pattern Focused Therapy can be considered an evidence-informed therapy approach because it incorporates this key component.

Finally, a therapist or trainee can confidently engage in the evidence-based practice of Pattern Focused Therapy, assuming that the therapist has sufficient expertise to provide a treatment approach which is supported by sufficient research evidence. At this point in time, and because a key component of it is empirically supported, Pattern Focused Therapy appears to have more value in evidence-based practice than many conventional therapy approaches.

## Case Illustration: Pattern Focused Therapy Session

This case illustrates the practice of Pattern Focused Therapy. Specifically, it shows how the four components of this approach are easily and seamlessly incorporated in the fourth session of a relatively brief six-session treatment.

### Background Information

Eliana is a 21-year-old, single, Hispanic female who sought therapy at her university counseling center which had a policy of initially offering up to six sessions of individual therapy that could be extended if indicated.

Eliana presented as mildly to moderately depressed and socially isolative during the initial assessment. Symptoms included low mood, difficulty falling asleep and staying asleep, fatigue, and difficulty concentrating. As a result, she took a brief leave of absence from coursework midway through the second semester of her junior year and moved out of her dorm and back to her parents' home. Because she misses the DSM-5 diagnosis of Major Depressive Disorder by one criterion, a diagnosis of Other Specified Depressive Disorder with mild anxious distress is given. Similarly, because she was one criterion short of the diagnosis of Avoidant Personality Disorder, Avoidant Personality Style was noted. Her PHQ-9 score at the time of this evaluation was 10, which is on the border of mild and moderate depression.

### Case Conceptualization

Eliana reports a lifelong history of social isolation, and she appears to move away from others to be safe and avoid rejection and criticism. This avoidant pattern can be understand in light of deficits in relational and coping skills and her history of being teased by her older brother and kids in her neighborhood and school. She views herself as vulnerable and inadequate, while viewing others as critical, demanding, hurtful, and distrustful. As a result, she avoids close relationships and so reduces her vulnerability to rejection. She also has some notable protective factors and strengths: she has described a secure attachment to her grandmother, and she is intelligent, insightful, articulate, consistently maintained an A average in college courses until the semester she dropped out and is reasonably motivated to change.

She identifies as Mexican American and is highly acculturated with no indication of acculturative stress. She believes that the root of her issues is because of her inability to use relational skills in interpersonal relationships and her limited healthy coping skills. Both personality and cultural factors appear to be operative and cultural dynamics are not likely to negatively impact the therapeutic relationship, given that the therapist is a supportive female. Treatment progress does not appear to be dependent on cultural factors, nor are culturally sensitive interventions indicated at this time.

Given her relatively high level of functioning and, at her request, there was mutual agreement on a six-session course of psychotherapy with the provision of additional sessions if indicated. The first-order change goal is to decrease her mild-moderate depressive symptoms. The second-order change goal is to shift her maladaptive pattern to a more adaptive one. Pattern Focused Therapy will focus on replacing or shifting her maladaptive pattern and related thoughts and behaviors so that she can feel safer connecting with others who are reasonably trustworthy.

Treatment obstacles may include "testing" behavior; difficulties with self-disclosure; and fear of being criticized and negatively evaluated by the therapist. Given her protective factors and strengths, treatment prognosis appears to be relatively good.

## Course of Treatment

Eliana has completed three sessions of the planned six-session therapy. A good working therapeutic alliance began in the initial session and Eliana has become increasingly comfortable with her female therapist and the pattern focused therapy process. She has responded well to three ultra-brief CBT interventions: behavioral activation for depressive symptoms in the first session, breath retraining for her anxiety symptoms, and assertive communication for increasing assertiveness in the second. She also responded well to the Query Sequence which was implemented in the second session. Routine monitoring of progress involves the PHQ-9, the Mood Scale, the ORS, the SRS, and she continues with improvements noted over the first three sessions.

## Plan for Session 4

This is the fourth of six sessions with reasonable progress made on both first-order and second-order treatment goals. It begins by reviewing the mutually agreed upon homework in the last session to find an opportunity to communicate more assertively with her parents. Also her scores on the PHQ-9, the Mood Scale, the ORS, and the SRS will be reviewed. The Query Sequence will be used to process a recent troublesome situation in light of her avoidance pattern. Mutual agreement on relevant homework activity between now and the next session will be reached.

## *Transcription: Session 4*

THERAPIST: Can we start the session by discussing your PHQ-9 and ORS scores? (Sure). I see that your PHQ-9 is now 7. That's great! I also see that your ratings for behavioral activation activities are really good also. (Progress monitoring—PHQ-9; homework: behavioral activation)

ELIANA: Yeah, I'm have a bit more energy and my mood is up more. (Pause) I think I'll continue with the same behavioral activation activity. I'm up to walking two miles a day. I'm feeling better, finally.

THERAPIST: Great! It also looks like there are positive changes in your overall ORS scores from our last session. In particular, your scores for individual wellbeing (5 to 6) and interpersonal wellbeing being (4 to 6) are higher. What has changed from our last meeting that contributes to your higher wellbeing scores? (Progress monitoring—ORS)

ELIANA: My relationship with my parents has been getting better because I have been communicating my feelings more. I've also signed up to start some classes this fall so I can resume my plan to finish my degree. I've been trying some relaxation techniques that we spoke about too, to help me relax more, like the breathing exercises.

THERAPIST: That's excellent. Sounds like your assertive communication practice efforts are working well and you've become more effective in communicating with your parents. (Pause) Glad to hear that you recognize how your practice of breath retraining is paying off. (Pause) And, it's wonderful that you are starting school again too because I know how important this was to you. (Review homework: assertive communication and breath retraining)

ELIANA: Yeah, it is so good that these interventions are making a difference. I guess it was worth all the hard work and having to stretch myself and taking the risk to be more assertive and communicative with my parents.

THERAPIST: This means that your pattern is shifting to be more adaptive. Congratulations on your hard work. It's paying off! (Pause). Might there be anything else that has contributed to your higher scores on the ORS this week?

ELIANA: Um, no, that's pretty much it. Um ... I have been trying to be more social with others. To network a bit too. I know it can help shift my pattern to be less avoidant, but I still feel a little hesitant to socialize with others.

THERAPIST: I agree. Shifting from an avoidant pattern to a more adaptive one is a process. We can continue to work together on you being more at ease around others. Is that okay with you? **(Query-Pattern)**

ELIANA: Yeah, it's becoming clearer that I need to work more on reducing and replacing my avoidant pattern.

THERAPIST: Great! Let's start with your homework from last session in which you agreed to increase socializing with one of your friends. How did that go?

ELIANA: Last week my best friend, Jackie, invited me to a mixer to socialize and network with others. I'm trying to change my ways of avoiding others and agreed to go and see how it turns out. Otherwise, normally I would have declined the offer to go out and just stay home and be a homebody.

THERAPIST: Okay, so you agreed to go to a mixer with your friend and how did it turn out for you?

ELIANA: So, it was a mixer at a restaurant downtown and there were a lot of people there. It seemed to be a good turnout for the restaurant because a lot of people attended the event there. Jackie and I got a table and we ordered dinner at the restaurant. She had other people there that she knew and called them over to our table and she introduced them to me and vice versa. But I noticed that when they sat down and joined us it was like I had nothing to say to them. I ended up not saying too much to them and when they asked me questions to try and talk to me or, I guess, just include me into the conversation, I had short responses with them to end the conversation quick. I didn't even really notice I was doing that until my friend told me how I was acting at the mixer afterwards. I guess it comes natural for me to just sit back and be behind the scenes and quiet. It's just ... I don't know ... it's hard for me to trust people like that. I kind of just keep my business to myself.

THERAPIST: Yes, I remember in the past when we discussed your difficulties in socializing at events because it is hard for you to trust others. How did you feel about not being able to socialize the way you want to at that mixer?

ELIANA: I definitely felt frustrated. It's like I know that I want to be able to get better at doing this by now but it's hard sometimes. I find myself isolating myself all over again when I try to socialize with people at events. I don't know why it's that way. It took a lot just to get me there.

THERAPIST: Well, let's look at it this way, you definitely made some progress because you actually attended the event with your friend whereas before you would have just stayed home instead.

ELIANA: Yeah, you're right. Before that's exactly what I would've done.

THERAPIST: Did anything else happen that night? Or was it specific to that situation at the table with your friend and her associates? **(Query-1)**

ELIANA: Well, a guy approached me and tried to talk to me, but I kind of just did the same thing and kind of pushed him away too. It's like I want to talk to guys too and get to know someone, but there I go again avoiding interactions with people. I was anxious and it was difficult to continue the conversation with him so once again I just kept it real short until the conversation kind of just trailed off and came to an end and he walked away.

THERAPIST: What were you thinking in both situations with the friend's associates and the guy that approached you for conversation? **(Query-2)**

ELIANA: Well, when my friend's associates came over to the table and sat down to chat, I was thinking, "Yeah, this is awkward." And when the guy approached me, I was thinking, "Okay, I have nothing to say to this guy." Both situations were really out of my element because I'd rather just stay home and catch something on TV or just do something else at home.

THERAPIST: In both situations, it seems like you were trying to avoid interacting with new people.

ELIANA: Yeah. I mean, just like we spoke about before, I am trying to change that, but I still need to work on that.

THERAPIST: Yeah, I agree that it's a gradual process. We can discuss ways in which you can do things to help you become better at socializing with new people and not have to feel anxious and mistrustful of others.

ELIANA: Yeah, that's true. I have a hard time seeing the positives sometimes.

THERAPIST: What were your behaviors in the situation, such as what did you say or do when you were at the event? **(Query-3)**

ELIANA: Um, I, kind of, was short with people when they were trying to talk to me, and I guess my facial expression didn't show enthusiasm to socialize with them at the restaurant.

THERAPIST: Okay, so to avoid interactions with others at the restaurant you were very brief in your responses and your facial expression did not indicate that you were pleased to continue socializing with others.

ELIANA: Yeah, that's pretty much it, that's all I did.

THERAPIST: What did you want to get out of that situation at the restaurant? **(Query-4)**

ELIANA: Well, I just wanted to be able to socialize with people without being distant and anxious about interacting with them.

THERAPIST: Okay, so you want to be able to be more confident and less anxious about interacting with people that you do not know well. Is that correct?

ELIANA: Yes, I just want to be able to do this without having such a hard time doing it, you know, like socializing with new people.

THERAPIST: What actually happened at the restaurant? **(Query-5)**

ELIANA: I just ended up not interacting the way that I want to learn how to interact with others. I was brief with people and I didn't show that I wanted to socialize with people. I was more comfortable with my best friend only because I've known her for many years, but when it comes to meeting new people, I'm not as comfortable.

THERAPIST: It sounds like you didn't get the outcome that you wanted. What do you think? **(Query-6)**

ELIANA: Yeah, I agree that it didn't turn out the way that I wanted it to. I wish that I could have just spoken to the people without being like that. I kind of feel bad too because I didn't want my friend to think that I was being rude to her friends. I don't know what they were thinking about the way I was acting, but it probably wasn't good.

THERAPIST: Did you let your friend know about how you felt and that you didn't mean to come off that way to her friends?

ELIANA: Yes. When she brought it to my attention about how I interacted with them, I let her know that. She said she understood, but still I kind of felt bad for doing that around her friends, you know?

THERAPIST: Don't beat yourself up about it because you did explain to your friend why you were behaving that way and you said that she understood as well.

ELIANA: Yeah, that's true, it didn't turn out bad because Jackie did say it was okay. I guess maybe I just feel bad that I can't socialize like everyone else does.

THERAPIST: Well, you're trying to do something about it and that's what counts. You may not be able to socialize and network the way you want now, but it's just a matter of not being able to do it yet. I have confidence in you that you'll gradually learn how to be more social in situations that require interaction with others you may not know well.

ELIANA: Thanks. I appreciate you saying that.

THERAPIST: We can look at this situation and review your thoughts and behaviors and see if it could have turned out differently that night and possibly for future events as well. OK? **(Query-7)**

ELIANA: Yeah, let's do that. I definitely need to learn how to change that.

THERAPIST: Your first thought was "This is awkward." Did it help or hurt you in getting what you wanted out of the interactions at the restaurant? **(Query-8)**

ELIANA: It definitely hurt me because I already put it in my head that it was going to be awkward and look what happened, it ended up being awkward.

THERAPIST: Yes, this is true when you put negative thoughts in your head. In a sense you're already expect the situation to turn out negatively. It seems that you fulfilled what you were thinking of the situation.

ELIANA: Yeah, you're right, that's exactly what happened. I do that a lot too. I think negative about something and expect things to go wrong too. And I really want to change that too. I know that it's not good to think that way, but sometimes I can't help it.

THERAPIST: Okay, so what thought could you have had instead of thinking that interacting with them will be awkward that would helped you get the outcome that you wanted?

ELIANA: I mean, I guess I could have just thought that it would not be awkward to talk to them ... yeah, I could have just thought that the interaction with her friends will turn out to go well instead of thinking that it is awkward.

THERAPIST: Yeah, that could definitely work in this situation with her friends and other situations where you are interacting with new people by thinking that the interactions are going to be positive.

ELIANA: Also, I could think that this will be a good opportunity to network with other people.

THERAPIST: Right, that would be a good opportunity to network with people for opportunities that may be beneficial to you.

ELIANA: Yeah, I need to start networking with people more because there may be opportunities that I'm missing out on.

THERAPIST: That's true, you never know who you might meet as far as opportunities go. You may meet the right person who can help you pursue your goals further.

ELIANA: Yeah, exactly.

THERAPIST: Let's move on to your second thought which was that you had nothing to say when the guy approached you. Did that help or hurt you in getting what you want out of the situation? **(Query-8)**

ELIANA: It hurt me because I ended up looking standoffish and, I mean, it possibly could have led to something else by getting to know each other, maybe possibly being able to date someone. You know, I wouldn't like to start dating but I have to work on being able to keep the conversation going and feeling more relaxed. I guess I just always have my guard up when it comes to trying to let people in. That just seems to be the way that it always goes.

THERAPIST: Yes, if you were trying to get to know someone to possibly date, then I could see how this hurt you in this situation. Do you think that you would be able to let your guard down just a bit to get to know other people?

ELIANA: Uh, maybe I could, but I mean I'd have to practice that though, because I've been hurt in the past and that's why I keep that guard up against other people because I don't want that to happen again.

THERAPIST: It seems that we can't control others hurting us, but is being hurt worth putting up a strong guard to prevent you from forming relationships with people?

ELIANA: Well, I guess, no, it's not worth it because then I won't meet someone new.

THERAPIST: Right, avoiding interactions with others will not lead to a new relationship with a guy because it will create distance.

ELIANA: Yeah, that's true. And I do that often too, distancing myself.

THERAPIST: So, what could you have thought instead of thinking that you have nothing to say to this guy, to get what you wanted out of the situation?

ELIANA: I guess I could have just thought, okay, well, I do have something to say with people instead of thinking I don't.

THERAPIST: By thinking that you do have something to say, how would you have used that in the situation with that guy?

ELIANA: I mean, I guess I could have found some common ground between us to keep the conversation going. I guess I wasn't really paying attention to what we had in common because I was anxious and wanted the conversation to be over quickly.

THERAPIST: Okay, that's great. Next time when you interact with others you can find common ground to make the conversation flow easier.

ELIANA: True. I can definitely do that in the future.

THERAPIST: So, let's review the alternative thoughts that you came up with. Your first alternative thought was to think that interactions with others will be positive and that it could be an opportunity to network with others. Your second one was that you could think that you do have something to say when you interact with others. Do you feel that you can see yourself using these thoughts in future interactions with others?

ELIANA: Yeah, I can see myself doing it and I know it will require some practice though, but it can be done.

THERAPIST: Right, and it is okay that from time to time you may have negative thoughts, but to realize when you have them and how they impact the way you interact with others.

ELIANA: I'm seeing that more clearly now.

THERAPIST: Let's move on to the behaviors. Did your first behavior which was to be brief or short in conversation with others, did that help or hurt you in getting what you wanted in that situation? **(Query-9)**

ELIANA: That ended up hurting me.

THERAPIST: And how did this hurt you?

ELIANA: Well, I guess because being short with them didn't necessarily help keep the conversation going to socialize with others and have a good time at the event.

THERAPIST: So, what might you have done differently to get to interact well with others in that situation?

ELIANA: I could have not been so short with her friends when I was trying to interact with them.

THERAPIST: Right, right, you could have continued the conversation instead of being short with her friends and that way you could have gotten to know them better and possibly hang out with her and her friends in the future.

ELIANA: Yeah, I definitely need to be more social to have fun at these events.

THERAPIST: Your second behavior which was having a facial expression that did not seem enthusiastic to interact with others, did that help or hurt you in getting what you wanted in that situation? **(Query-9)**

ELIANA: I could have just had a positive expression on my face when I was talking to her friends.

THERAPIST: Right, and a more positive expression would let them know that you are interested in engaging in conversation with them and they would be equally pleased to continue the conversation with you.

ELIANA: Yeah, that's true. I need to gage my facial expressions to know when I'm looking standoffish versus looking happy or more pleasant.

THERAPIST: Do you see yourself doing that in future conversations by not being short with people and paying attention to your facial expressions?

ELIANA: Yeah, I think I can do this if I practice doing them.

THERAPIST: Great. Can you see yourself practicing this more adaptive pattern in interactions between now and when we meet next? We can review your experiences then. Would that be OK?

ELIANA: Yes, I do.

THERAPIST: So, how important is it for you to make those changes in your adaptive pattern? On a scale from 0–10, where 0 is not at all important, and 10 is extremely important, where would you say you are? **(Query-10–1)**

ELIANA: I'd say 9 or 10.

THERAPIST: And on that 10-point scale, how confident are you that you will make some changes in it this week? **(Query-10–2)**

ELIANA: That'd be a 6.

THERAPIST: Can you see yourself practicing this more adaptive pattern in interactions between now and when we meet next? (Yes) We can review your experiences then. Would that be OK?

ELIANA: Yeah, I can do that till we see each other next time. I definitely need to practice them. That's for sure.

THERAPIST: Okay, so let's take a few moments to complete the SRS so that I may gage how the session was today. (Progress monitoring—SRS) Eliana fills out form and hands it back.

THERAPIST: Okay, well, I see that the scores (38) are pretty consistent with last week's (38), which are pretty high. Is there anything that you'd like to see differently in our sessions?

ELIANA: No, I think you covered everything that we need to talk about during sessions. And, I do feel heard by you; and it is becoming easier to trust you.

THERAPIST: So glad to hear that. Thanks. (Pause) Do you have any questions or concerns about this session and the technique we used?

ELIANA: No.

THERAPIST: Okay. So, when we meet next, we can discuss your use of the new alternatives you learned in this session when you interact with others. Does that make sense, and do you agree that would be a reasonable homework activity? (Homework)

ELIANA: Yes, it makes sense, and I'm ready to do it. (Pause) It means I'm going to have to stretch myself and move out of my comfort zone.

## Commentary

This transcription represents a fairly typical session of Pattern Focused Therapy and demonstrates how the four components of this approach are incorporated. It began with a review of scores on screeners and outcome measures, and the agreed upon homework assignment. This allowed the therapist to assess the effectiveness of the ultra-brief interventions introduced in previous sessions. Of note is that Eliana is quite engaged in the therapeutic process, has reduced her depressive symptoms (PHQ-9 = 7), reports being more assertive with her parents, and experiences some shift to a more adaptive pattern. Her scores on the two MI questions suggest that shifting to a more adaptive pattern is very important to her (score of 10) while her confidence in making this change (score of 6) is moving in the right direction. Subsequent sessions presumably will focus on her level of confidence.

## Conclusion

The practice of Pattern Focused Therapy appears to have considerable appeal for the everyday practice of therapy today. This focused approach is easily learned and effectively practiced by both novice and experienced therapists. Since 2012, this approach has been fully implemented in a graduate psychotherapy training program (Sperry, 2016; Sperry & Sperry, 2018), and initial data shows it to be effective and successful in achieving treatment goals in clients. Furthermore, because it incorporates a key component of a recognized empirically supported (evidence-based) treatment, Pattern Focused Therapy can be considered an evidence-informed therapy approach.

# References

American Psychological Association (2018). *Psychological treatments*. Washington, DC: American Psychological Association. Retrieved from www.div12.org/treatments/

APA Presidential Task Force on Evidence-Based Practice. (2006). Evidence-based practice in psychology. *The American Psychologist*, 61(4), 271–285.

Fraser, J. S., & Solovey, A. D. (2007). *Second-order change in psychotherapy: The golden thread that unifies effective treatments*. Washington, DC: American Psychological Association.

McCullough, J. (2000). *Treatment for chronic depression: Cognitive behavioral analysis system of psychotherapy*. New York, NY: Guilford Press.

McCullough, J., Schramm, E., & Penberthy, K. (2014). *CBASP as a distinctive treatment for persistent depressive disorder: Distinctive features*. New York, NY: Routledge.

Meier, S. (2015). *Incorporating progress monitoring and outcome assessment into counseling psychotherapy: A primer*. New York, NY: Oxford University Press.

Miller, W., & Rollnick, S. (2013). *Motivational interviewing: Helping people change*, 3rd ed. New York, NY: Guilford Press.

Sackett, D., Richardson, W., Rosenberg, W., Haynes, R., & Brian, S. (1996). Evidence based medicine: What it is and what it isn't. *British Medical Journal*, 312, 71–72.

Sperry, L. (1988). Biopsychosocial therapy: An integrative approach for tailoring treatment. *Journal of Individual Psychology*, 44, 225–235.

Sperry, L. (2000). Biopsychosocial therapy: Essential strategies and tactics. In J. Carlson & L. Sperry (Eds.). *Brief therapy with individuals and couples*. Phoenix, AZ: Zeig, Tucker & Theisen.

Sperry, L. (2005). A therapeutic interviewing strategy for effective counseling practice: Application to health and medical issues in individual and couples therapy. *The Family Journal*, 13(4), 477–481.

Sperry, L. (2006). *Psychological treatment of chronic illness: The biopsychosocial therapy approach*. New York, NY: Brunner/Mazel.

Sperry, L. (2010). *Highly effective therapy: Developing essential clinical competencies in counseling and psychotherapy*. New York, NY: Routledge.

Sperry, L. (2016). Pattern-focused psychotherapy. In L. Sperry (Ed.). *Mental health and mental disorders: An encyclopedia of conditions, treatments, and well-being*. 3 vols. (pp. 816–818). Santa Barbara, CA: Greenwood.

Sperry, L., & Binensztok, V. (2019). *Ultra-brief cognitive behavioral interventions: A new practice model for mental health and integrated care*. New York, NY: Routledge.

Sperry, L., Brill, P., Howard, K., & Grissom, G. (1996). *Treatment outcomes in psychotherapy and psychiatric interventions*. New York, NY: Brunner/Mazel.

Sperry, L., & Sperry, J. (2012). *Case conceptualization: Mastering this competency with ease and confidence*. New York, NY: Routledge.

Sperry, J., & Sperry, L. (2018). *Cognitive behavior therapy in professional counseling practice*. New York, NY: Routledge.

# Chapter 4

# Ultra-Brief Therapeutic Interventions

As already noted, Pattern Focused Therapy is characterized by a unique core therapeutic strategy and the incorporation of an ultra-brief intervention. Its core therapeutic strategy is the Query Sequence which focuses primarily on second-order change, particularly shifting from a maladaptive pattern to a more adaptive one. Ultra-brief interventions focus primarily on first-order change goals, such as symptom reduction, self-management, or relational improvement. The Pattern and Query Sequence are described in detail in Chapter 3.

This chapter describes 12 of the most commonly used brief therapeutic interventions that I have found to be both very useful and essential in everyday clinical practice, particularly in the context of short-term therapy.

Each of these interventions is designed to produce changes in behaviors and presenting symptoms in a short time frame. Because many of them can be quickly introduced and implemented in a session, these focused interventions are quite compatible with the trend toward short-term therapy practiced in mental health and integrated case settings. Furthermore, these interventions can easily be incorporated into therapists' "therapeutic arsenal," irrespective of their theoretical orientation. Each of these interventions is defined and described, including their indications and how they can be incorporated into the therapeutic process. The chapter begins with a description of brief interventions.

## Brief Interventions and Brief Intervention Protocols

The term "brief therapeutic intervention" has yet to be clearly defined in terms of a specific time frame. However, the term "ultra-brief therapeutic intervention" has been defined as "specific cognitive behavioral methods that can be utilized in very brief, i.e., ultra-brief time frame of 10 to 20 minutes" (Sperry & Binensztok, 2019, p. 18). Typically, such interventions are implemented within a single treatment session.

A related designation, "ultra-brief treatment protocols" (Otto & Hofmann, 2010) refers to the number of sessions of treatment; typically five sessions as compared to the customary delivery of psychotherapies which range from 12–20 sessions (Otto, Tolin, Nations, Utschig, Rothbaum, Hofmann, & Smits, 2012). In primary care settings, short-term therapy is often delivered in 6–8 individual or group sessions, instead of 16–18 individual or group sessions in conventional mental health settings. Not surprisingly, the reason why session durations can be short (20–30 minutes) is because ultra-brief interventions are used to achieve a specific therapeutic outcome in a given session. Table 4.1 lists these interventions. Near the end of the chapter is a section entitled "Key Resources." It includes valuable resources that therapists may find invaluable in learning more about these interventions.

## Assertive Communication

Assertive communication is a behavioral intervention to teach individuals to express emotions, opinions, and needs more clearly and appropriately (Sperry & Binensztok, 2019). Its aim is to increase an individual's ability to express thoughts, feelings, and beliefs in a direct, honest, and appropriate manner without violating the rights of others. Specifically, it involves the ability to say "no," to make requests, to express positive and negative feelings, and to initiate, continue, and terminate conversations (Alberti, 2008). Lack of assertive behavior is usually related to specific skills deficits but may also be related to interfering emotional reactions and thoughts. A variant of assertive communication is compassionate assertiveness which is a way to express needs and deal with conflict while keeping a kind heart, i.e., being compassionate. In short, mindfulness is a key component of this form of assertive communication,

*Table 4.1* Ultra-brief therapeutic interventions

- Assertive Communication
- Behavioral Activation
- Behavioral Rehearsal
- Breath Retraining
- Cognitive Defusion
- Cognitive Disputation
- Habit Reversal
- Limit Setting
- Mindfulness
- Relapse Prevention
- Stimulus Control
- Thought Stopping

(Vavrichek, 2012). Assertive communications training can occur in individual sessions, group therapy, as well as in other small contexts, such as support groups.

Used alone or as an adjunct to other interventions, assertive communication is useful for clients presenting with stress, bullying, anxiety, depression, eating disorders, substance abuse, and autism spectrum disorders. It is also useful in increasing self-esteem in sexual abuse survivors and improving interpersonal skills in clients with disabilities. It is not recommended for clients whose difficulty in communicating arises from chronic depression, in which case, the depression should be treated first (Segal, Williams, & Teasdale, 2013). Providers should also be aware of views of assertiveness in non-Western cultures.

Here is how this intervention can be incorporated into the therapeutic process. Initially, the therapist performs a careful assessment to identify the following: situations of concern to the individual; current assertiveness skills; personal and environmental obstacles that need to be addressed, such as difficult significant others or limited social contexts; and personal and environmental resources that can be drawn on. Next, the therapist formulates an intervention plan. If appropriate behaviors are available but not performed because of anxiety, the focus may be on enhancing anxiety management skills. Discrimination training is required when skills are available but are not performed at appropriate times. If skills deficits are present, skills training is indicated. Then, the intervention is introduced. For skills training, the therapist teaches the individual specific skills via modeling, behavioral rehearsal, feedback, and homework. Modeling effective behavior in specific situations is accomplished by using one or more of the following methods: in vivo demonstration of the behavior by the therapist, written scripts, videotapes, audiotapes, or films. In behavior rehearsal, the individual is provided opportunities to practice the given skill in the clinical setting. After that, the therapist provides positive feedback following each rehearsal in which effective verbal and non-verbal reactions are noted and specific changes that could be made to enhance performance are identified. Homework assignments involve tasks that the individual agrees to carry out in real-life contexts. Finally, the length of assertion training depends on the domain of social behaviors that must be developed and on the severity of countervailing personal and environmental obstacles. If the response repertoire is narrow, such as refusing requests, and the obstacles minor, only a few sessions may be required. If the behavior deficits are extensive, additional time may be required even though only one or two kinds of social situations are focused on during the intervention.

## Behavioral Activation

Behavioral activation is a behavioral intervention to help individuals break cycles of inactivity and avoidance by substituting more activating behaviors (Sperry & Sperry, 2018). This technique aims to break the self-perpetuating cycle of inactivity often accompanying depression and avoidance conditions. As individuals reduce pleasurable activities, they receive less positive reinforcement, leading to worsened depression and further reduction of activities. Similarly, individuals who avoid necessary tasks may be left with a sense of defeat that worsens their mood symptoms. Behavioral activation emphasizes the role of environmental factors over internal causes in depression and avoidance conditions. The focus is on increasing activity, rather than analyzing cognitions. By scheduling both pleasant and necessary activities weekly, the individual increases pleasure, motivation, and self-efficacy. Small changes reinforce the individual and help lead to increasingly challenging activities.

Behavioral activation was initially used with depressive disorder. More recently, it has been utilized with various avoidance conditions such as Avoidant Personality Disorder, Social Anxiety Disorder, and other anxiety disorders.

Here is how this intervention can be incorporated into the therapeutic process. First, the therapist teaches the client about cycles of inactivity and explains how the client's avoidant behavior reinforces his or her symptoms. Then the therapist and client discuss how the client's current inactivity and avoidant behavior have been contributing to his or her symptoms. The intervention and its rationale are then explained. Next, the therapist helps the client make three lists—one of the activities the client currently engages in, one of the necessary tasks the client needs to perform but has been avoiding, and one of pleasurable activities the client can potentially engage in. The therapist may give the client a handout of possible activities to choose from.

During the first week, the client chooses one or two activities that take no longer than 15–20 minutes each to complete. It is important that the client begins by setting small goals and not taking on too much at once. The chosen activities should include both pleasurable and necessary tasks. When beginning, the client should choose easier activities. This can also be achieved by breaking down a larger task into several small tasks. Next, the therapist helps the client schedule the activities for the week, choosing a specific day and time for each. Back-up activities should also be identified to increase the likelihood that activities will be completed. The therapist gives the client a handout to track the completion of tasks. The client is asked to rate each activity on a scale from 0–10 for level of completion and amount of pleasure derived. Then, the client brings the activity log to the next session, in which the activities are reviewed. Each activity is reviewed separately, and the client is asked to explain his or her ratings for completion and pleasure. The therapist asks what was good and what was not good about each activity. Finally, over the next few sessions, the client increases the number of activities completed each week, as well as the duration and complexity of activities.

## Behavioral Rehearsal

Behavioral rehearsal is a behavioral intervention to help individuals identify and practice behaviors that are more useful and appropriate in social settings (Sperry & Binensztok, 2019). Behavioral rehearsal helps individuals build appropriate social skills through modeling, practice, and feedback. The individual identifies social skill deficits and the therapist helps generate behaviors that would be more effective in social settings. The therapist models appropriate verbal and nonverbal behaviors for the client to learn. The client is encouraged to be an active participant, giving the therapist feedback and suggestions. The therapist then role-plays a situation, allowing the client to practice the new social skills. Skills should be easy to learn and implement. The therapist uses praise and constructive feedback to help the client improve the new skills.

Behavioral rehearsal can be used with clients of various ages and developmental levels. It is useful as an adjunct technique to help clients practice the new techniques and skills they learn in therapy before implementing them in real-world settings. Therapists should take cultural and contextual factors into account before teaching and modeling targeted behaviors.

Here is how this intervention can be incorporated into the therapeutic process. First, the therapist helps the client identify the social skill deficit to be targeted. The client may identify a specific situation in which he or she is unsure of behaviors to implement. Next, the therapist explains the process and benefits of behavioral rehearsal and elicits the client's permission to engage in the intervention. The therapist describes and then models appropriate social skills for the targeted situation. Next, the therapist asks the client for feedback and suggestions and modifies the modeling accordingly. Then, the therapist role-plays the situation with the client, allowing the client to practice the new skills. After the role-play, the therapist praises the client for his or her efforts and provides constructive feedback. Finally, the role-play may be repeated, incorporating this feedback.

## Breath Retraining

Breath retraining, also known as controlled breathing, is a behavioral intervention used to slow an individual's breathing and restore regulated breathing rhythms, resulting in reduced stress-related symptoms (Sperry & Binensztok, 2019). Breath retraining is used to train individuals to regulate their breathing rate. Shallow or rapid breathing patterns can increase stress and panic, while regulated deeper breathing patterns can lead to a more relaxed state by calming the parasympathetic nervous system response. Purposely engaging in controlled breathing can also interrupt negative thought patterns and give an individual a sense of control over symptoms. Diaphragmatic breathing is the primary method of teaching individuals how to take slow, deep inhales and exhales from the abdominal area, rather than the chest. Diaphragmatic breathing should slow respiration to about half of the typical rate—about six to eight breaths per minute. The individual may place a hand on their stomach in order to gain feedback on the depth of the breaths. Paced respiration is another technique for controlling breathing. With this method, the individual inhales and exhales at a paced rate, often by counting or by using a pacing instrument like a metronome. The individual may be instructed to position his or her lips in a way that facilitates slowed breathing, i.e. pretending to blow on a spoonful of soup.

This technique can be used with individuals suffering from symptoms associated with panic, stress, anxiety, chronic pain, insomnia, and headaches, among other concerns. It is useful for children, adolescents, and adults. Breath retraining is often combined with other techniques like progressive muscle relaxation, guided imagery, or cognitive restructuring.

Here is how this intervention can be incorporated into the therapeutic process. First, the therapist asks the client to breathe normally and observes the client's normal breathing pattern. Next, the therapist then explains the role of breathing in the client's presenting symptoms, and also explains how controlled breathing can help alleviate symptoms. Then the therapist teaches the client to take slow, smooth, deep breaths that originate in the abdomen. The therapist may model the diaphragmatic breath for the client. The therapist can instruct the client to position his or her lips in such a way that breathing is slower and smoother. The therapist can use examples like, "Imagine you are blowing bubbles or blowing on a spoonful of hot soup." The therapist instructs the client to take six to eight breaths per minute. Inhales and exhales can be paced by counting. Finally, the therapist instructs the client to practice the breathing technique between sessions and when symptoms arise.

## Cognitive Defusion

Cognitive defusion is a mindfulness-based method for distancing oneself from troublesome thoughts, rather than disputing, restructuring, or replacing them (Sperry & Binensztok, 2019). Cognitive defusion is a core technique in Acceptance and Commitment Therapy. It is based on the premise that individuals "fuse" with negative thoughts and judgments, leading to distressing feelings. Cognitive defusion is used to help the client accept distressing thoughts instead of disputing them, which may serve to reinforce these thoughts. This technique teaches individuals to treat thoughts as just thoughts and not attach feelings or judgments to the thoughts. The individual is encouraged to see himself or herself as not comprised of his or her thoughts but that thoughts are a separate entity from the person. The individual is also encouraged to change the language used to address the thoughts. Language can be used to separate oneself from the distressing thoughts. For example, the person can say, "I am having an anxious thought," rather than, "I am anxious," or "I can't stand it." The individual can repeat distressing thoughts over and over again until they lose their meaning, thus changing the person's perspective on the thoughts. One or more of these methods can be used with the goal of the individual not fusing with the thoughts, thus weakening their hold on the individual. Cognitive defusion can be used to treat depression, anxiety, substance abuse, eating disorders, and impulse control disorders.

Here is how this intervention can be incorporated into the therapeutic process. First, the therapist helps the client identify a problematic situation and the client's thoughts associated with the problem. Then, the therapist helps the client understand the nature of thoughts and how they tend to come and go and do not comprise who the person is. It can be helpful for the therapist to explains how language influences thoughts and the way the individual defines his or her experiences accordingly. The therapist can use metaphors to explain this. The therapist explains how language reinforces thoughts and behaviors. Next, the therapist helps the client defuse from thoughts by teaching the client to notice them without judgment and label them differently. Finally, the client is asked to practice cognitive defusion by labeling thoughts without judgment and interaction.

## Cognitive Disputation

Cognitive disputation is a cognitive-behavioral intervention that uses logic to assist individuals in identifying the irrationality of their maladaptive thoughts (Sperry & Sperry, 2018). Cognitive disputation is based on the understanding that cognitions lead to feelings and behaviors and it focuses on challenging individuals' maladaptive beliefs. The therapist disputes the client's irrational beliefs by using logic, with the aim of teaching the client to challenge his or her own thoughts without the help of a therapist. Thoughts can be disputed using Socratic questioning, an approach based on Aaron T. Beck's cognitive therapy, focusing on logical errors or cognitive distortions, i. e. catastrophizing, all-or-nothing thinking. The therapist can also directly dispute the thoughts, an approach based on Albert Ellis' Rational Emotive Behavior Therapy, focusing on one's beliefs that things "should" or "must" be a certain way for situations to be bearable. Both approaches encourage the client to test their thoughts against reality, with Beck's method encouraging clients to view their thoughts as testable hypotheses rather than facts. Clients learn to become aware of their thoughts by recording them, as well as events that may later help dispute irrational thoughts.

Cognitive disputation is useful for treating depression, anxiety, eating disorders, substance abuse, and marital distress. It is contraindicated for individuals who have limited cognitive capacity, including those with intellectual disability, borderline intellectual functioning, dementia, psychosis, or who engage primarily in preoperational or emotional thinking.

Here is how this intervention can be incorporated in the therapeutic process. First, the therapist helps the client identify maladaptive thoughts, and explains that thoughts may be specific to a situation or more generalized. Next, the client is asked to document thoughts as homework. Then, the therapist explains the rationale for cognitive disputation and explains how thoughts influence feelings and behaviors. The therapist then illustrates how this intervention works by disputing the client's maladaptive thoughts, using logic to demonstrate how the thoughts are irrational. Either Socratic questioning or disputation is used to convince the client that the thoughts are irrational. The therapist may ask the client to view the thought as a hypothesis and test it against reality. Then, the client is asked how much he or she believes the thought on a scale from 0–10 where 0 is not at all and 10 means totally. After gathering evidence for and against the belief, the therapist asks the client to again rate how much he or she believes the thought on the same scale. Finally, the client is given homework to continue to identify maladaptive thoughts as they arise. The therapist asks the client to journal the daily occurrences to provide a basis for disputing other beliefs and then practices disputing his or her own thoughts between sessions.

## Habit Reversal

Habit reversal is a behavioral intervention used to reduce tics, stuttering, hair-pulling, and skin-picking by engaging in a competing response which then suppresses the unwanted behavior (Sperry & Sperry, 2018). Habit reversal is intended to reduce the occurrence of compulsive behaviors, such as hair-pulling, by replacing those behaviors with inconspicuous, opposing behaviors. Instead of breaking or stopping a negative habit, it substitutes it with a better or incompatible one (Sperry, 2011). Habit reversal therapy is comprised of four stages: (1) building awareness; (2) developing a competing response; (3) increasing motivation; and (4) skill generalization. In the awareness stage, the client increases awareness of the behavior by describing it or performing it in a mirror, as well as identifying situations in which the behavior frequently occurs. In the competing response stage, the client learns a behavior that is incompatible with the unwanted behavior. The competing response should be the opposite of the unwanted behavior and inconspicuously performed in social situations. The competing behavior should also induce isometric tension of the muscles involved in the unwanted behavior and be practiced for several minutes at a time. In the motivation stage, the client explores reasons to discontinue the unwanted behavior, including times when the behavior has proved embarrassing or inconvenient. The client's friends and family are asked to encourage the client's reduction of the unwanted behavior and the client controls the unwanted behavior in front of trusted people. Finally, in the generalization phase, the client rehearses the competing behavior in other situations.

Habit reversal is useful in treating tic disorders, hair-pulling disorder, skin-picking disorder, stuttering, and other habits like nail biting, teeth grinding, scratching, and oral-digital habits. It can be used with children, adolescents, and adults. Habit reversal is not indicated for clients with borderline intellectual functioning or intellectual disability.

Here is how this intervention can be incorporated into the therapeutic process. First, the therapist helps the client become aware of the unwanted behaviors. The client either describes the behavior in detail or observes himself/herself performing the behavior while looking in a mirror. Then, the therapist can also point out when the behavior occurs during sessions until the client becomes more aware of the behavior. Next, the therapist helps the client identify warning signs for the oncoming behavior, such as urges, physical sensations, or thoughts. Situations in which the behavior is most likely to occur are also identified. Similarly, the therapist helps the client identify a competing behavior that is the opposite of the unwanted behavior and is inconspicuous in public. For example, the behavior may involve putting one's hands in one's pockets or pinching one's forearm. Next, the client practices the competing behavior for several minutes at a time. Then, the therapist works with the client to write a list of problems, inconveniences, and embarrassments caused by the unwanted behavior. Outside the session, the client enlists family and friends for support and demonstrates suppression of the unwanted behavior in front of them. These individuals are enlisted to praise the person for control of the behavior. Next, the therapist helps the client symbolically rehearse performing the competing behavior in different areas of the client's life. Finally, the client practices the competing behavior in different contexts.

## Limit Setting

Limit setting is a behavioral intervention to establish the boundaries of positive and acceptable client behavior. The aim of limit setting is to foster therapy-enhancing behaviors that facilitate the achievement of first- and second-order change goals while limiting treatment-interfering behaviors. Typical treatment-interfering behaviors include: (1) coming late for sessions, missing a session, unnecessarily delaying or failing to make payment; (2) harmful behavior to self or others, including parasuicidal behaviors; inappropriate verbal behavior, such as abusive language; (3) dominating treatment by excessive or rambling speech; (4) efforts to communicate with the therapist outside the treatment context (i.e., unnecessary phone calls); inappropriate actions such as hitting or unwanted touching, breaking or stealing items; or (5) failure to complete assigned therapeutic tasks or homework. In short, limit setting exists in therapy to protect and enhance the therapeutic experience.

Limit setting is a common intervention with personality-disordered clients who have difficulty maintaining boundaries, as well as appreciating and anticipating the consequences, especially the negative consequences, of their actions (Sperry, 2016). Setting limits and setting boundaries are considered a life skill in Dialectical Behavior Therapy which has developed specific guidelines for limit setting (Linehan, 2015). Furthermore, limit setting is a therapeutic intervention that is quite useful in outside treatment settings as well.

Here is how this intervention can be incorporated into the therapeutic process. First, the therapist observes or anticipates the treatment-interfering behaviors. Next, the therapist begins implementing limit setting by setting the limit. The limit is specified in "if ___ then ___" language. It is crucial that the therapist states the limit in a neutral, non-critical tone and non-judgmental language. Then, the therapist explains the rationale for the limit. After that, the therapist specifies or negotiates with the individual the consequences for breaching the limit. Finally, the therapist responds to any breaches of the limit setting. Because individuals can and do test limits—whether for conscious or unconscious reasons—more commonly in the early phase of treatment, limit testing should be expected. The therapist should be prepared to respond by confronting and/or interpreting it; enforcing the consequences, and discussing the impact of the breach on treatment; or predicting that such testing may reoccur.

## Mindfulness

Mindfulness is an intervention which helps individuals to focus on the present without judgment (Sperry & Sperry, 2018). The result is that it can reduce stress, anxiety, mood symptoms, and mindless action. Mindfulness originated in the Buddhist tradition and is used to mediate physical, emotional, and behavioral symptoms. It can facilitate individuals to build awareness and observation of thoughts, sensations, and mood states without active engagement with or judgment of them. The individual becomes aware of bodily sensations, emotional states, thoughts, and mental images, while practicing remaining fully present in the moment. Instead of attempting to escape these sensations, the individual views them as objective facts. For example, one might observe physical symptoms of anxiety and describe, "My throat feels tight right now." Observation of thoughts and feeling states should be non-judgmental and the participant should bring all attention to the current experience. Individuals are encouraged to cultivate mindful attention in daily activities. As mindfulness practice evolves, individuals habituate to unpleasant sensations and thoughts. Mindfulness is thought to relieve distressing thoughts, improve self-management, and allow individuals to recognize impending relapse or mood symptoms so they can implement coping skills to manage these occurrences.

Mindfulness can be used for chronic pain, medical problems, anxiety disorders, mood disorders, eating disorders, substance abuse, and personality disorders. It has been reported that the mindfulness exercise of loving kindness is not recommended for clients who present with chronic depression (Segal, Williams, & Teasdale, 2013). Mindfulness can be applied as a skills training method, as a meditative technique, or as a component of other interventions. Though typically taught in a group setting, mindfulness instruction may take place in a one-on-one format.

Here is how this intervention can be incorporated into the therapeutic process. First, the therapist teaches the client to observe his or her thoughts without labeling or describing them. Next, the therapist assigns homework for the client to continue observing thoughts, feelings, and sensations. The therapist then teaches the client to observe sensations without judgment through an activity like mindful eating, in which he/she focuses on the smells, texture, temperature, and physical sensations during the experience. The client is asked to describe thoughts and sensations as they arise, i.e. "The tomato is watery," without making judgments, i.e., "I don't like it." After that, the therapist helps the client practice making a running commentary on events and experiences without judgment. Finally, the therapist assigns homework for the client to practice giving full attention to experiences, either in daily meditation or during everyday activities.

## Relapse Prevention

Relapse prevention is a behavioral intervention that originally taught individuals to maintain sobriety while coping with everyday stressors and temptations, but more recently is used to maintain therapeutic gains with most presentations (Sperry & Sperry, 2018). After completing treatment for substance use issues, individuals are tasked with maintaining sobriety while facing stressors and obstacles. Individuals may find it challenging to avoid relapsing if their judgment is still affected by continued use. Relapse prevention helps clients develop coping skills and self-efficacy. The approach is based on the premise that when facing a stressful event, an individual's coping skills are the main determining factor between relapse and maintained sobriety. Employing effective coping mechanisms in the face of distressing events leads to increased self-efficacy and a decreased risk of relapse. Relapse prevention uses relapse education, which teaches individuals to identify warning signs and high-risk situations, learn effective coping skills, challenge irrational beliefs, form more realistic expectations, and create a toolkit that includes social support, self-care, and avoidance of relapse triggers.

Relapse prevention is useful for individuals in recovery from substance abuse and other addictive behaviors, such as eating disorders, overeating, smoking, and self-harm. More recently, it is being used to maintain therapeutic gains with nearly all mental health conditions in conjunction with most therapeutic approaches. It is a key intervention in Pattern Focused Therapy.

Here is how this intervention can be incorporated into the therapeutic process. First, the therapist assesses the client's patterns of use or behavior, coping skills, self-efficacy, expectations, and readiness for change. Then, the therapist educates the client on relapse and the benefits of a relapse prevention plan. Next, the therapist helps the client make a list of the client's high-risk situations, and stressful events that can potentially trigger the unwanted behavior. After that, the client and therapist discuss the high-risk situations and how they lead to use. Next, the therapist helps the client identify and challenge irrational beliefs about use since clients use such irrational beliefs to provide emotional relief in difficult situations. Then, the client and therapist make an inventory of relapse warning signs, including major stressors as well as a culmination of small stressors, and the client is taught to address initial small stressors rather than waiting to reach his or her breaking point. Then, the client is encouraged to keep a log of warning signs. Similarly, the client and therapist devise a list of supportive efforts to ensure the plan is maintained. These may include continued therapy, attending 12-step meetings, a list of supportive people to call, a list of people and places to avoid, the use of a sponsor, and improved self-care. Finally, the client commits to a lifestyle change that supports his or her recovery, including caring for his or her health, exercise, positive social interactions, etc.

## Stimulus Control

Stimulus control is a behavioral intervention to identify factors, i.e., stimuli, that precede a behavior to be changed and then taking steps to alter the factors to bring about the desired result (Sperry & Binensztok, 2019). Stimulus control works by using an individual's ability to associate a stimulus with a consequence. The stimulus then works to control the individual's behaviors. A stimulus can be an object, activity, image, or place. Stimulus control can be achieved when a stimulus is paired with either a pleasant or unpleasant experience, or when a behavior is reinforced or punished in the presence of a stimulus. For example, a person who gets food poisoning after eating chicken, may then avoid chicken entirely, with the dish serving as the stimulus and its consumption as the behavior being controlled. The stimulus then serves as a trigger for a specific behavior or response.

Stimulus control can be used to increase any desired behavior and decrease any undesired behavior. Originally used as an essential intervention for alcohol use disorders and other addictions, it is now a mainstay treatment for insomnia and obesity. Potentially, there are many other conditions in which it could be applied. In short, it is a simple and easy to implement intervention that is too often underutilized in clinical practice.

Here is how this intervention can be incorporated into the therapeutic process. First, the therapist helps the client identify a targeted behavior that the client would like to either increase or decrease. Then, the therapist then explains how stimuli become behavioral triggers and how stimulus control can be used to modify behaviors. Next, possible triggers of the targeted behavior are identified as the therapist asks about contributing thoughts, feelings, behaviors, and environmental factors, including specific individuals. Then, the client is directed to monitor those target behaviors and keeps a log of occurrences to identify all possible triggers. When they meet again, the client and therapist review the triggers and agree on which triggers will be controlled. Finally, the therapist helps the client devise a plan for controlling each specific trigger. For example, a client with insomnia may find that she cannot fall asleep on days when she answers work emails before bed. Once the client identifies triggers and agrees that she would like to control them, the therapist helps her identify ways to control each trigger. She identifies having her notebook computer next to her bed as the main trigger. Her plan is to stop answering work emails before bedtime by removing the computer from her bed stand, she effectively controls the stimulus which is the trigger for her difficulty in falling asleep.

## Thought Stopping

Thought stopping is a behavioral intervention to block or eliminate ruminative or intrusive thought patterns that are unproductive or anxiety-producing (Sperry, 2016). It may also have the effect of increasing the individual's sense of control and reducing distress. This intervention is usually introduced and demonstrated by the therapist. It is then practiced and applied by the individual. As a result of applying this intervention, the individual increases his sense of control.

Thought stopping can be used for obsessive thoughts associated with obsessive-compulsive disorder, psychotic symptoms, depression, panic, generalized anxiety, tobacco use, drug and alcohol use, and body dysmorphic disorder. It can be used as either a stand-alone or auxiliary treatment.

Here is how this intervention can be incorporated into the therapeutic process. First, the therapist instructs the client on the similarities between normal and obsessive/intrusive thoughts. An agreement is reached to try to reduce the duration of the intrusive thoughts, thus making them more "normal" and increasing the client's sense of control. Then the therapist and client draw up a list of three obsessional thoughts and several specific triggering scenes. Next, a list of up to three alternative thoughts (i.e., interesting or relaxing thoughts) is made. For example, a scene from a movie, lying on a sandy beach, or taking a walk through the woods. Each obsessional thought is rated for the discomfort it produces on a scale of 1–10 (1 = lowest, 10 = highest). Then the therapist demonstrates how to block obsessional thoughts and substitute an alternative thought. The therapist directs the individual to close his or her eyes and become relaxed with the instruction to raise a hand when the obsessional thought is first experienced. For example: "Sit back and relax and let your eyes close. I'll mention a specific triggering scene to you, and then describe you experiencing an obsessional thought. As soon as you begin to think the thought, raise your hand, even if I'm only describing the scene." The therapist then describes a typical triggering scene, and as soon as the individual raises a hand, the therapist says "Stop!" loudly. The therapist asks the client whether the obsessional thought was blocked and whether the individual was able to imagine the alternative scene in some detail. The discomfort arising from that obsessional thought is then rated on the 1–10 scale. Next, the therapist then leads the client in practicing thought stopping with different triggering scenes and alternative thoughts, and the discomfort ratings are recorded. Practice continues until the individual can sufficiently block and replace the obsessional thought. After that, the procedure is modified so that following the therapist's description of the triggering scene and obsessive thought, the client says "Stop!" and describes the alternative scene. Next, the therapist gives an intersession assignment (homework) to the client for 15 minutes of practice a day at times when the client is not distressed by intrusive thoughts. A log is kept with ratings of 1–10 made of the distress and vividness evoked by the intrusive thought. Finally, after a week of practice, the therapist prescribes the intervention to be used to dismiss mild to moderately distressing thoughts as they occur. The client is instructed that as his or her sense of control increases, the thoughts, when they occur, will become less distressing (on the 1–10 scale) until the individual experiences little or no concern about them.

## Conclusion

This chapter describes 12 brief interventions that can easily and effectively be incorporated into Pattern Focused Therapy or other therapy in both mental health and integrated care settings. Chapter 5, Chapter 6, Chapter 7, and Chapter 10 will illustrate the use of such interventions over the course of successful therapies. The interested reader will find 20 ultra-brief therapeutic interventions described with clinical illustrations in the book by Sperry and Binensztok (2019) as well as other sources of brief interventions (Sperry, 2016; Sperry & Sperry, 2018).

## Key Resources

### Assertive Communications

Alberti, R. (2008). *Your perfect right: Assertiveness and equality in your life and relationships*. 9th ed. San Luis Obispo, CA: Impact Publications.

Segal, Z., Williams, J., & Teasdale, J. (2013). *Mindfulness-based cognitive therapy for depression*. 2nd ed. New York, NY: Guilford Press.

Vavrichek, S. (2012). *The guide to compassionate assertiveness*. Oakland, CA: New Harbinger Press.

## Behavioral Activation

Beck, J. (2011). *Cognitive behavior therapy: Basics and beyond.* 2nd ed. New York, NY: Guilford Press.
Martell, C. R., Addis, M. E., & Jacobson, N. S. (2001). *Depression in context: Strategies for guided action.* New York, NY: Norton.
Veale, D. (2008). Behavioral activation for depression. *Advances in Psychiatric Treatment, 14,* 29–36. http://dx.doi.org/10.1192/apt.bp.107.004051
Veale, D., & Willson, R. (2007). *Manage your mood: A self-help guide using behavioural activation.* London: Constable & Robinson.

## Behavioral Rehearsal

Wolpe, J. (1990). *The practice of behavior therapy.* New York, NY: Pergamon Press.
Wolpe, J., & Lazarus, A. A. (1966). *Behavior therapy techniques: A guide to the treatment of neuroses.* New York, NY: Pergamon Press.

## Breath Retraining

Lehrer, P. M., Woolfolk, R. L., & Sime, W. E. (2007). *Principles and practice of stress management.* 3rd ed. New York, NY: Guilford Press.
Mirgain, S., Singles, J., & Hampton, A. (n.d.). The power of breath: Diaphragmatic breathing clinical tool. Retrieved from http://projects.hsl.wisc.edu/SERVICE/modules/12/M12_CT_The_Power_of_Breath_Diaphragmatic_Breathing.pdf

## Cognitive Defusion

Hayes, S., & Smith, S. (2005). *Get out of your mind and into your life: The new acceptance and commitment therapy.* Oakland, CA: New Harbinger.

## Cognitive Disputation

Beck, J. (2011). *Cognitive behavior therapy: Basics and beyond.* 2nd ed. New York, NY: Guilford Press.
Ellis, A., & MacLaren, C. (1998). *Rational emotive behavior therapy: A therapist's guide.* San Luis Obispo, CA: Impact.

## Habit Reversal

Azrin, N. H., & Peterson, A. L. (1988). Habit reversal for the treatment of Tourette syndrome. *Behaviour Research and Therapy, 26*(4), 347–351. doi:10.1016/0005-7967(88)90089-7.
Sperry, L. (2011). Switch and snap techniques: Breaking negative habits and reducing distress. In H. Rosenthal (Ed.), *Favorite counseling and therapy homework assignments* (pp. 309–311). New York, NY: Routledge.
Woods, D. W., & Miltenberger, R. G. (1995). Habit reversal: A review of applications and variations. *Journal of Behavior Therapy and Experimental Psychiatry, 26*(2), 123–131. doi:10.1016/0005-7916(95)00009-0.

## Limit Setting

Green, S. (1988). *Limit setting in clinical practice.* Washington, DC: American Psychiatric Press.

Linehan, M. (2015). *Skill training manual for treating borderline personality disorder.* 2nd ed. New York, NY: Guilford Press.

Sharrock, J., & Rickard, N. (2002). Limit setting: A useful strategy in rehabilitation. *The Australian Journal of Advanced Nursing, 19*(4), 21.

## Mindfulness

Crane, R. (2009). *Mindfulness-based cognitive therapy: Distinctive features.* New York, NY: Routledge.

Forsyth, J. P., & Eifert, G. H. (2007). *The mindfulness and acceptance workbook for anxiety.* Oakland, CA: New Harbinger Publications.

Linehan, M. (2015). *Skill training manual for treating borderline personality disorder.* 2nd ed. New York, NY: Guilford Press.

Segal, Z., Williams, J., & Teasdale, J. (2013). *Mindfulness-based cognitive therapy for depression.* 2nd ed. New York, NY: Guilford Press.

## Relapse Prevention

Bowen, S., Chawla, N., & Marlatt, G. A. (2011). *Mindfulness-based relapse prevention for addictive behaviors: A clinician's guide.* New York, NY: Guilford Press.

Gorski, T., & Miller, M. (1986). *Staying sober: A guide for relapse prevention.* Aspen, CO: Independence Press.

Marlatt, G. A., & Donovan, D. (2005). *Relapse prevention: Maintenance strategies in the treatment of addictive behaviors.* 2nd ed. New York, NY: Guilford Press.

## Stimulus Control

Bootzin, R. R. (1972). A stimulus control treatment for insomnia. *Proceedings of the American Psychological Association, 7,* 395–396.

Perlis, M. L., Jungquist, C., Smith, M. T., & Posner, D. (2006). *Cognitive behavioral treatment of insomnia: A session-by-session guide.* New York, NY: Springer.

## Thought Stopping

McKay, M., Davis, M., & Fanning, P. (2012). *Thoughts and feelings: Taking control of your moods and your life.* 4th ed. Oakland, CA: New Harbinger Publications.

Wolpe, J. (1990). *The practice of behavior therapy.* New York, NY: Pergamon Press.

Wolpe, J., & Lazarus, A. A. (1966). *Behavior therapy techniques: A guide to the treatment of neuroses.* New York, NY: Pergamon Press.

Yamagami, T. (1971). The treatment of an obsession by thought-stopping. *Journal of Behavior Therapy and Experimental Psychiatry, 2*(2), 133–135. doi:10.1016/0005-7916(71)90028-0.

## References

Alberti, R. (2008). *Your perfect right: Assertiveness and equality in your life and relationships.* 9th ed. San Luis Obispo, CA: Impact Publications.

Linehan, M. (2015). *Skill training manual for treating borderline personality disorder.* 2nd ed. New York, NY: Guilford Press.

Otto, M., Tolin, D. F., Nations, K. R., Utschig, A. C., Rothbaum, B. O., Hofmann, S. G., & Smits, J. A. (2012). Five sessions and counting: Considering ultra-brief treatment for panic disorder. *Depression and Anxiety, 29*(6), 465–470.

Otto, W., & Hofmann, S. G. (2010). *Avoiding treatment failures in the anxiety disorders.* New York, NY: Springer.

Segal, Z., Williams, J., & Teasdale, J. (2013). *Mindfulness-based cognitive therapy for depression.* 2nd ed. New York, NY: Guilford Press.

Sperry, J., & Sperry, L. (2018). *Cognitive behavior therapy in professional counseling practice.* New York, NY: Routledge.

Sperry, L. (2011). Switch and snap techniques: Breaking negative habits and reducing distress. In H. Rosenthal (Ed.), *Favorite counseling and therapy homework assignments* (pp. 309–311). New York, NY: Routledge.

Sperry, L. (2016). *Cognitive behavior therapy of DSM-5 personality disorders.* 3rd ed. New York, NY: Routledge.

Sperry, L., & Binensztok, V. (2019). *Ultra-brief cognitive behavioral interventions: The cutting-edge of mental health and integrated care practice.* New York, NY: Routledge.

Vavrichek, S. (2012). *The guide to compassionate assertiveness.* Oakland, CA: New Harbinger Press.

Chapter 5

# Outcomes Assessment and Indicators of Successful Treatment

In the era of accountability, therapists are not only expected to provide successful treatment but are increasingly expected to demonstrate that their provided treatment is effective. Two perspectives have surfaced on how to achieve such expectations. The first is "evidence-based practice," based on the empirically-demonstrated effects of a specific treatment intervention with specific psychological indications. The second is "practice-based evidence," wherein therapist-client collaboration and feedback are the focus of clinical effectiveness rather than specific treatment interventions (Sperry, Brill, Howard, & Grissom, 1996; Rousmaniere, 2017).

From the latter perspective, ongoing assessment throughout the course of therapy is of crucial importance where therapists monitor the processes and outcomes of treatment. This chapter emphasizes the latter perspective. The focus of research, until recently, was on the overall assessment of outcomes in treatment. More recently, it has since shifted to ongoing assessment, i.e., session-by-session monitoring of the progress of therapy called progress monitoring and routine outcome monitoring (Rousmaniere, 2017). As already noted, outcomes assessment and incorporating feedback are the fourth key component of Pattern Focused Therapy.

The chapter begins with a discussion of outcomes assessment, progress monitoring, and routine outcome monitoring, and their clinical value. It reviews some key research findings and applications to everyday clinical practice. Then, it describes several common outcome measures and screeners that are essential to clinical practice. Finally, it describes seven indicators of what highly effective therapists do to achieve successful therapeutic outcomes.

## Outcomes Assessment, Progress Monitoring, and Routine Outcome Monitoring

Let's begin with some technical definitions. Outcomes assessment is the use of measures to collect clinical data about the amount and type of change clients experience from the beginning to the end of therapy. Progress monitoring is the use of outcome measures that produce clinical data to monitor client change or non-change during the course of therapy (Rousmaniere, 2017). Routine outcome monitoring adds another element to progress monitoring in that it measures clients' progress not simply to evaluate change or non-change but, if necessary, to adapt treatment (van Sonsbeek, Hutschemaekers, Veerman, & Tiemens, 2014).

Therapists are not especially adept at predicting the strength of their client-therapist relationship nor predicting treatment outcomes. Instead, research has suggested that client ratings are more accurate at predicting the client-therapist alliance and treatment outcomes than those of their therapists (Orlinsky, Rønnestad, & Willutzki, 2004). The client's subjective experience of progress in the early treatment process is also a superior predictor of treatment success than all other predictors or measures, according to research (Orlinsky, Rønnestad, & Willutzki, 2004). How, then, can a therapist evaluate or accurately assess a client's treatment response? A simple answer is to measure and monitor both the alliance and outcomes of treatment.

A key premise of psychotherapy outcomes research is that therapists can use feedback to improve their clinical effectiveness (Sperry, Brill, Howard, & Grissom, 1996). Research has consistently shown that therapists who receive feedback on their ongoing work with clients outperform those who do not. Their treatment effectiveness increases significantly, as does the quality of their therapeutic relationships. In a study by Whipple et al. (2003), therapists who had access to feedback on their clients' progress and information about the therapeutic alliance were able to achieve significant changes with their clients, had fewer results of treatment dropout, and their clients were less likely to deteriorate. Another study examined the relationship between clients and therapists that were at risk of adverse outcomes. Therapists who received formal feedback in the study were 65% more likely to accomplish positive treatment results than those who did not get feedback (Whipple et al., 2003). A study including in excess of 6,000 clients reported that therapists who used formal feedback measures on an ongoing basis had significantly higher rates of retention and doubled the positive effects overall in comparison to therapists who did not have such feedback (Miller, Duncan, Brown, Sorrell, & Chalk, 2006). Although it was not a randomized controlled trial (RCT), the results reported in this study are noteworthy due to its notably large sample size. Finally, Shimokawa, Lambert, and Smart (2010) examined clients who were on-track for positive outcomes versus clients who were predicted to be treatment failures. They reported on the effects of feedback on these clients. Their review included over 4,000 clients and compared the treatment-as-usual conditions to feedback-assisted treatments in six RCTs. Results indicated that the condition in which therapists received feedback was far superior to treatment-as-usual clients, by approximately 20–30% of the clients. The feedback provided an advantage as it enabled therapists to identify and treat clients differently than in the treatment-as-usual condition. The results of the feedback also reduced the rates of deterioration to 5.5%, adding evidence of its substantial benefit.

Three predictions can be made when both the therapist and the client are aware of how the client rates the therapeutic relationship and the progress of treatment: (1) the therapeutic relationship is more likely to be effectively developed and maintained; (2) the client is more likely to stay in treatment; and (3) there are more positive treatment outcomes. Therefore, the monitoring of treatment outcomes and processes is absolutely crucial to providing effective therapy. This section will provide a description of various ways of assessing the therapeutic relationship and ensuring the ongoing examination of treatment processes and outcomes.

## *Clinical Value of Progress Monitoring*

Inconsistent and limited therapist performance is a major reason for giving feedback. A study of over 6,000 clients treated in routine practice found that only about a third improved or recovered while approximately two-thirds did not improve or recover (Hansen, Lambert, & Forman, 2002). Some therapists rarely have a single client who deteriorates, while others experience consistently high rates. Failures are usually due to therapist failure to identify deterioration or those who are not improving. Regularly assessing and monitoring outcomes has become indispensable in identifying clients who are not doing well, and in improving therapists' performance by increasing awareness of clients' progress. Such systems regularly track progress using measures which clients complete throughout treatment and which provide immediate feedback to therapists which is then used to inform treatment decisions (Lambert, Whipple, & Kleinstäuber, 2018).

Two extraordinary studies were published in 2018 that have significant implications for psychotherapy practice. Both have immediate clinical applications for therapists wishing to increase their expertise and clinical effectiveness. The first summarizes the meta-analytic results and clinical practice implications of fitting or tailoring treatment to specific client characteristics, such as attachment style, coping style, culture, gender identity, reactance level, religion and spirituality, sexual orientation, stages of change, and therapy preferences. These findings are from the APA Task Force on Evidence-Based Relationships and Responsiveness and its 28 recommendations for fitting psychotherapy to an individual client (Norcross & Wampold, 2018).

The second study is a systematic review and meta-analysis that examines the impact of measuring, monitoring, and feeding back information on client progress to therapists while providing psychotherapy. It considers the effects of the two most frequently studied routine outcome monitoring practices: The Partners for Change Outcome Management System, i.e., the ORS and SRS, and the Outcome Questionnaire System, i.e., the OQ-45. All three of these are described in detail in the following section.

Both attempt to enhance routine care by assisting therapists in recognizing problematic treatment response and then increasing collaboration between therapist and client to overcome poor treatment response. A total of 24 studies were analyzed. Two-thirds of the studies found that these two progress monitoring systems were superior to treatment-as-usual offered by the same therapists. Their use reduced deterioration rates and nearly doubled clinically significant change rates in clients who were predicted to have a poor outcome.

The practice implications of using either OQ-45 or ORS/SRS monitoring in routine practice is made clear by this study. The first is that these feedback systems provide therapists a most effective means of helping clients improve as well as preventing deterioration or lack of change among the two-thirds of clients who would otherwise do poorly. The second implication is that routine outcomes monitoring can further optimize treatment outcomes in the other third of clients. Across the 24 studies of both systems, results did not seem to depend on the presenting problem and diagnosis.

There are two questions therapists and trainees are increasingly asking about tracking client progress. The first is: Does tracking clients' response to treatment improve the overall outcome? Based on this meta-analysis, the answer is "yes." Both progress monitoring approaches for tracking a client's mental health vital signs were found to improve outcomes compared with treatment without such monitoring. The second is: How does it work? The answer is that these progress monitoring systems help therapists prevent treatment failure as well as optimize positive outcomes because therapists using them become more responsive to the client's needs and difficulties.

Finally, another key article focuses on some practical considerations in incorporating progress monitoring in everyday psychotherapy. It reviews the benefits, obstacles, and challenges that can hinder and have hindered implementation of routine outcome monitoring in clinical practice (Boswell, Kraus, Miller, & Lambert, 2015).

## Outcome Measures and Screeners

There are several psychometrically-sound outcomes measures and screeners available. This section describes 15 such measures. Some are primarily outcome measures: ORS, SRS, Polaris MH, and the OQ-45 which are described first, while the others serve both screening and outcomes monitoring functions. Screeners or screening instruments are "assessment tools that are easily administered, and scored, and provide useful insight into a client's presenting problem" (Sperry & Binensztok, 2019, p. 91).

### Session Rating Scale (SRS)

The Session Rating Scale (SRS; Duncan et al., 2003), is a 4-item instrument which measures the therapeutic alliance, that is short and easy to administer. The client is provided with four horizontal lines (measuring 10 cm long) printed on a sheet of paper. The first line is used to measure to what extent the client felt respected and understood. The second line indicates how much the therapist addressed what the client wanted to talk about. The third line measures the "fit" of the therapy approach for the client. On the fourth line, the client provides an indication on the level of satisfaction with the session. The client completes the scale immediately following the end of the session (Miller et al., 2006). The SRS is free of charge and available to individual mental health professionals by license accessible at: www.heartandsoulofchange.com/.

### Outcomes Rating Scale (ORS)

The Outcomes Rating Scale (ORS; Miller et al., 2003) is a brief and easy-to-administer measure that assesses the client's outcomes. The client is provided a sheet of paper containing four lines that are 10 cm in length. The client is asked to indicate on the line how things went based on how they feel; their relationships; ratings of social life and work life; and the overall well-being. This scale is given to the client to fill out prior to the start of the session. However, it may be administered after the first meeting (Miller Duncan, Sorrell, & Brown, 2005). The ORS is free of charge and available to individual mental health professionals by license accessible at: www.heartandsoulofchange.com/

### Polaris MH

Polaris MH is a comprehensive outcomes and diagnostic system. Like its predecessor, COMPASS-OP (Howard, Kopta, Krause, & Orlinsky, 1986; Howard, Moras, Brill, Martinovich, & Lutz, 1996; Sperry et al., 1996), Polaris MH is a psychometrically sophisticated, computer-based assessment system. Polaris MH provides both treatment process and outcomes feedback, in addition to a number of diagnostic and critical indicators. Like other comprehensive treatment outcomes measures, Polaris MH provides the following outcomes information and indicators: suggested treatment focus; treatment progress; client satisfaction with treatment; and, therapeutic alliance. Polaris MH also provides the following information and indicators: severity and nature of the patient's symptoms; the impact of the patient's problems upon his/her life functioning; the presence of co-morbid conditions: chemical dependency, psychosis, and bipolar disorder; presence of critical conditions (e.g., suicidality, psychosis, violence).

The Polaris-MH measures three domains: Subjective Well-Being, Symptoms, and Functional Impairment. The Symptoms scale is a composite of sub-scale scores: depression, anxiety, post-traumatic stress disorder, obsessive-compulsive, somatization, panic, phobia, and an overall scale of symptomatic distress. The three sub-scales of Functional Impairment are personal, social, vocational, as well as a scale of overall functioning. Polaris-MH also assesses for general health problems, substance abuse, psychosis, and bipolar disorder. In addition, it measures resilience, meaning, treatment motivation, satisfaction with treatment. and the therapeutic alliance or bond.

Polaris-MH consists of three measures or questionnaires. The Patient Intake form provides detailed information for treatment planning. The Patient Update form provides information concurrently with treatment about the client's condition, progress, and satisfaction with treatment. The Brief Patient Update form provides a global mental health status indicator, and the severity of symptoms of depression. Polaris-MH also provides Reports that provide information for clinical decision support, i.e., individual patient reports, and for outcomes assessment, i.e., program-level aggregate data (Lueger, 2006).

## OQ-45

The OQ-45 (Lambert, Gregersen, & Burlingame, 2004) is probably the most commonly used commercial treatment outcomes measure today. It is a brief, 45-item, self-report outcome and tracking instrument that is designed for repeated measurement of client progress through the course of therapy and following termination. It measures client functioning in three domains: symptom distress; interpersonal functioning; and social role. Functional level and change over time can be assessed which allows treatment to be modified based on the changes noted. The OQ-45 also contains risk assessment items for suicide potential, substance abuse, and potential violence at work. It has been translated into more than ten languages and is based on normative data and has adequate validity and reliability. It can be administered and scored in either electronic or paper format. Access to the OQ-45.2 version is available at www.agapepsych.com/serfiles/1059203/file/Updated%20Forms%20(01_2018)/OQ-45_2.pdf.

### The Patient Health Questionnaire-9 (PHQ-9)

The Patient Health Questionnaire-9 (PHQ-9) is a 9-item questionnaire that corresponds to the nine DSM-5 criteria for Major Depressive Disorder. Each question is rated on a 4-point scale from 0–3 where 0 = not at all, 1 = several days, 2 = more than half the days, and 3 = nearly every day. A tenth question asks how any symptoms the client rated between 1 and 3 have interfered with the person's ability to function at work, at home, and with other people. Clients rate their experiences for the previous two weeks. The scoring for the PHQ-9 is as follows:

   0–4 = minimal or none
   5–9 = mild
   10–14 = moderate
   15–19 = moderately severe
   20–27 = severe.

The PHQ-9 is useful for screening, diagnosis, treatment planning, and progress monitoring. The first two questions of the PHQ-9 are referred to as the PHQ-2 and are used for screening since they assess for depressed mood and lack of pleasure, and at least one of those symptoms must be present for the diagnosis to be met. The full instrument is required for diagnosis and progress monitoring (Martin, Rief, Klaiberg, & Braehler, 2006).

### *The Columbia Suicide Severity Rating Scale (C-SSRS)*

The Columbia Suicide Severity Rating Scale (C-SSRS) is a questionnaire used to assess suicidal ideation and risk. It consists of several forced choice (yes/no) questions and several multiple choice and free response questions. The C-SSRS assesses whether clients are having thoughts of suicide, the intensity of those thoughts, whether clients have taken any steps to create a suicide plan and prepare for suicide, and whether the client has attempted suicide previously. There is also a computer-automated version of this measure (Mundt et al., 2010).

### *The Mood Scale*

The Mood Scale is very brief measure of an individual's overall experience, in the moment, of a down mood and depression. Instructions for its use are simple and straightforward. Ask the client to rate their overall feeling of nervousness and anxiousness at a particular point in time on a scale of 0–10, where 0 is the worst mood possible and 10 is the best possible mood (Sperry, 2010).

A mood of 3 or less is considered severe, 4–5 is considered mildly depressed, 6–8 is considered euthymic or normal, and higher is considered happy and upbeat. The Mood Scale is useful for progress monitoring.

## Subjective Units of Distress (SUDS)

The Subjective Units of Distress scale is a useful, informal tool to rate a client's level of anxiety or panic. Developed by Joseph Wolpe (1969), clients can be rated on a 0–10 or a 0–100 scale. This scale is useful for both clients and providers to assess the intensity of symptoms and the distress and disturbance they cause for clients. It is also a useful measure to monitor progress through therapy and after interventions. The instructions are simple: On a 1–100 scale where 1 represents the most calm and serenity you can imagine and 100 represents the most severe distress you can imagine, give the number that best indicates how you currently feel (or in a specific past situation). With a minimum amount of practice in SUDS, clients can quickly and accurately rate and communicate their distress to a therapist. The widespread use of this self-rating assessment reflects its clinical utility.

## Generalized Anxiety Disorder-7 (GAD-7)

The Generalized Anxiety Disorder-7 (GAD-7) is a 7-item questionnaire that corresponds to the DSM-5 criteria for Generalized Anxiety Disorder (Lowe et al., 2008). Each question is rated on a 4-point scale from 0–3 where 0 = not at all, 1 = several days, 2 = more than half the days, and 3 = nearly every day. Clients rate their experiences for the previous two weeks. The scoring for the GAD-7 is as follows:

0–4 = minimal or none
5–9 = mild
10–14 = moderate
15–21 = severe.

The first two questions of the GAD-7 are referred to as the GAD-2 and can be used to screen for anxiety but the full instrument is required for diagnosis and progress monitoring. The GAD-7 has also been shown to be useful in screening for Panic Disorder and Social Anxiety (Bardhoshi et al., 2016).

## The PCL PTSD Checklist

The PCL PTSD Checklist is a 17-item questionnaire widely used as a PTSD screening instrument. Respondents are asked about the severity with which a particular symptom has affected them within the last month. Each question is rated on a 5-point scale where 1 = not at all, 2 = a little bit, 3 = moderately, 4 = quite a bit, and 5 = extremely. The PCL includes subscales for Reexperiencing, Avoidance, and Hyperarousal, and is available for civilians (PCL-C) and members of the armed forces (PCL-M). Both instruments are available to the public and used by the Department of Veterans Affairs (Bardhoshi et al., 2016).

### The Anxiety Scale

The Anxiety Scale is very brief measure of an individual's overall experience, in the moment, of anxiety and panic. Instructions for its use are simple and straightforward. Ask the client to rate their overall feeling of nervousness and anxiousness at a particular point in time on a 1–10 scale: where 1 = feeling you were going to die or have a heart attack or go crazy, and where 10 = being perfectly calm and anxiety-free (Sperry, 2010). The Anxiety Scale is useful for progress monitoring.

### The Insomnia Severity Index

The Insomnia Severity Index (ISI) is a 7-item questionnaire that corresponds to the DSM-5 criteria for insomnia (Morin, Belleville, Bélanger, & Ivers, 2011). Each question is rated on a 5-point scale from 0–4 where 0 = none, 1 = mild, 2 = moderate, 3 = severe, and 4 = very severe. Questions assess difficulty in falling and staying asleep, as well as implications for mood and daily functioning. The scoring for the ISI is as follows:

   0–7 = no clinically significant insomnia
   8–14 = subthreshold insomnia
   15–21 = clinical insomnia (moderate severity)
   22–28 = clinical insomnia (severe).

### The Drug Abuse Screening Test

The Drug Abuse Screening Test (DAST) is a 28-item forced-choice (yes/no) self-report questionnaire that assesses problem drug use and its associated consequences. The DAST enquires about use of prescribed and over-the-counter drugs in excess of directions and the non-medical use of drugs (Cocco & Carey, 1998).

### The PEG Pain Scale

The PEG Pain Scale is a 3-item instrument used to assess pain intensity and interference. Each question is rated on an 11-point scale from 0–10 where 0 = no pain, and 10 = pain as bad as you can imagine. Clients are asked to rate their average level of pain in the past week, the extent to which the pain has interfered in their enjoyment of life in the past week, and the extent to which the pain has interfered with general activity in the past week (Krebs et al., 2009).

## The Current Opioid Misuse Measure (COMM)

The Current Opioid Misuse Measure (COMM) is a 17-item instrument used to assess a patient's misuse of medication by determining its effect on social, emotional, and general functioning. Each question is rated on a 5-point scale from 0–4, where 0 = never, 1 = seldom, 2 = sometimes, 3 = often, 4 = very often. This patient self-report instrument also measures contextual factors such as emotional volatility and recent history of arguments. These questions are meant to measure the effect of medication misuse on the client's functioning, but may not necessarily point to medication abuse. This screening tool is best paired with an interview about how the client is using medications (Butler et al., 2007).

## Seven Indicators of Successful Therapy

There has yet to be clinical or research consensus on exactly how significant and enduring client change is effected. Clearly, using feedback to inform therapy makes a difference. But, there is more to it. Some have speculated it can be used as well as to provide qualitative and quantitative research to identify the differences between how highly effective therapists and average therapists function. Dr. Marvin Goldfried contends that there are four principles of change and distinct methods that highly effective therapists consistently utilize that average therapists do not (Goldfried, 1980). Approximately 32 years later, he remains convinced that these four defining principles define how master therapists work, based on his and others' research (Goldfried, 2012). The four indicators are: (1) enhance the therapeutic alliance; (2) enhance positive expectations and client motivation; (3) increase client awareness; and (4) facilitate corrective experiences. Based on my observations of other highly effective therapists, three additional indicators can be added: (5) identify patterns and focus treatment; (6) facilitate first-, second-, and third-order change; and (7) increase therapist expertise. Each of these indicators is described in this section.

### 1. Enhance the Therapeutic Alliance

The therapeutic alliance refers to both the relationship and bond between the client and therapist and the agreed-upon goals and methods of therapy. A productive therapeutic alliance, in which clients can trust the therapist to be competent and concerned about their best interests, is associated with effective therapy. Therapeutic alliances are not consistent from client to client. A therapist may have an easier time developing a therapeutic alliance with a motivated client and a more difficult time developing an effective alliance with a defiant one. The latter would require significant effort and investment on the part of the therapist. The therapist's experience and skills in developing the therapeutic alliance are reflected in the outcomes of therapy, provided that the strong therapeutic alliances are associated with effective therapy. Enhancing the alliance not only becomes an inviting factor, creating more involvement on the part of the client, but it may also facilitate willingness to engage in the painful or difficult processes of change (Goldfried, 2012).

## 2. Enhance Positive Expectations and Client Motivation

For therapy to work, the clients entering the process need a reasonable expectation it can help them. They also need to have some motivation for change. These two prerequisites are essential for effecting therapeutic change. Several factors can influence the prerequisites in a positive or negative way. For instance, seeking information about panic attacks and discussing the process of change with a friend or a trusted family member can increase both motivation and expectation. Subsequently, this individual may be more motivated to change after experiencing another panic attack or a related symptom than a teenager who is acting out is sent to therapy by his or her parents. When motivation or expectations are suboptimal, it becomes the therapist's priority to increase these prerequisites, as they are essential for change (Goldfried, 2012). Unsurprisingly, known master therapists excel at this task. Whether employing motivational interviewing (MI) or other similar interventions, these therapists increase the credibility of both the clinician and the process of therapy as they enhance the client's readiness and motivation for change.

## 3. Increase Client Awareness

Increasing the client's awareness is another prerequisite for change. Awareness is needed in effecting change, irrespective of the therapeutic orientation employed. However, the degree of awareness and its kind may differ, depending on the presenting problem and the client's personality:

> Some clients may be unaware of how their thinking is influencing their feelings, others may be unaware of how their emotional reaction results in behavior, and still others how their behavior negatively impacts on others. Thus, individuals who are unaware of their anger, and also their tendency to

withdraw when angry are unaware of how this emotion-action link adversely affects their relationships with others.

(Goldfried, 2012, p. 20)

Therapeutic considerations such as time, frequency, and nature of thoughts, feelings, and behaviors must be involved in increasing the client's awareness. The operative dynamics and determinants of the case can be identified with a clear and accurate case conceptualization. In effect, such case conceptualization can provide the therapist a basis for increasing the client's awareness of factors affecting their life.

## 4. Facilitate Corrective Experiences

Profound and enduring change necessitates more than marginal insight or simple behavior change. This type of change can, and often does, require a corrective experience, in which the individual experiences a relationship or event in an unexpected way. These are not just ordinarily helpful events in therapy. Instead, they are significant events that disprove past experiences and have substantial effects on the individual (Castonguay & Hill, 2012). Corrective experiences are central to the transformative processes of many psychotherapy approaches and they represent second-order change. In order for this kind of experience to occur, the client must "take a risk behaving differently, often in the presence of some skepticism and apprehension. By experiencing a positive outcome, thinking (e.g., expectations that something bad will happen) and emotion (e.g., anxiety) will start to change as well" (Goldfried, 2012, pp. 20–21). A clear indication of a corrective experience is noted

> when clients report a between-session experience with the tone of surprise in their voice – either because they behaved in a way that was different for them or because of the unexpected positive consequences that followed what they did. At other times, the [corrective experience] may result from an ongoing interaction with a supportive and affirming therapist.
> 
> (Goldfried, 2012, p. 21)

Highly effective therapists are capable of facilitating corrective experiences.

## 5. Identify Patterns and Focus Treatment

As already noted, pattern is one of the key components of Pattern Focused Therapy. Not surprisingly, effective therapists can more quickly, accurately, and effortlessly identify maladaptive patterns than novice therapists and trainees. This capability is predictable given the amount of time and extensive experience needed to develop the expertise for identifying the complex recognition of patterns (Ericsson, 2006).

For effective therapists, pattern is the heart of case conceptualization. A focused, accurate, and thorough case conceptualization is required in order to plan, guide, and effect change (Sperry, 2010). For average therapists, this process can require one or two sessions and involve eliciting considerable amounts of information on the case. However, master therapists can typically conceptualize cases in their initial meeting with the client and base determinations on the recognition of patterns. Thereafter, they test out the conceptualization and modify accordingly, if necessary. The process is intuitive and swift for master therapists, whereas for trainees and beginning therapists, it tends to be much more deliberate and slower (Sperry & Sperry, 2012).

The focus of treatment provides the course for the process and targets in order to replace a maladaptive pattern with a more adaptive pattern (Sperry, 2010). It also provides needed stabilization for the process, regularly maintaining the focus and efforts on change. Positive treatment outcomes are associated with the ability to track and maintain a treatment focus, which master therapists are unsurprisingly capable of accomplishing. Chapter 9 provides a more in-depth description and illustration of the process of case conceptualization, including emphasis on the importance of the treatment focus and pattern recognition.

### 6. Facilitate First-, Second- and Third-Order Changes

There are a host of strategies that can be utilized in order to manage life concerns. Some strategies are career counseling, personal counseling, crisis counseling, coaching, case management, and psychotherapy. Presumably, psychotherapy is a strategy that primarily aims at effecting profound and enduring change. In order to fully appreciate the impact of psychotherapy, it can be useful to conceptualize change processes in terms of orders of change. Good and Beitman (2006) have identified three orders of change: first, second, and third order. In first-order change, clients endeavor to achieve stability, reduce symptoms, and manage small changes. Normally, strategies such as case management, crisis counseling, and career counseling assist in symptom reduction or a temporary resolution for given life problem. These strategies can effect stability but not personality or pattern transformation. Second-order change occurs when clients change or modify a maladaptive pattern to a more adaptive one. This order of change can be deemed transformative (Fraser & Solovey, 2007). Finally, in third-order change, clients become their own therapists. That is, they can facilitate change on their own, without help or guidance. Profound and enduring change is not possible without second- and third-order change. Whether or not they are acquainted with the change orders, renowned master therapists are experts in effecting all three orders of change.

## 7. Increase Therapist's Expertise

Three questions are central to psychotherapy research as well as psychotherapy practice. The first question: Is psychotherapy effective? was posed by Hans Eysenck (1952). It has taken five decades to definitively answer that question. Today, both the efficacy and effectiveness of psychotherapy have been well established. But, despite the consistent findings substantiating psychotherapy's worth, a second question arose: How does psychotherapy work? Unfortunately, the question remains unanswered largely because of the ideological feud between advocates of the common factors (process) position and advocates of specific factors (evidence-based or empirically supported treatments) position. Even though a compromise position emerged—integrative approaches where both common and specific factors are combined—it has not resolved a number of theoretical and research issues. The hope was that

> knowing how psychotherapy works would give rise to a universally accepted standard of care which, in turn, would yield more effective and efficient treatment. However, if the outcome of psychotherapy is in the hands of the person who delivers it, then attempts to reach accord regarding the essential nature, qualities, or characteristics of the enterprise are much less important than knowing how to best accomplish what they do.
> (Miller, Hubble, Chow, & Seidel, 2013, pp. 90–91)

As it is currently framed, it is not the therapeutic alliance nor a specific intervention that determines whether therapy is effective and successful. Rather, it is how the therapist expertly develops and maintains the alliance and effectively tailors the intervention to the client that makes the difference. Available research supports this new perspective. It documents that therapist expertise is probably the most robust predictor of psychotherapy outcome rather than the therapeutic alliance (common factors) or a treatment intervention (specific factors). Indeed, the variance of outcomes attributable to therapists (5–9%) is greater than the variability among treatments (0–1%), the alliance (5%), and the superiority of an empirically supported treatment to a placebo treatment (0–4%) (Miller et al., 2013, p. 90; Wampold, 2005; Lutz et al., 2007; Duncan, 2010).

During this same time frame, a more focused question emerged: Why are some therapists better than others? Mounting research has already begun to provide an answer to this third question, but at the same time addresses the second question. The reality is that therapist expertise and the acquisition of expertise are already changing psychotherapy research and practice (Barkham, Lutz, Lambert, & Saxon, 2017).

Research on expertise in psychotherapy, also called the therapist effect, is under way, as are innovative training programs to increase therapist expertise. Seeking client feedback with outcomes instruments to inform therapy and engaging in deliberate practice are ways of increasing clinical effectiveness and expertise (Rousmaniere, 2017).

Deliberate practice involves three elements. First, the performance of well-designed tasks at an appropriate level of difficulty. Second, useful feedback. Third, opportunities for repetition and correction of errors (Ericsson, 2006). In leaning new skill sets and competencies, deliberate practice involves engaging in increasingly difficult elements of the skill or competency. Seeking constant feedback in various forms is another essential component of deliberate practice. This includes directly asking clients for feedback as well as using standard outcome measures to assess and monitor clients' progress. Then, it requires using the feedback to alter the course or direction of treatment.

> Being open to feedback is part of deliberate practice. Another part of turning experience into expertise is the use of reflection ... There must be a feedback loop so that the individual can learn from the practice. When therapists are fully licensed and working alone, they can fall victim to not learning from their own practitioner experience if there is no deliberate practice feedback system that includes self-reflection and self-monitoring of oneself as a practitioner.
> (Jennings, Skovholt, Goh, & Lian, 2013, p. 241)

In other words, "[d]eliberate practice is essential to developing expertise, it is not optional" (Sperry & Carlson, 2014, p. 191). Finally, professional training in the near future will increasingly emphasize the development of evidence-based therapists at least as much as, if not more than, learning how to perform one or more evidence-based treatment approaches (Barkham, Lutz, Lambert, & Saxon, 2017).

## Conclusion

The first section of this chapter addressed the role of outcomes assessment and the use of this feedback to inform and improve treatment. The second section described 15 commonly used outcome measures and screeners. Finally, the third section addressed seven indicators of successful therapy and suggested that highly effective therapists differ from less effective therapists and trainees by using these indicators. Essentially, highly effective therapists foster therapeutic alliances, foster positive expectations and motivation in their clients, increase their clients' awareness, facilitate corrective experiences, quickly identify patterns and maintain the focus of treatment, facilitate first-, second-, and third-order change, and work to increase their therapeutic expertise, including deliberate practice. Of course, routine outcomes monitoring is a necessary element of therapeutic effectiveness, but it is not of itself sufficient. It appears that being a highly effective therapist assumes routine outcome monitoring and engaging in these seven indicators.

## References

Bardhoshi, G., Erford, B. T., Duncan, K., Dummett, B., Falco, M., Deferio, K., & Kraft, J. (2016). Choosing assessment instruments for posttraumatic stress disorder screening and outcome research. *Journal of Counseling & Development*, 94, 184–194.

Barkham, M., Lutz, W., Lambert, M. J., & Saxon, D. (2017). Therapist effects, effective therapists, and the law of variability. In L. G. Castonguay & C. E. Hill (Eds.), *How and why are some therapists better than others?: Understanding therapist effects*. Washington, DC: American Psychological Association.

Bordin, E. S. (1994). Theory and research on the therapeutic working alliance: New directions. In A. O. Horvath & L. S. Greenberg (Eds.), *The working alliance: Theory, research, and practice* (pp. 13–37). New York, NY: John Wiley & Sons.

Boswell, J. F., Kraus, D. R., Miller, S. D., & Lambert, M. J. (2015). Implementing routine outcome monitoring in clinical practice: Benefits, challenges, and solutions. *Psychotherapy Research*, 25(1), 6–19.

Butler, S., Budman, S., Fernandez, K., Houle, B., Benoit, C., Katz, N., & Jamison, R. (2007). Development and validation of the current opioid misuse measure. *Pain*, 130(1–2),144–156.

Castonguay, L., & Hill. C. (Eds.). (2012). *Transformation in psychotherapy: Corrective experiences across cognitive-behavioral, humanistic, and psychodynamics approaches*. Washington, DC: American Psychological Association.

Cocco, K., & Carey, K. (1998). Psychometric properties of the Drug Abuse Screening Test in psychiatric outpatients. *Psychological Assessment*, 10(4), 408–414.

Duncan, B. (2010). *On becoming a better therapist*. Washington, DC: American Psychological Association Press.

Duncan, B. L., Miller, S. D., Sparks, J. A., Claud, D. A., Reynolds, L. R., Brown, J., & Johnson, L. D. (2003). The Session Rating Scale: Preliminary psychometric properties of a "working" alliance measure. *Journal of Brief Therapy*, 3(1), 3–12.

Ericsson, K. A. (2006). The influence of experience and deliberate practice on the development of superior expert performance. In K. A. Ericsson (Ed.), *Cambridge handbook of expertise and expert performance* (pp. 685–705). New York, NY: Cambridge University Press.

Eysenck, H. J. (1952). The effects of psychotherapy: An evaluation. *Journal of Consulting Psychology*, 16, 319–324.

Fraser, J., & Solovey, A. (2007). *Second-order change in psychotherapy: The golden thread that unifies effective treatments*. Washington, DC: American Psychological Association.

Goldfried, M. (1980). Toward the delineation of therapeutic change principles. *American Psychologist*, 35(11), 991.

Goldfried, M. (2012). The corrective experiences: A core principle for therapeutic change. In L. Castonguay & C. Hill (Eds.). *Transformation in psychotherapy: Corrective experiences across cognitive-behavioral, humanistic, and psychodynamics approaches* (pp. 13–29). Washington, DC: American Psychological Association.

Good, G., & Beitman, B. (2006). *Counseling and psychotherapy essentials: Integrating theories, skills, and practices*. New York, NY: Norton.

Hansen, N. B., Lambert, M. J., & Forman, E. V. (2002). The psychotherapy dose-response effect and its implications for treatment delivery services. *Clinical Psychology: Science and Practice, 9,* 329–343.

Howard, K. I., Kopta, S. M., Krause, M. S., & Orlinsky, D. E. (1986). The dose-effect relationship in psychotherapy. *American Psychologist, 41*(2), 159–164.

Howard, K. I., Moras, K., Brill, P. L., Martinovich, Z., & Lutz, W. (1996). Evaluation of psychotherapy: Efficacy, effectiveness, and patient progress. *American Psychologist, 51*(10), 1059–1064.

Jennings, L., Skovholt, T. M., Goh, M., & Lian, F. (2013). Master therapists: Explorations of expertise. In M. H. Rønnestad & T. M. Skovholt (Eds.), *The developing practitioner: Growth and stagnation of therapists and counselors* (pp. 213–246). New York, NY: Routledge.

Krebs, E., Lorenz, K., Bair, M., Damush, T., Wu, J., Sutherland, J.., ... & Kroenke, K. (2009). Development and initial validation of the PEG, a three-item scale assessing pain intensity and interference. *Journal of General Internal Medicine, 24*(6), 733–738.

Lambert, M. J., Gregersen, A. T., & Burlingame, G. M. (2004). The Outcome Questionnaire-45. In M. E. Maruish (Ed.), *The use of psychological testing for treatment planning and outcomes assessment: Instruments for adults* (pp. 191–234). Mahwah, NJ: Lawrence Erlbaum Associates Publishers.

Lambert, M. J., Whipple, J. L., & Kleinstäuber, M. (2018). Collecting and delivering progress feedback: A meta-analysis of routine outcome monitoring. *Psychotherapy, 55*(4), 520–537.

Livesley, W. (2003). *Practical management of personality disorder.* New York, NY: Guilford Press.

Löwe, B., Decker, O., Müller, S., Brähler, E., Schellberg, D., Herzog, W., & Herzberg, P. Y. (2008). Validation and standardization of the Generalized Anxiety Disorder Screener (GAD-7) in the general population. *Medical Care, 46*(3), 266–274.

Lueger, R. J. (2006). Technology to support the clinical management of psychotherapy cases: Commentary on the Polaris-MH. *Pragmatic Case Studies in Psychotherapy, 2*(3), 1–7.

Lutz, W., Leon, S. C., Martinovich, Z., Lyons, J. S., & Stiles, W. B. (2007). Therapist effects in outpatient psychotherapy: A three-level growth curve approach. *Journal of Counseling Psychology, 54,* 32–39.

Martin, A., Rief, W., Klaiberg, A., & Braehler, E. (2006). Validity of the brief patient health questionnaire mood scale (PHQ-9) in the general population. *General Hospital Psychiatry, 28*(1), 71–77.

Meier, S. (2015). *Incorporating progress monitoring and outcome assessment into counseling and psychotherapy: A primer.* New York, NY: Oxford University Press.

Miller, S. D., Duncan, B. L., Brown, J., Sorrell, R., & Chalk, M. B. (2006). Using formal client feedback to improve retention and outcome: Making ongoing real-time assessment feasible. *Journal of Brief Therapy, 5,*5–22.

Miller, S. D., Duncan, B. L., Brown, J., Sparks, J., & Claud, D. (2003). The outcome rating scale: A preliminary study of the reliability, validity, and feasibility of a brief visual analog measure. *Journal of Brief Therapy, 2*(2), 91–100.

Miller, S. D., Duncan, B. L., Sorrell, R., & Brown, G. S. (2005). The Partners for Change Outcome Management System. *Journal of Clinical Psychology, 61,* 199–208.

Miller, S. D., Hubble, M. A., Chow, D. L., & Seidel, J. A (2013). The outcome of psychotherapy: Yesterday, today and tomorrow. *Psychotherapy, 50*(1), 88–97.

Morin, C. M., Belleville, G., Bélanger, L., & Ivers, H. (2011). The Insomnia Severity Index: Psychometric indicators to detect insomnia cases and evaluate treatment response. *Sleep, 34*(5), 601–608.

Mundt, J., Greist, J., Gelenberg, A., Katzelnick, D., Jefferson, J., & Modell, J. (2010). Feasibility and validation of a computer-automated Columbia-Suicide Severity Rating Scale using interactive voice response technology. *Journal of Psychiatric Research, 44*(16), 1224–1228.

Norcross, J. C., & Wampold, B. E. (2018). A new therapy for each patient: Evidence-based relationships and responsiveness. *Journal of Clinical Psychology,* 74(11), 1889–1906.

Orlinsky, D. E., Rønnestad, M. H., & Willutzki, U. (2004). Fifty years of psychotherapy process-outcome research: Continuity and change. In M. J. Lambert (Ed.), *Bergin and Garfield's handbook of psychotherapy and behavior change.* 5th ed. (pp.307–389). New York, NY: Wiley.

Rousmaniere, T. (2017). *Deliberate practice for psychotherapists: A guide to improving clinical effectiveness.* New York, NY: Routledge.

Shimokawa, K., Lambert, M. J., & Smart, D. (2010). Enhancing treatment outcome of patients at risk of treatment failure: Meta-analytic and mega-analytic review of a psychotherapy quality assurance system. *Journal of Consulting & Clinical Psychology,* 78, 298–311.

Sperry, L. (2010). *Highly effective therapy: Developing essential clinical competencies in counseling and psychotherapy.* New York, NY: Routledge.

Sperry, L., & Binensztok, V. (2019). *Ultra-brief cognitive behavioral interventions: The cutting-edge of mental health and integrated care practice.* New York, NY: Routledge.

Sperry, L., Brill, P. L., Howard, K. I., & Grissom, G. R. (1996). *Treatment outcomes in psychotherapy and psychiatric interventions.* New York, NY: Routledge.

Sperry, L., & Carlson, J. (2014). *How master therapists work: Effecting change from the first through the last session and beyond.* New York, NY: Routledge.

Sperry, L., & Sperry, J. (2012). *Case conceptualization: Mastering this competency with ease and confidence.* New York, NY: Routledge.

Van Sonsbeek, M. A., Hutschemaekers, G. G., Veerman, J. W., & Tiemens, B. B. (2014). Effective components of feedback from Routine Outcome Monitoring (ROM) in youth mental health care: Study protocol of a three-arm parallel-group randomized controlled trial. *BMC Psychiatry,* 14(1), 3. doi:10.1186/1471-244X-14-3.

Wampold, B. E. (2005). Establishing specificity in psychotherapy scientifically: Design and evidence issues. *Clinical Psychology: Science & Practice,* 12, 194–197.

Whipple, J. L., Lambert, M. J., Vermeersch, D. A., Smart, D. W., Nielsen, S. L., & Hawkins, E. J. (2003). Improving the effects of psychotherapy: The use of early identification of treatment failure and problem-solving strategies in routine practice. *Journal of Counseling Psychology,* 58, 59–68.

Wolpe, J. (1969). *The practice of behavior therapy.* New York, NY: Pergamon Press.

# Chapter 6

# The First Session

During the first session of Pattern Focused Therapy, the client gets a sense of the therapy experience as well as a map of the process. It is the most critical session and largely determines both the course and outcome of therapy (Sperry & Carlson, 2014). In my experience, several essential tasks must be accomplished in this session in order to achieve successful treatment outcomes in short-term therapy in mental health or integrated care settings (Sperry & Binensztok, 2019a). In the past, these essential tasks might have been spread out over two or three sessions. But when the course of therapy is relatively brief—six or fewer sessions—this session tends to be highly structured in order to quickly and efficiently elicit key clinical information, establish a treatment focus and goals, and socialize the client to the therapy process, to name just three of these tasks.

The chapter begins with a description of these essential tasks. Then, the case of Jerrod is offered to illustrate the initial session in Pattern Focused Therapy. A transcription of segments and commentary is provided. The remaining sessions of this completed and successful therapy are presented in Chapter 7 and Chapter 8.

## Essential Tasks of the Initial Session

Here is a preview of the eight tasks. Informed consent is the first task. Within this task, the client is informed about the type of the treatment, as well as his rights and responsibilities. Then, the clinician begins to establish an effective therapeutic relationship by joining the client in an atmosphere characterized as safe, mutual, and nonjudgmental. While it begins in the initial session, establishing and then maintaining an effective therapeutic alliance continues throughout the course of treatment. Another key task is assessment. Three crucial components of assessment are required in the initial session: (1) collecting sufficient data to formulate a diagnosis; (2) completing a functional assessment; and (3) identifying the client's pattern. Brief screening instruments are useful in completing the initial assessment as well as assessing and monitoring clinical progress. An effective assessment is the basis for identifying the client's basic pattern and developing an accurate case conceptualization. Accurately identifying the pattern is essential to developing and maintaining an effective therapeutic alliance and implementing interventions that will achieve treatment goals.

Another task that is important in the initial session is socializing the client to the treatment context. This includes a thorough explanation of what treatment involves, its intended effects, and what is expected of both the therapist and the client. This discussion typically leads to mutual agreement of first- and second-order goals. Additionally, it is crucial for some change to be facilitated within the first session. This can take the form of instillation of hope or a reduction of some of the client's distress. Finally, the client is assigned homework to complete and present for the following session. Let us now describe the eight tasks in more detail.

## *1. Develop and Foster the Therapeutic Alliance*

One of the most critical tasks in the first session is to begin to establish the therapeutic alliance. Increases in treatment compliance, decreases in premature termination, and the improvement of treatment outcomes have all been linked to strong therapeutic alliances (Horvath & Luborsky, 1993; Sperry, 2010a). The term "therapeutic alliance" is used interchangeably with "therapeutic relationship." However, this is inaccurate as the alliance is greater and more inclusive than the relationship. The therapeutic relationship is the bond between the client and therapist. The alliance, on the other hand, includes the client-therapist bond, agreement on goals for treatment, and mutual agreement on the methods for treatment (Bordin, 1994). The client must feel comfortable, understood, and hopeful about therapy in order to form a bond with the therapist. This influences the client and encourages them not only to have sensitive conversations, but also to modify their ways of thinking, feeling, and behaving (Sperry & Carlson, 2014).

The client's preferred approach and expectations for treatment must also be identified. While some clients may verbalize their specific hopes and desires for therapy, others may not. Therefore, structured questions can aid in developing mutually agreed upon goals. Furthermore, some clients prefer to engage in concrete action to control or reduce symptoms, while others show a preference for mutual exploration. An effective collaboration and assessment of the client's needs are part of the therapist's capacity to form an effective therapeutic alliance.

Even a strong and established therapeutic alliance is susceptible to ruptures and strains. Therefore, the therapeutic alliance must be monitored throughout. Ruptures in the therapeutic alliance are considered a factor that interferes with treatment and can affect treatment outcomes in a negative manner (Sperry, 2010b).

The Session Rating Scale (SRS) (Duncan et al., 2003) is administered at the end of each session in order to monitor and evaluate the therapeutic alliance. For instance, the SRS may uncover some disappointment on behalf of the client that a specific topic was not covered within the session. This can lead to a productive clarification of the client's needs and inform the therapist about the expectations of the client, leading to modification in subsequent sessions. While the therapeutic alliance may be strained or ruptured otherwise, understanding and agreement facilitated by the use of a monitoring tool can preserve the therapeutic alliance.

## 2. Secure Informed Consent

Typically, informed consent involves signing a form that explains confidentiality and its limits, fees, risks and benefits, the rights of the client to terminate therapy, and a description of the protocol for treatment. Presumably, the client is provided the opportunity to asks questions and seek clarification before signing the treatment consent form (Sperry, 2008).

In Pattern Focused Therapy, informed consent is understood as a process not simply an event, i.e., signing a consent form prior or during the first session. In fact, it is viewed as an ongoing process of client assent, the client must be provided a thorough outline of rights and involvement in therapy in a statement. The statement should explain confidentiality and its limits, fees, risks and benefits, the rights of the client to terminate therapy, and a description of the protocol for treatment. The client must be provided with the opportunity to asks questions and seek clarification before signing the treatment consent form.

In the case of Jerrod that is introduced in this chapter and continues in Chapter 7 and Chapter 8, the client was referred for medication evaluation by his family. However, he wanted psychotherapy instead. He stated that if psychotherapy was "not working sufficiently" he would consider adding medication to psychotherapy, which is called combined treatment. Accordingly, the informed consent needed inclusion of the consideration of combined treatment. Throughout the discussion of the terms of treatment, it was mutually agreed upon by both therapist and client that if his moods did not improve, evaluation for medication treatment would be scheduled. This became a documented agreement.

## 3. Begin Assessment

Initial session assessment is focused on identifying possible diagnoses, as well as presenting problems and concerns, and pattern. Additionally, the precipitants, predisposing, and perpetuating factors are elicited. One of the main reasons for conducting an initial assessment is to identify the client's pattern and formulate an accurate case conceptualization (Sperry, 2010b).

The therapist asks structured questions to rule out comorbid conditions and pencil in possible diagnoses. Structured and focused questions, as opposed to open-ended questions, are used purposefully to accomplish an assessment and have sufficient time remaining to accomplish other first session tasks. Symptom disorders and personality disorders are ruled in or out based on an evaluation of the severity of symptoms and impairment. Pattern identification is crucial in the first session. Diagnostically, the therapist must determine whether the client's pattern is severe enough to warrant the diagnosis of a personality disorder. As noted in Chapter 2, with sufficient practice, a full diagnostic assessment can be completed in as little as 15 minutes.

Functional assessment enhances the diagnostic assessment. This assessment focuses on the degree to which the client's presenting problem or concerns affect his or her daily life. It also distinguishes components that can alleviate or worsen the problem. These components can be physical, environmental, social, behavioral, or cognitive in form and make up the focus of the functional assessment (Sperry & Binensztok, 2019b).

Finally, screening instruments can aid the diagnostic assessment and function as a monitor for assessing changes over time. The Patient Health Questionnaire (PHQ-9) (Kroenke & Spitzer, 2002) is one of the most useful and frequently used screeners in mental health and integrated care settings. It specifically screens and monitors levels of depression. This 9-item questionnaire, which corresponds to the nine DSM-5 diagnostic criteria, is rated on a 4-point Likert-type scale. Clients are asked to rate their experiences for the length of two weeks prior to the session. A final tenth question assesses how any of the indicated symptoms that the client rated between 1 and 3 interfere with the ability of the client to function at work, at home, and with other people. Depression severity is indicated according to scores on the PHQ-9 such as: minimal or none (0–4); mild (5–9); moderate (10–14); moderately severe (15–19); and severe (20–27). The client is asked to complete the PHQ-9 at the outset of every session on a weekly basis.

## 4. Identify Pattern

A key outcome of an effective assessment is the identification of pattern, because pattern is the heart of the case conceptualization and the basis for planning and implementing effective interventions. It also provides the therapist critical information in fostering an effective therapeutic alliance. It also forms the basis for establishing mutual goals and anticipating potential problems and challenges throughout the therapy process (Sperry & Sperry, 2012).

Pattern is also central to establishing and maintaining an effective therapeutic alliance. It should be noted that agreement on the second and third components of the alliance, i.e., goals and methods or interventions, requires knowledge of relevant personality dynamics, particularly the client's maladaptive pattern in order to develop an effective case conceptualization and tailored treatment goals and interventions. Failure to identify the client's maladaptive pattern in the first session and to discuss how it will be central to the treatment process decreases the value of the therapeutic alliance, in engaging the client in the treatment process, and effecting change. Chapter 2 elaborates pattern and case conceptualization.

## 5. Socialize to Treatment

An overview of Pattern Focused Therapy begins with the client in the first session. Additionally, the therapist explains the main purpose and focus of the therapy as well as the expectations for the client. The protocol is also explained, and the client is allowed to ask questions. Then, the therapist prompts the client to determine if they are willing to proceed with the process that has been laid out. This process instills a sense of autonomy in the client and fosters clinician credibility as well as credibility for the indicated approach. If done correctly and successfully, this process also increases the client's hopefulness (Sperry, 2010b).

## 6. Agree on Treatment Goals

The first session offers an adequate context to discuss and establish first-order, second-order, and third-order goals with the client. The goals established must be realistic, measurable, and achievable. The client's agreement to the set treatment goals is crucial. They must understand the goals, view them as attainable, and commit to working to achieve them.

- *First-order goals.* First-order goals are mainly shorter-term goals. They essentially help the client reduce their symptoms and return to baseline—a previous level of functioning—and in resolving the presenting problem. For Jerrod, this includes reducing depressive symptoms, while increasing activity and functioning in social settings.
- *Second-order goals.* Second-order goals are longer-term goals. They include changes in the client's personality dynamics. In this approach, that is a shift from a maladaptive to a more adaptive pattern. Therefore, an adaptive pattern must be agreed upon in the first session. The adaptive pattern is commonly the reverse of the maladaptive pattern (Sperry & Carlson, 2014). In the case of Jerrod, for instance, the maladaptive pattern is characterized as

over-conscientiousness, to the point of reduced effectiveness. Therefore, it follows that his adaptive pattern is to be reasonably conscientious while maintaining effectiveness. Accordingly, he agrees to work toward a second-order goal of becoming more reasonably conscientious.

- *Third-order goals.* Third-order change is comprised of pattern change that is originated and carried out independently by the client. Third-order change evidences that the client has attained the capability of acting as their own therapist. Therefore, they identify and alter maladaptive responses independently. This type of goal should be the ultimate goal of therapy as it shows that clients can respond to internal and external challenges without the aid of a therapist. Building client awareness is the primary goal toward moving in the direction of third-order change. As clients become more aware of their patterns, behaviors, responses, and consequences, they are more likely to respond effectively. Additionally, clients must increasingly assume responsibility for their responses. Third-order change is extremely unlikely to happen on its own. Therapists must purposefully aid clients in gaining awareness and modifying responses (Sperry & Carlson, 2014). Third-order change is not commonly addressed in the first session, but instead is discussed throughout the process of therapy. However, the two processes of increasing awareness and encouragement do begin in the first session, and they are important in preparing the client for post-therapy.

## 7. Effect Initial Change

Effecting some change in the first session helps to build the clinician's credibility as well as credibility toward the methods. It also helps the client become more hopeful about the potential outcomes of therapy. Distressed clients are likely to return for further sessions if some change is achieved in the first session (Sperry & Carlson, 2014). Some strategies for achieving this initial change are: offering a reframe of the client's problem, emotional first aid, a brief intervention, or even a novel strategy, such as a paradoxical suggestion.

## 8. Agree on Homework

Clinicians practicing Pattern Focused Therapy routinely utilize ultra-brief interventions. These interventions can be introduced in the first session in order to effect change. They are also utilized as practice or homework between sessions. Most treatment approaches use homework because they help to supplement and increase in-session treatment progress. In Pattern Focused Therapy, homework is not simply between-session activities but also training in third-order change. In other words, homework becomes the training ground for clients to begin learning what it means to be their own therapist. Accordingly, the between-session activities that make up homework must be agreed upon mutually and not simply assigned by the therapist (Sperry & Sperry, 2018).

## Pattern Focused Therapy: Illustrative Case of Jerrod

The application of Pattern Focused Therapy is demonstrated in the case of Jerrod. It is a planned, six-session therapy with a male client presenting with moderate depression. A Student Health Services physician referred Jerrod to the university's Counseling and Psychological Services (CAPS) for psychotherapy because Jerrod expressed concern about the side effects of antidepressant medications. However, he showed some willingness to consider medications in the case that psychotherapy alone did not sufficiently alleviate his depressive symptoms.

### Background

Jerrod is a 26-year-old biomedical engineering graduate student with low mood, a reduction in pleasure in activities that he previously found pleasurable, isolation, and decreased motivation. Jerrod's symptoms reportedly began three weeks prior to the first session due to stress and responsibilities. As a result, he began to isolate from his peers. He also reported feeling fatigue and stated that this was the first time he had felt this down. He expressed concerns that his current issues may thwart his plans to become a successful lawyer. Such worries led to undue guilt about his performance and mood while undertaking school-related tasks. Jerrod has two siblings, each two years apart. He is the oldest son and described his parents as holding very high standards and routinely having his siblings compare themselves to him in order to strive for good behavior.

### Diagnostic Impression

Jerrod scored a 12 on the Patient Health Questionnaire-9 (PHQ-9) which indicates a moderate level of depression. However, he did not meet sufficient criteria for the DSM-5 diagnosis of Major Depressive Disorder. Instead, the diagnosis of Other Specified Depressive Disorder (311) is given (American Psychiatric Association, 2013). Jerrod also exhibits an obsessive-compulsive personality style as the evaluation found him to be one criterion short for the diagnosis of Obsessive-Compulsive Personality Disorder.

### Case Conceptualization

Jerrod comes to treatment presenting with low moods, reduced pleasure, guilt about school performance, and decreased motivation. He meets the criteria for

Other Specified Depressive Disorder. The described symptoms have resulted in decreased social and school function and isolation from friends and peers, due to the precipitating factor which has been an extreme and debilitating focus on academic studies. Over-conscientiousness and perfectionism comprise his maladaptive pattern, to the point of impairment and ineffectiveness. His predisposition is likely explained by the following factors: biologically, he may be genetically predisposed to depression, given a paternal uncle who also suffers from depression. Psychologically, obsessive-compulsive personality features make up his personality pattern and style. He holds self-other schemas such as "I cannot possibly make mistakes because I am responsible for getting things right;" and a world-view of "Life is unjust and stressful. I have to keep an eye on everything to make sure nothing goes wrong." His life strategy seems to be: "I have to be perfect, so I have to work extremely hard and keep up with my parents' expectations." Skills deficits such as limited coping skills and poor time management have also been identified. Socially, Jerrod's history has been riddled with extremely high parental expectations, social isolation, and struggles with socializing with his siblings due to perceived parental pressures. Social isolation, unreasonable expectations for himself, and highly demanding coursework at college make up his perpetuating factors. Culturally, Jerrod identifies as middle-class Caucasian of Euro-American background. His cultural explanation is that he is under significant stress and that he wants to be treated without medications.

First-order treatment goals include increasing social connectedness and reducing symptoms of depression. Second-order treatment goals will include shifting to a more reasonably conscientious and effective interpersonal style that will comprise a more adaptive pattern. Keeping in mind his obsessive-compulsive pattern, Jerrod is likely to resist getting in touch with "soft" feelings, and instead strive to talk and explain his way through his presenting problems. He may also present with significant ambivalence at the point of termination. However, given his low moderate level of depression and motivation for treatment, his prognosis is good, and it is reasonably likely that he can achieve symptom remission. Accordingly, he is an appropriate client candidate for six sessions of individual therapy at CAPS with the provision for two more sessions if indicated.

## *Session Plan*

The general plan for this session is to accomplish the eight therapeutic tasks. More specifically, background information will be elicited as well as completion of a brief diagnostic evaluation Scores on a number of screening and monitoring measures will also be gathered. The client's maladaptive pattern will be identified and shared and first- and second-order change goals will be mutually agreed upon.

## Transcription

THERAPIST: Hi, Jerrod. Welcome. Nice to meet you. (smiles and shakes hands with client)

JERROD: Hi, very nice meeting you as well.

THERAPIST: I want to tell you a bit about our first therapy session—it's going to be a bit different from the rest. Today I'm going to be asking you a number of questions. I want to get a better understanding of what you've been going through and how you've been feeling. Does that sound alright?

## Commentary

Both verbal and nonverbal communication are used in the initial interaction to develop rapport. The therapist requests the client's permission to continue to instill a sense of autonomy and collaboration, thus beginning to build the therapeutic alliance. Asking Jerrod for permission to continue also fosters an egalitarian relationship that de-emphasizes some of the power of the therapist in the therapist-client dynamic.

JERROD: Sure. That sounds okay.

THERAPIST: Great. Can you tell me a bit more about why you're seeking therapy?

JERROD: Yeah. (Pause) I haven't been feeling like myself lately. School has been really hectic and stressful. I feel like I'm overwhelmed and tired all the time. The other day I missed a deadline for a project which is very not like me. I was disappointed, but I was too exhausted to get things in on time.

THERAPIST: Sounds like you've had a rough go at it in the recent past. I'm sorry to hear that. Can you tell me a bit about your mood lately?

JERROD: Uh, it's been pretty low. I'm down all the time. I feel like I'm dragging through my days.

THERAPIST: And how often have you felt that way?

JERROD: Every day, basically. Sometimes a bit better, but in general pretty low.

THERAPIST: What about things you typically find pleasant? Are you still doing those?

JERROD: Not really. I haven't been going to the gym. I have no energy for it. I get so busy with school that I'm not seeing my friends. I don't feel like doing anything.

THERAPIST: So, you're not finding as much pleasure in those things anymore?

JERROD: Yeah. I haven't really liked or wanted to do anything lately. Everything is gray. I wasn't even into it the last time I forced myself to go out with my friends. I was supposed to do something with them this weekend, but I didn't go.

THERAPIST: So, you've mentioned that you feel exhausted a lot of the time. Can you tell me more?

JERROD: About feeling tired? Yeah, I'm tired all the time. I sleep in sometimes and I still wake up feeling tired and dragging. It's hard to focus on things so I've been putting a lot off in the things I have to do.

THERAPIST: So, you feel tired a lot of the time and have been struggling with concentration.

JERROD: Exactly.

THERAPIST: How about your sleep? How has that been?

JERROD: Well, I'm oversleeping a lot in the past few weeks. If I'm feeling tired in the morning, I just go back to sleep. I've slept through my alarm a couple of times and the other day when I woke up it was 11 o'clock and I had missed my morning class. And I was still tired!

THERAPIST: It must be really frustrating to feel tired all of the time with so many responsibilities.

JERROD: It is. It's been hard.

THERAPIST: And how long has this been going on?

JERROD: Like three weeks. It feels like much longer though. It's been rough.

THERAPIST: And have you ever gone through a rough patch like this before?

JERROD: Not really. This is the first time.

THERAPIST: Have you ever been to a psychotherapist or psychiatrist before in your life?

JERROD: No.

THERAPIST: Have you ever had any psychiatric medications prescribed?

JERROD: No. I've never been prescribed or taken anything.

THERAPIST: I see. And how has your everyday life been affected by these symptoms?

JERROD: Like I said, I don't do anything I like. I'm in bed all the time. I don't go out with my friends. I'm missing study group and classes, which are important to me. I've been really worried about my grades. I'm pre-law so my courses are really difficult right now. Law school is going to weigh heavily on these courses, and I feel like I'm failing. I'm going to mess up my career. I haven't even told my parents though because I don't want them to find out I'm struggling in class.

THERAPIST: I see. So, you have been isolating, missing important classes and events, and struggling to keep up with schoolwork. You're worried that this all will affect your career and your prospects of getting into law school.

JERROD: Exactly. I feel really guilty about slacking off. I mean, I'm still doing what I can to keep my grades up, but I know I could do better. I'm down about it all the time.

THERAPIST: Okay. You're also feeling guilty even though you have been keeping up and managing.

JERROD: Yes, absolutely.

THERAPIST: It seems like this has been a very difficult experience for you. I appreciate you answering these questions. I'd like to ask you a few more, if that's okay.

JERROD: Sure. Go ahead.

THERAPIST: Thanks. You said that you've been through some changes recently and your energy and sleep patterns have been off. Have you had any weight loss or weight gain recently?

JERROD: No, not really any change.

THERAPIST: So, no weight changes. Have you ever felt like you had extra bouts of energy and you didn't need to sleep as much?

JERROD: No. It's the other way around. I have no energy most of the time. I had a lot of energy before.

THERAPIST: How about any mood swings? Sometimes going up and sometimes down?

JERROD: Not really. I wouldn't say mood swings. Some things get me frustrated, but never up and down like that.

THERAPIST: Okay. How about any major changes in your life? Like breakups or loss in your family?

JERROD: No. I've been here for more than a year. Nothing big has happened

THERAPIST: Any events that might have made you feel scared or out of control?

JERROD: No.

THERAPIST: Would you also describe yourself as a nervous person?

JERROD: Um, well, sometimes I get a bit worried about missing deadlines and things like that. I wouldn't really say I'm a nervous person, though.

THERAPIST: So, schoolwork is your most typical worry. Are there any other things you worry about?

JERROD: No. Not really.

THERAPIST: You said that you had been staying away from social situations and other people. Have you ever struggled in social situations, like speaking in public for a presentation?

JERROD: No, I'm actually good at presentations. I enjoy it. I've just been stressed out and busy. I've been too tired and didn't really care about being with other people recently.

THERAPIST: Okay, I see. Can you tell me if there are any places, you're afraid to go or things you're afraid of doing?

JERROD: No. I don't really have anything like that.

THERAPIST: How about any specific fears, like flying or heights?

JERROD: Not really. I really don't like frogs, but it's not like a phobia or anything.

THERAPIST: Okay. Have you ever been in a situation in which you thought you might die, stop breathing, or have a heart attack?
JERROD: No. Never.

## Commentary

The therapist and Jerrod continued to work through the diagnostic evaluation. The DSM-5 diagnosis of Major Depressive Disorder was ruled in, while anxiety and stress-related disorders were ruled out (American Psychiatric Association, 2013). The therapist exhibited warmth and active listening, regularly reflecting Jerrod's thoughts and feelings. This allowed the therapist to develop and enhance the therapeutic alliance. The session continues as other diagnostic conditions are ruled out.

THERAPIST: Have you had any repetitive thoughts of something bad happening, or any repetitive behaviors that you feel you need to do?
JERROD: No. I'm organized and some of my friends have joked that I'm kind of predictable because I stick to my routines, but not so much lately. I don't have any rituals or anything like that.
THERAPIST: So, with your routines—do you find it hard to break those routines if something comes up spontaneously?
JERROD: It's hard, but I can do it. Like if I had thought about organizing my work, I can head out with my friends for a bit and then get to it later. But it is a struggle.
THERAPIST: So, you have struggled with flexibility at times?
JERROD: Yes, that's pretty much it.
THERAPIST: I just have a few more questions. Have you ever experienced anything strange or unusual?
JERROD: I can't think of anything. No.
THERAPIST: Okay, have you ever felt like you lost touch with reality, heard voices, or thought that people were trying to hurt you?
JERROD: No.
THERAPIST: Has anyone ever told you that you had strange ideas?
JERROD: No.
THERAPIST: Have you ever felt like your mind was playing tricks on you?
JERROD: Um, what?
THERAPIST: Like any experiences where you felt like you were outside of your body? Or having a period from your life that you can't recall?
JERROD: No. That sounds terrible. Definitely not.
THERAPIST: And how has your memory been lately?
JERROD: It's been fine. I mean I've had a hard time focusing like I mentioned but I don't think my memory has suffered too much.
THERAPIST: So, no memory decline?

JERROD: No. Not at all.

THERAPIST: I see. You've told me that there hasn't been any weight fluctuation. Have you ever had any issues with food, like overeating or eating too little? Has that ever been a problem?

JERROD: No. I try to eat healthy but I'm not too strict with it. I also don't starve or anything like that.

THERAPIST: Have you ever felt like you didn't have control of how much you were eating? Eating too much in one sitting?

JERROD: No, never.

THERAPIST: Have you ever restricted your food intake?

JERROD: No, I haven't.

THERAPIST: How about any behaviors like throwing up what you ate or using laxatives?

JERROD: No way.

THERAPIST: You mentioned that you liked going to the gym. Any issues with over-exercising?

JERROD: No.

THERAPIST: Okay. Any drug or alcohol use?

JERROD: I don't really drink much—only once in a while with my friends. I don't like it all that much. I don't enjoy the feeling. And I've never used drugs. Some of my friends in the past have offered me ADHD drugs to help me study but I stayed away from it. That stuff is not for me.

THERAPIST: Okay. So, there's no chance that what's been going on with you recently has anything to do with any substance?

JERROD: No. No chance.

THERAPIST: Any prescription or medications over the counter?

JERROD: I don't take any medications. I mean, like Advil every once in a while, if I have a headache. I take some allergy medicine sometimes—the non-drowsy kind.

THERAPIST: Have you been diagnosed with any physical or medical conditions?

JERROD: No, I'm healthy. I had a physical recently. The doc said everything was fine.

THERAPIST: It's good to hear that. Given that you've been struggling quite a bit lately, have you had any thoughts of harming yourself or thought that you didn't want to live anymore?

JERROD: No, absolutely not. Nothing like that.

THERAPIST: Okay, how about hurting someone else?

JERROD: No way. Never.

THERAPIST: And how would you describe yourself as a person, Jerrod?

JERROD: Um, I guess I'd say I'm focused. I'm organized and I like to focus on school and my work. I like to be active and play softball.

THERAPIST: And you had mentioned that some people have complained about your routines. Is that pretty common for you?

JERROD: Yeah, I guess. I mean my friends get on my back about it—if they want to go someplace but it's the day I typically clean up around the house, they tease me about it, "Lame!" and stuff like that. But I don't think it's that bad. I can usually reschedule if I have to.

THERAPIST: So, do you ever find yourself so narrowly focused on organizing, making a list, or attending to the details that you lose track of your original intent?

JERROD: Oh, for sure! Yes! That sounds just like me. In my first year here, I was so focused on some of the details of one of my assignments that I did the thing wrong and ended up with a B minus. It was terrible. I overdid it on one detail, and I missed the entire point of the assignment.

THERAPIST: Okay, so it sounds like you overcomplicated one portion of it and you completed the assignment incorrectly?

JERROD: Yeah.

THERAPIST: Then, it sounds like you can get in your own way. This could be called a pattern of conscientious perfectionism. There's also an element of pleasing others. Does this sound right? **(maladaptive pattern is shared)**

JERROD: (Pause) Well, I've never really thought about it like that, but yeah. That happens. I'm very organized and get annoyed when people are sloppy. People just don't care about the details, or maybe I just care too much. I've been called a perfectionist before. I can see that. I also want others to think well of me and so I guess I do try to please them too.

THERAPIST: I see. And it sounds like being organized and paying close attention has worked for you in the past—they're useful traits! Do you think it could be even more helpful if you could find a balance between being conscientious and perfectionistic while still maintaining some flexibility and being effective? **(second-order change goal)**

JERROD: Yes. Absolutely. That would be awesome. I've gotten pretty frustrated in the past. I'd do something and think "Why did I do that? What's wrong with me?" I should have been able to realize that getting focused on one small detail wasn't helping anything.

THERAPIST: Right. And it might've saved you some time and trouble.

JERROD: Yeah. I want to be more efficient.

THERAPIST: Is it also a pattern for you to avoid social situations or things that you find pleasurable because you're focused on your work?

JERROD: Well, yeah. I started doing that when I got overwhelmed and falling behind. But it hasn't been a problem for me before. Typically, I can schedule stuff in and have fun with people.

THERAPIST: It's good to hear that. Do you ever find yourself hanging on to things that you wanted to throw out? Even if those things have no value or are worn out?

JERROD: No. I throw things out all the time. I like things clean and I don't keep junk around.

THERAPIST: Right. And you mentioned that you get frustrated with other people if they're not as organized as you. Has this ever become an obstacle in working with others? For instance, if you have to delegate tasks, do you think that others might not do it as well?

JERROD: Um, yeah that's hard for me. People have told me that I nitpick a lot. I like group work, especially if I know the people in the group, but sometimes that is a struggle. Yes.

THERAPIST: How about handling money? Are you a big spender? Or do you tend to save your money?

JERROD: Well, I don't have much to spend right now. My parents help me out. But I do plan and save a lot. I also like going shopping and going to the movies.

THERAPIST: Okay, so you have a pretty good balance between saving and spending?

JERROD: Yeah.

## Commentary

Additional DSM-5 diagnoses were ruled out throughout the screening. Jerrod's responses are indicative of obsessive-compulsive personality style. The Major Depressive Disorder diagnosis was made earlier in the evaluation. The maladaptive pattern of over-conscientiousness and perfectionism to the point of decreased effectiveness became more pronounced. Obsessive-compulsive personality disorder was ruled out, as Jerrod did not meet full criteria. Jerrod's decreased social interest and increased sense of discouragement can be explained by his maladaptive pattern. There are several rigidly self-imposed rules and criticism about high achievement expectations. This reduces the ability to remain flexible and engage with others, exacerbating symptoms of depression. The core beliefs seem to be that perfection is of the utmost importance in order to be worthwhile.

THERAPIST: Can you tell me a bit about your family? What was it like growing up in your home?

JERROD: Sure. I'm the oldest of three. I have a little brother and younger sister. My sister is four years younger than me and my brother is two years younger. My childhood was fine. We always had what we needed. I had violin lessons. I was in many sports. But there was a lot of pressure because I always did well, and my brother and sister were told to look up to me. My parents expected me to do very well in school because I had to be a good example for them.

THERAPIST: Okay. So, your parents provided for you well, but also placed a lot of expectations on you from a very young age.

JERROD: Yeah.

THERAPIST: And how would you describe their relationship? Your parents?

JERROD: Oh, they get along fine. They have a good relationship. You know, some fights here and there but for the most part good.

THERAPIST: Okay, and who made the big decisions in your family?

JERROD: I think my parents did a good job sharing those responsibilities. My dad was the breadwinner and my mom worked part-time for some time. She stayed at home for a few years.

THERAPIST: And how did they work out their problems or conflicts?

JERROD: Um, like I said—some arguments—but for the most part they worked things out well. Some things seemed like they never worked out though. My mom complained a lot that my dad worked too much. My dad typically complained that my mom made him late for things because she took so long getting ready. He says she's terrible with time management.

THERAPIST: Do you think there was an expectation that you would take on any career when you grew up?

JERROD: Yeah. Law, medicine, or business. My parents told me early on. They said that liberal arts majors are typically unemployed right out of college. I mean, I don't mind it because I was on the debate team in high school. I wanted to go to law school either way.

## Commentary

Closed-ended questions were used to assess family dynamics. Although there were not as many instances of reflective statements, the therapist remained nonjudgmental and warm throughout which led Jerrod to feel comfortable disclosing information and deepening the developing alliance between Jerrod and the therapist.

THERAPIST: Very good, Jerrod. I appreciate you answering my questions. This process has helped me obtain a better understanding of your symptoms and concerns. Also, I think I have a better idea of how these issues have been affecting your daily life, what it was like for you growing up, and your current career goals. I'd like to formally discuss the informed consent agreement and a bit about what your hopes are for our work together in the coming weeks.

Subsequently, the therapist and Jerrod discussed the informed consent. The therapist informed Jerrod that informed consent spans more than just signing the form. It is also a process of "permission seeking" that could emerge in further sessions if the focus of the treatment changes.

## Commentary

Jerrod showcased good cooperation, responding with early recollections and family constellation. Jerrod's emotions and experiences were reflected, validated, and restated throughout. The therapist showed appreciation for Jerrod's willingness to share and explained the rationale for the processes thus far and how they helped the therapeutic process. Then, the therapist requested permission to proceed with the therapeutic goals, which enhanced the therapeutic alliance and clinician credibility. It also served to preserve the relationship and avoid triggers for Jerrod's maladaptive pattern. Jerrod and the therapist set goals collaboratively and informed consent was discussed. One final consideration was the inclusion of medication combined with therapy if therapy alone did not alleviate the symptoms. Then, Jerrod signed the informed consent form.

JERROD: I'd like to shake off this mood. I'd like to feel better and be motivated to actually do my work. I also want to get back to playing softball and doing other things I like.

THERAPIST: I agree that we should focus on your depressive symptoms as well as increasing your level of energy. This is so that you can get back to enjoying things you used to like, like playing softball. **(first-order change goal)**

JERROD: Yeah, I'd like that. I hope that's possible but I'm worried that I'm going to keep feeling this way. I also hope that therapy will work because I only want to use medication as a last resort.

THERAPIST: I hear you. And I think there's a good chance that we can achieve your goals working together.

JERROD: It's good to hear that.

THERAPIST: Before, we talked about a pattern of perfectionism and narrow focus on details. This was happening to the point where it was getting in the way of you being effective. Is that also something you'd like to work on in here?

JERROD: (Pause) Yes, I really would. I like that I'm organized and like you said, that's worked for me well so far, but I want to be effective and not let it get in my way.

THERAPIST: Right. Well, I think these goals we've set are achievable. We can dedicate the next few weeks to helping you achieve them and start feeling better, becoming more flexible and getting more accomplished. Does that sound alright?

JERROD: Yeah. That sounds awesome. I like that there's a plan in place. It makes me feel a bit better.

THERAPIST: I'm happy to hear that. So, what do you say we spend a few minutes discussing your energy levels and motivation?

JERROD: Yeah. We can do that.

THERAPIST: Great. You know, sometimes when people feel like you have been feeling, they tend to stop doing the things that they find enjoyable. This can result in inactivity cycles. So, the less they do, the less energy they have to get involved with things.

JERROD: Interesting. Yeah, I can see that.

THERAPIST: You mentioned that you were active before. The technique I'd like to suggest is called behavioral activation. That means that by intentionally being active, you begin to activate more energy and feel less depressed. You can start feeling positive feelings by starting your physiology. A different way of saying this is acting "as if" you were motivated or energetic. This way, you feel a surge of energy and feel more motivated. Does that make sense?

JERROD: Yeah. Sure, but does that actually work?

THERAPIST: Actually, yes. (Pause) Why don't we schedule some gradual activities? It's best to start small. You don't want to plan something you're not actually going to do. Even something small like taking a walk for 10 minutes can start to snowball into bigger effects.

JERROD: Yeah, like with exercising, it's not good to take on too much all at the same time.

THERAPIST: Exactly. So, what would be two activities that you could complete in 15–20 minutes this week? Something that you typically like to do.

JERROD: Well, I like taking saunas. But I haven't been doing much of either lately even though it usually makes me feel really good.

THERAPIST: That sounds great. Do taking saunas have a soothing effect on you?

JERROD: Yeah, it also seems to invigorate me.

THERAPIST: Getting both results sounds like it would help with your symptoms. It's very encouraging that you have things that you can do that are enjoyable. Have a look at this list of some other things that people find enjoyable. (Hands list) This typically gives people some ideas. Can you tell me if anything stands out for you?

JERROD: This is quite a list. And, yeah, things like taking walk to the park stand out, and reading a novel. I also like collecting coins. I've been collecting since I was a kid.

THERAPIST: Oh, that sounds very interesting. Have you been to one of those coins shows they hold at the Coliseum?

JERROD: Yes. I actually went last year and got some new ones, but I've been putting it off. I don't actually know why. Probably because I'm so busy. (Pause) But if I had to choose, I'd go for a sauna at the university fitness center.

THERAPIST: Well, great! Is that something that you would consider doing for 20 minutes this coming week?

JERROD: Yes, I can totally do that for 20 minutes

THERAPIST: And when will you do that this week?

JERROD: I can do it on Thursday. I have a little time then.

THERAPIST: Ok, great. Can you think of a backup plan in case something comes up and you can't get to that?

JERROD: Well, I like to read and there's this book on my nightstand. I can read for 15–20 minutes.

THERAPIST: That sounds great. And how about that second activity?

JERROD: I can go through my coin collection and make a list of what I might add to it.

THERAPIST: Ok, sounds good. Would that take you about 15–20 minutes?

JERROD: Yeah.

THERAPIST: And when do you want to plan on doing that?

JERROD: I'd say Friday.

THERAPIST: Good. What about a backup for that activity?

JERROD: Well, I think my backup for that would be to take a walk to the mall and back. It's about 2 miles each way.

THERAPIST: Good. So, your first activity is to take a sauna at the fitness center on Thursday. Then, on Friday, you'll take a bath for about 15–20 minutes using your new products. That sounds great. Feel free to keep this list and take a look at it if needed. Also, I'd encourage you to give yourself permission to try other things throughout the week if the thought comes up. If not, the planned activities should be a good start.

JERROD: Ok. Yeah. I can do that.

THERAPIST: It's also important for us to track your progress. I'm going to give you this log. Give each activity two ratings, on a scale from 0–10. The first rating will address the extent to which you completed the activity—all, some, or not at all. Then, rate how much enjoyment you got from it, 0 would be none at all, and 10 would be the most possible enjoyment. Does that sound doable?

JERROD: Yeah. Seems pretty simple.

THERAPIST: OK, great. I really think you're going to get some positive results.

JERROD: You know, I think I will get positive results.

THERAPIST: Okay. Now, would you mind filling out the SRS form? This is so that we can keep an eye on if you're getting what you want from our sessions.

JERROD: Sure. (Pause while he fills it out)

THERAPIST: Okay. I see you noted that you're satisfied with what we talked about.

JERROD: Yeah. I think this was good for me. I feel better now than when we started.

THERAPIST: I'm happy to hear that and I look forward to our work together.

## Commentary

Jerrod seemed receptive to the behavioral activation intervention His statement: "You know, I think I will get positive results" and that he feels better than at the start of the session suggest that Jerrod is feeling a sense of hopefulness, and are both indications that the task of effecting a small change in the session was met.

THERAPIST: Before we wrap up, can you rate on a scale from 0 to 10, 0 being not at all and 10 being the most, how important it is for you to attain the goals we discussed? **(Query-Pattern & Query-10–1)**

JERROD: A 10. I don't like how I've been feeling, and I want to get back to my old self.

THERAPIST: I see. So, it's very important for you. Good. And on that same scale, can you rate your level of confidence? **(Query Pattern & Query-10–2)**

JERROD: Well, for that I'd say about a 6. It's hard for me to see it happening.

THERAPIST: . Before we end, I'd like to give you something to do between now and our next session. Would that be alright?

JERROD: Yeah. That sounds fine.

THERAPIST: This is a daily mood rating sheet. It's divided into two hours chunks on the left column. Please write in the dates of the week on top. During this upcoming week, pay close attention to how you feel—your moods specifically—and jot it down every two hours. You can write in as much as you want to describe how you're feeling. Does that sound okay?

JERROD: Yeah. I think I can do that.

THERAPIST: And, finally, please fill out the Session Review Scale. It's four items that review our session today. It looks to assess if you were able to get what you came here for. Is that okay?

JERROD: Yes. Sure. (Pause while form is filled out)

THERAPIST: (After reviewing the SRS and scoring it as 38 out of 40) So, here you have indicated that you were satisfied with our session and that we talked about what you wanted to talk about.

JERROD: Yeah, we did. (Pause) I thought I was going to be much more nervous and that this was going to be a more painful process, but I got over my nerves easy. It was easy to talk to you.

THERAPIST: I'm so happy to hear that. (Pause) I also think you did really well, and I look forward to working with you. Do you have any other questions before we close?

JERROD: No, not really.

THERAPIST: Okay, then have a great rest of your week and I'll look forward to seeing you next week.

JERROD: Thanks, you too. I'll see you then.

## Commentary

Jerrod's responses on the importance and confidence rating were surprisingly high in this first session, especially given his depressive presentation. Presumably, these responses reflect increases in hope and trust in the therapeutic process. Additionally, relatively high SRS scores are suggestive of his approval of the alliance with the therapist, not just the bond, but goals and methods. Given this indication of relatively strong alliance, there is a high likelihood that he will return for the follow-up session and therefore there was no need for an ultra-brief intervention.

It is important to note that the therapist did not trigger—wittingly or unwittingly—Jerrod's maladaptive pattern in the session. This might have surfaced if the therapist had commented in a way that was perceived as critical or demanding and resulted in a strain or rupture to the alliance. If that had occurred, it would be the therapist's responsibility to repair the alliance or risk having the client feel insufficiently safe or confident to return for the second session (Sperry, 2010a).

## Chart Note

The client presents with depressive symptoms and PHQ-9 score of 12, which suggests moderate depression. He merits the DSM-5 diagnosis of Other Specified Depressive Disorder (311) and exhibits an obsessive-compulsive personality style. A maladaptive pattern of conscientious perfectionism and pleasing was identified and discussed. It was mutually agreed that our therapy would focus on reduction of depressive symptoms and shifting to a more adaptive pattern. Behavioral activation and monitoring were agreed upon as homework. Consent form was signed and therapeutic alliance appears positive and appropriate for a first session and reflects his confidence in achieving therapeutic change.

## Conclusion

In Pattern Focused Therapy, the eight essential tasks described above are the focus of the first session. These tasks were illustrated using the case of Jerrod. This case showcases how the therapeutic alliance was fostered and also highlighted that his maladaptive pattern was identified. and first- and second-order change goals were mutually established. The other five essential tasks were also accomplished, including effecting some initial change in the first therapeutic encounter. In my experience, when all the tasks are achieved in the first session, it is highly predictive of the client engaging in therapy, and specifically returning for the second session.

As noted at the beginning of this chapter, the case of Jerrod will continue in Chapter 7 and Chapter 8, from the second session through termination in the sixth session.

## References

American Psychiatric Association. (2013). *Diagnostic and statistical manual of mental disorders*, 5th ed. Arlington, VA: American Psychiatric Association.

Bordin, E. S. (1994). Theory and research on the therapeutic working alliance: New directions. In A. O. Horvath & L. S. Greenberg (Eds.), *The working alliance: Theory, research, and practice* (pp. 13–37). New York, NY: John Wiley & Sons.

Duncan, B., Miller, S., Parks, L., Claud, D., Reynolds, L., Brown, J., & Johnson, L. (2003). The Session Rating Scale: Preliminary properties of a "working" alliance measure. *Journal of Affective Disorders*, 49, 59–72.

Horvath, A. O., & Luborsky, L. (1993). The role of the therapeutic alliance in psychotherapy. *Journal of Consulting and Clinical Psychology*, 61, 561–573.

Kroenke, K. & Spitzer, R. L. (2002). The PHQ-9: A new depression and diagnostic severity measure. *Psychiatric Annals*, 32, 509–521.

Sperry, J., & Sperry, L. (2018). *Cognitive behavior therapy in professional counseling practice*. New York, NY: Routledge.

Sperry, L. (2008). *The dictionary of ethical and legal terms and issues: The essential guide for mental health professionals*. New York, NY: Routledge.

Sperry, L. (2010a). *Highly effective therapy: Developing essential clinical competencies in counseling and psychotherapy*. New York, NY: Routledge.

Sperry, L. (2010b). *Core competencies in counseling and psychotherapy: Becoming a highly competent and effective therapist*. New York, NY: Routledge.

Sperry, L., & Binensztok, V. (2019a). *Learning and practicing Adlerian therapy*. San Diego, CA: Cognella.

Sperry, L., & Binensztok, V. (2019b). *Ultra-brief cognitive behavioral interventions: The cutting-edge of mental health and integrated care practice*. New York, NY: Routledge.

Sperry, L., & Carlson, J. (2014). *How master therapists work: Effecting change from the first through the last session and beyond*. New York, NY: Routledge.

Sperry, L., & Sperry, J. (2012). *Case conceptualization: Mastering this competency with ease and confidence*. New York, NY: Routledge.

# Chapter 7

# The Middle Sessions

The middle sessions in Pattern Focused Therapy are directed at effecting major change in the client. These sessions implement the treatment plan developed in the initial session for both first-order change goals and second-order change goals. Specifically, these sessions target reduction of symptoms (first-order change) and shifting to a more adaptive pattern (second-order change). While not the primary focus of these sessions, third-order change is a secondary target. Depending on the practice setting, the number of middle sessions may be as short as two or three sessions or considerably longer. In the case of Jerrod, the usual practice policy for therapy was for six sessions. This included an initial and two ending sessions ,leaving three middle sessions. This chapter analyzes the middle phase of Jerrod's therapy: sessions 2, 3, and 4. It provides transcription selections from these three sessions along with commentary. Since Pattern Focused Therapy is focused and intentional, a "session plan" with a given structure is specified prior to the session.

## Session 2

### Session Plan

The plan included getting a current PHQ-9 score and as well as reviewing the Mood Scale rating chart, the ORS, and the behavioral activation assignment. Then, a recent situation is processed with the Query Sequence to assist in shifting Jerrod's maladaptive pattern to a more adaptive one. If another ultra-brief intervention is indicated, it is introduced. Finally, additional behavioral activation activities and others are assigned. Continued monitoring with the PHQ-9, the Mood Rating Scale, the Outcomes Rating Scale, and the Session Rating Scale is done in order to more effectively tailor the treatment process. Here is the transcription of all of session 2.

THERAPIST: Hi, Jerrod. It is nice to see you again.
JERROD: Thanks. Nice to see you too.

THERAPIST: I see that your PHQ-9 is 10, an improvement since the first time we met. Very good. What was it like doing your Mood Rating Chart this past week?
JERROD: All right. I was able to fill it in each day. There were a couple of hours where I forgot but I was able to go back and fill it in. Basically, I was able to keep track.
THERAPIST: Looking at it, I see you wrote "annoyed" and "tired" a lot. Can you say more about that?
JERROD: Well, yeah—that's why I came here to start with. I was feeling tired all the time and didn't have any motivation. I didn't realize I wrote "annoyed" so much though. That's surprising.
THERAPIST: When do you feel annoyed? In what kind of situations?
JERROD: Typically, when I'm feeling a lot of pressure. For example, when I have an assignment due and my friends are going on about stupid stuff.
THERAPIST: So, you feel annoyed when you're already overwhelmed or stressed about things you have to do and your friends are demanding of you? Or they're wanting to discuss something trivial?
JERROD: Yes, exactly.
THERAPIST: Would it be okay to add another component to your mood chart between now and your next session? I'd like you to jot down the kind of situation you're in when you're recording your mood.
JERROD: Yeah—okay. That's fine.

## Commentary

Jerrod's notations on his mood chart reflect his perfectionistic pattern. Although he completed the assignment, he admitted there were some days he missed filling in the Mood Rating Scale log, so he later went back to fill in the blanks. Such "pleasing" behavior is congruent with his maladaptive pattern. Accordingly, the therapist praised Jerrod's efforts and highlighted how the pattern emerges when Jerrod feels demands are being made of him, as they were in the take home assignment. It is possible that his ambivalent motivation was triggered by the therapist's "demands" that he complete the assignment.

THERAPIST: How would you rate yourself right now on the Mood Rating Scale from 1–10?
JERROD: I would rate myself between 4 and 5.
THERAPIST: Alright. Looking over the ORS you just filled out, I see the areas needing the most improvement were individually and socially. Can you tell me more about that?
JERROD: I haven't been doing too hot individually. I'm still sad and low. Really tired too.

THERAPIST: That sounds tough. What about socially?

JERROD: Well, I haven't been seeing other people and I've been having a hard time in school. But that was still my highest score.

THERAPIST: So, socially you marked as the highest, but things were still pretty low overall. Can you say more?

JERROD: Yeah—I was just tired all the time. I felt like I was dragging, and I felt guilty about it. I didn't really get my work done—well, barely. I go to study group on Tuesdays, typically. I didn't even go the last week—and I usually get a lot out of it.

THERAPIST: I understand. I'm sorry to hear you didn't feel up to going, even though you usually enjoy the group. The symptoms you described also match today's PHQ-9 score.

## Commentary

These markers of mood and functioning are useful and necessary. However, Jerrod's response to engaging in the assigned therapeutic intervention will be particularly telling. Accordingly, the therapist with Jerrod will review the behavioral activation assignment from last session.

THERAPIST: Could we review your behavior activation log?

JERROD: Yeah, sure.

THERAPIST: You had scheduled activities such as taking a walk and sorting through your collection. You rated your first activity as a 10! Great!

JERROD: Yes, I did that one.

THERAPIST: And how did you rate it as far as the pleasure that you got from it?

JERROD: Like a 7. I felt very relaxed.

THERAPIST: Seven sounds very good. And what was your score on your second activity, which was to sort out your coin collection?

JERROD: To be honest, that one was only about a 6. I got really busy and I've had this collection since I was a kid. I couldn't really do it for 20 minutes.

THERAPIST: Well, a 6 is still pretty good. How did you enjoy doing that?

JERROD: I gave it a 6 as well. It took me back to my childhood and I liked that.

THERAPIST: Would you be willing to tell me what you found good about the activity?

JERROD: Sure. I mean, to hold the coins was really good because it took me back. My uncle gave me some of those and I liked remembering him. He's actually the one that started me in collecting.

THERAPIST: That sounds awesome. And what else did you enjoy about it?

JERROD: I kind of felt a sense of peace. Like I was meditating while I was sorting it through.

THERAPIST: Good. That sounds very reassuring. And what were some of the not so good things about the activity?

JERROD: I was disappointed because I didn't get to the rest of it. I had to stop with barely having completed any of it. I was frustrated.

THERAPIST: I can see how that could be frustrating for you.

JERROD: Yeah. I was upset.

THERAPIST: And has this ever happened before?

JERROD: All the time. I typically get caught up on the little things and miss the big picture. Or sometimes I don't get something right and I put it off forever, like on my assignments.

THERAPIST: I see. Sometimes you get caught up on the details and that takes you away from completing the work.

JERROD: Yes. Or even if I do finish, I'm obsessing about the one thing that I didn't do or do right.

THERAPIST: I see. And what do you think happens that takes your focus into those small details even if you find that not to be very productive?

JERROD: I just want things to be done right. I don't want to be a slob or have my things turn out sloppy.

THERAPIST: You want to do things the right way. That's admirable.

JERROD: Thanks.

THERAPIST: But maybe it doesn't always work out how you want it to?

JERROD: No, definitely not.

THERAPIST: So, do you think that there's a pattern here of conscientious perfectionism and pleasing? And this pattern gets in the way of being effective and completing your tasks? **(Query-Pattern)**

JERROD: Yeah—that sounds about right. (Pause) Just this last week there was another example of that.

THERAPIST: Yeah? Would you be willing to tell me more? **(Query-1)**

JERROD: The best possible outcome would be for my professor to let me turn my paper in without any penalty.

THERAPIST: Ah, yes. That sounds like a pretty ideal outcome. Is that something that you can control?

JERROD: Um, no. I see.

THERAPIST: Yes. I agree with you there. What might've been a best possible outcome in your control in this given situation?

JERROD: Maybe just turning in the paper on time? It was a small mistake and if I had turned it in, I wouldn't have worried about it anymore. I would've just been done.

THERAPIST: Okay—so you wanted to get it in on time regardless of that small mistake. Then that would be a weight off. Right?

JERROD: Yeah. I would've wanted that.

## Commentary

The Query Sequence continued with elicitation of his thought and interpretations. His desired outcome (Query-4) was to turn his paper in on time and be done with it.

THERAPIST: I see. And what actually happened? **(Query-5)**
JERROD: Well, instead, I stressed about it and turned it in late.
THERAPIST: You wanted to turn your paper in on time, but instead you went home to fix it and turned it in late.
JERROD: Yeah.
THERAPIST: Did you get what you wanted out of this situation? **(Query-6)**
JERROD: No. In fact, I ended up even more stressed out about it.
THERAPIST: It must have been really stressful to have to turn the paper in late after putting in all the work.
JERROD: Yes, I was really disappointed.
THERAPIST: So, would you be okay with reviewing this situation and seeing how it might've turned out otherwise? **(Query-7)**
JERROD: Yeah—that's fine.
THERAPIST: I think we should review your thoughts and behaviors and see if they follow your maladaptive pattern. Your first thought, for instance, was "I'm going to fail if this is how I turn in the paper." Was that thought helpful or hurtful in getting your desired outcome? **(Query-8)**
JERROD: Uhm—hurtful.
THERAPIST: It was hurtful—how was it hurtful?
JERROD: I felt like I couldn't recover. Like everything was already messed up.
THERAPIST: So, it sounds like it affected your confidence.
JERROD: Yeah.
THERAPIST: Does it seem like that's related to your pattern of perfectionism?
JERROD: Yeah. I mean, that happens a lot. I struggle with letting things go and I work on them nonstop.
THERAPIST: Right. And this is an obstacle to being effective—like in this example, getting the paper in on time?
JERROD: Yes, that's it. Also, when I was sorting through my collection.
THERAPIST: So, it makes sense that your pattern is related to these unhelpful thoughts. Can you think of an alternative thought that might have been more helpful?
JERROD: I could've just thought I did my best or that it wasn't so big a mistake.
THERAPIST: I see. So, considering that you did your best or that it wasn't such a grave mistake—that would certainly fit with a more adaptive pattern that we could call "reasonably conscientious while maintaining effectiveness." Make sense?
JERROD: (Pause) Yeah. Makes sense.

THERAPIST: Now, how would that adaptive pattern and thought have been more helpful to you in getting your paper in on time?

JERROD: I could've just been more relaxed about it instead of freaking out.

THERAPIST: So, it might've taken the wind out of the sails of catastrophizing the situation?

JERROD: Yes, that's a perfect way of saying it. I think everything is the end of the world when it comes to situations like that.

THERAPIST: I see. And, your second thought was, "This paper is a disaster." Right? In getting what you wanted, was that helpful or hurtful?

JERROD: Well, that definitely hurt me as well—it just made me think more and more how things were completely hopeless.

THERAPIST: And you started to blame yourself?

JERROD: Yeah, I did. That's where things end up when I think like that.

THERAPIST: Is your mood affected by that at all?

JERROD: (Pause) Of course, I mean, I feel guilty and depressed. Like all I ever do is fail.

THERAPIST: So, you feel like a failure and very guilty about it?

JERROD: Yeah.

THERAPIST: I think it makes sense that these thoughts and feelings are connected, leading to some feelings of depression. Do you think it might also be related to your pattern of being overly conscientious and perfectionistic? Especially when that gets in the way of what you want?

JERROD: Yeah, I see that it stresses me out and I feel guilty and like a failure. I see how that leads to me feeling depressed.

THERAPIST: Then, it sounds like you're making a connection between the level of conscientiousness and the guilt and feelings of depression, is that accurate?

JERROD: Yeah—exactly. I start focusing on a small detail and I feel like I'm going to fail. It's all connected, and it affects my mood and makes me feel hopeless.

THERAPIST: So, it also affects your motivation?

JERROD: (Pause) It really does a number on me. It affects my motivation, my mood, and even the outcome of my work.

THERAPIST: I see. And what's an alternative thought for "This paper is a disaster" that might've been more helpful?

JERROD: Maybe to consider that only one thing was wrong in my paper and that's pretty good?

THERAPIST: Hm. And how would that have been more helpful?

JERROD: It would've helped me get over one minor thing.

THERAPIST: Yes, it might've emphasized the size of the mistake and let you see all of the other good work in there.

JERROD: Yes, I worked really hard on that paper and I thought it was pretty good overall.

THERAPIST: Is that a realistic thought? Do you see yourself having a thought like that?

JERROD: Yeah. I mean, I hadn't thought about it before. I think this conversation will help me remember when I'm in another situation like that.

THERAPIST: Sure. Sounds good. Your third thought was "I have to go and change the paper." Was that thought helpful or hurtful in getting what you wanted?

JERROD: It was hurtful.

THERAPIST: And how did it hurt?

JERROD: I just got tunnel vision about changing it instead of seeing the big picture.

THERAPIST: Right, you had a narrow focus on the thing you didn't like.

JERROD: Yeah, exactly.

THERAPIST: And what would've been a more helpful alternative thought?

JERROD: I could've thought "It's too late now—it's fine as it is and I can just turn it in. No time for changes now."

THERAPIST: Okay, so you might've thought that it was too late to change one small detail.

JERROD: Yeah. I could've just turned it in and been done with it. I have other things I have to get to as well.

THERAPIST: Okay, so this alternative might've made it so that you could be more productive in your other responsibilities?

JERROD: Yes, exactly right.

THERAPIST: That sounds like a good alternative to me. It might've saved you a lot of stress too, it seems like.

JERROD: Very true.

THERAPIST: And it could've helped you zoom out and see the big picture as you're wanting to work on?

JERROD: Yeah, I don't want to get stuck on the minutiae all the time.

THERAPIST: I agree with that. Well, moving on to your behaviors—your first behavior of going over your paper again and again—was that helpful or hurtful in getting your paper in on time? **(Query-9)**

JERROD: It definitely hurt.

THERAPIST: So, it was hurtful? How?

JERROD: I started analyzing and overthinking everything. It just snowballed.

THERAPIST: OK, so you found yourself overthinking the task?

JERROD: Yeah.

THERAPIST: And if that was hurtful, what would've been a more helpful thing for you to do?

JERROD: Not looking at it anymore—just turning the thing in.

THERAPIST: Right. So, just going ahead and turning it in?

JERROD: Right.

THERAPIST: How do you think that would've been more helpful?

JERROD: I wouldn't have had a chance to second-guess myself if I'd just let it go. If I turned it in, that would've been it.

THERAPIST: I see. And is that realistic for you to do?

JERROD: Yea, I think. I just need to remember not to stress about it.

THERAPIST: Great. Now, your second behavior of not turning in the paper. Was that helpful or hurtful in getting it in on time?

JERROD: It was hurtful, obviously.

THERAPIST: Okay. What would have been a more helpful behavior? One that might've been along the lines of "reasonably conscientious while maintaining effectiveness"?

JERROD: (Pause) I should've reminded myself that I did my best and handed it in.

THERAPIST: Okay, so a reminder that you had done your best and committing to handing it in?

JERROD: Yeah. That would've made it, so I didn't second-guess myself or give me a chance to overthink it. I could've just said "it's done" and not looked back.

THERAPIST: Sounds like you're saying that it would be good to trust yourself more and give yourself fewer opportunities to over-analyze things.

JERROD: Yeah—that's what gets me in a pickle.

THERAPIST: When you overthink things?

JERROD: Yes.

THERAPIST: When you start overthinking, what happens?

JERROD: I start feeling bad because I get stuck thinking about how things should be. I feel like a failure.

THERAPIST: And that takes a toll on your mood, huh?

JERROD: (Pause) Yeah. Especially if I've worked hard on something, I feel bad about messing up.

THERAPIST: That must be very frustrating.

JERROD: It really is.

THERAPIST: Your last behavior was that you went back to edit the paper. Did that help or hurt in this situation?

JERROD: Obviously it hurt.

THERAPIST: I see—you wanted to get the paper in on time. What would have been an alternative behavior that might have been more helpful?

JERROD: Like I said, just leave it the way it was and turn it in.

THERAPIST: OK, so just go ahead and turn it in as it was?

JERROD: Yeah.

THERAPIST: It seems like that might've made a big difference. As we discuss this pattern of being overly conscientious to the point where it gets in the way of your effectiveness, on a scale from 0–10, where 0 is not at all important and

10 is the highest in terms of importance, how would you rate how important it is for you to work on changing this pattern? **(Query-10-1)**

JERROD: About an 8.

THERAPIST: So, an 8 is very important.

JERROD: Yeah. It really gets in the way—I don't want to change it completely because it really does work for me sometimes.

THERAPIST: So, you're saying you'd like to balance out some of its benefits while maintaining effectiveness?

JERROD: Yes. I want to do good work without overdoing it.

THERAPIST: I see. Now, in terms of confidence, using that same scale, how confident would you rate yourself on being able to become more "reasonably conscientious while maintaining effectiveness"? **(Query-10-2)**

JERROD: (Pause) Probably a 6.

THERAPIST: A 6 is very good. You're more than halfway there! What would need to happen for you to get to a 7 or an 8?

JERROD: I think if I do it one time. If I just turn the thing in, or if I can remember to not obsess over things. I'd feel more confident then.

THERAPIST: That makes sense. If you get some practice with it?

JERROD: Yes, that could definitely help.

THERAPIST: Excellent. You had some great ideas about how to come up with helpful alternatives. How was that for you?

JERROD: It was fine. I felt like I was getting the idea and it can help me overcome focusing too narrow. I could also see how it affects my mood.

THERAPIST: So, you got a lot of perspective from this. Lots of different ways to think about it?

JERROD: Yeah, it was good to talk about it and I was able to think about how much stress it causes.

THERAPIST: It sounds very stressful. I'm also glad you were able to see the links. Would you be okay if we discussed some of the behavioral activation activities we can plan for this week?

JERROD: Yeah—let's do it.

THERAPIST: Great. Any activities in particular that you have in mind for the week?

JERROD: I thought about some things but I'm not really sure. I don't know what I want to do.

THERAPIST: Well, what's one of your ideas?

JERROD: Well, I was going to see a comedian this week with some of my friends, but I don't know if that could count because it's more than 20 minutes.

THERAPIST: That can definitely count. It sounds like a great idea. Laughter can be great for wellness. When were you thinking of going?

JERROD: On Saturday—I bought the tickets a while back.

THERAPIST: How about another idea?

JERROD: Maybe just going outside since the weather is changing and it's been nice lately.

THERAPIST: Okay. And doing what kind of stuff outside?

JERROD: Like just going for a walk.

THERAPIST: Is that something you think you could enjoy?

JERROD: For sure. I used to take my dog all the time. I'd walk for about 5 minutes to the park and I like seeing the other dogs.

THERAPIST: You like dogs?

JERROD: Yeah, I really do. I want to get one when I finish school.

THERAPIST: So, you can take a walk to the dog park nearby for about 15–20 minutes?

JERROD: Yeah.

THERAPIST: And you'll schedule that for what day this week?

JERROD: Wednesday after class could work.

THERAPIST: So, it sounds like you have a pretty good plan for this week. On Wednesday, you'll take a walk to the park nearby and see the dogs. Then on Saturday, you'll go out with your friends to the comedy show. Are you willing to keep a log of these activities? Rate them from 0–10 in terms of completeness and how much pleasure you got from it?

JERROD: Yeah—I can definitely do that.

THERAPIST: Great. Well, before you go, would you mind filling out this form? I'd like to see if you're getting what you want out of our time together.

JERROD: Alright. Sure.

THERAPIST: You indicated that you were satisfied and that we talked about the things you wanted to talk about.

JERROD: Yeah. I wanted to discuss my issues at school and we definitely accomplished that. I also feel better about it.

THERAPIST: I'm really happy to hear that, Jerrod. I look forward to our next meeting.

## Commentary

Jerrod was quite responsive to the query sequence. His engagement is consistent with his conscientious perfectionism and pleasing pattern. He was also able to gain some insight into how his perfectionistic pattern affected not only his behaviors but also his mood. He also began to understand that engaging in negative self-talk, related to his perfectionistic standards, decreases his motivation and ability to focus. The therapist reinforces how the query sequence can help Jerrod become more aware and in control of his pattern. This is important because it not only increases credibility in therapy but also provides him the sense of control he wants. As a result, he can be more productive and effective.

## Session 3

### Session Plan

The plan included taking the PHQ-9 and reviewing the Mood Rating Chart, the ORS, the SRS, and the behavioral activation assignment. Then, a recent situation is processed that presumably will assist in shifting Jerrod's maladaptive pattern to a more adaptive one. If another ultra-brief intervention is indicated, it is introduced. Finally, additional behavioral activation activities and continued monitoring with the mood chart are assigned. As with other middle sessions, this third session reviews the PHQ-9 scores, the Mood Rating Chart log, the ORS, and the behavioral activation assignment log. The transcription starts with a troubling situation which Jerrod wants to therapeutically process.

THERAPIST: Could you describe a recent situation that we can process together? **(Query-1)**

JERROD: Yeah. One of my friends from the study group texted me and asked if I was OK. That was nice, but I also felt embarrassed that I was so unproductive.

THERAPIST: So, you felt embarrassed that you didn't go?

JERROD: Yes, I could really have used the help studying this week. We are covering some material that is very challenging. I should have gone. But I just could not bring myself to get up and go, and I didn't feel like I had the energy to get ready and walk all the way over there. So, I just stayed home and watched TV.

THERAPIST: So, it sounds like you typically enjoy going to the study group and you get a lot out of it, but this week you were too tired to go and stayed home instead. Then, you felt guilty because you weren't as productive. Is that correct?

JERROD: Yes.

THERAPIST: What happened after that?

JERROD: That was it. I stayed home.

THERAPIST: Could this be related to the pattern we've talked about? Being perfectionistic and overly conscientious?

JERROD: It could be. I've been worried a lot that I'm not performing as I should. I got really discouraged. And I felt hopeless—like either way I wasn't going to get what I wanted. What's the point? You know?

THERAPIST: Ok. So, your first thought was, "What's the point?" **(Query-2)**

JERROD: Yeah.

THERAPIST: I see. What's another thought you had?

JERROD: I thought that my peers were going to know that I'm unprepared. I thought I was wearing my lack of preparation and usually I'm ready and do really well. They'd think "What's wrong with him?"

THERAPIST: You were thinking that they would judge you for your lack of preparation?

JERROD: Yeah.

THERAPIST: So, you were thinking "They're totally going to know I'm unprepared and they're going to judge me for it."

JERROD: Yeah. Exactly. I hate that feeling.

THERAPIST: Was there another thought?

JERROD: That I totally messed up. I got frustrated with myself.

THERAPIST: So, your thoughts were "What's the point?," "They're going to judge me because I'm unprepared," and "I totally messed up."

JERROD: Yes, that sums it up.

THERAPIST: I see. And what are some of the things you did? What were your behaviors? **(Query-3)**

JERROD: Um, I didn't get my work ready—it's more about what I didn't do.

THERAPIST: You didn't get ready with your work.

JERROD: Yeah. I didn't shower either. I didn't get dressed.

THERAPIST: OK, so you didn't get ready to go. Was there anything else?

JERROD: Yeah, I stayed in my sweatpants watching TV.

THERAPIST: So, essentially, you were tired, so you didn't prepare, you didn't get ready to go, and you stayed home and watched TV.

JERROD: Yes, pretty terrible, huh?

THERAPIST: Well, I'm not sure yet. What did you want to get out of the situation? **(Query-4)**

JERROD: I wanted to go. It would've made me feel better and I would've gotten a lot out of it.

THERAPIST: So, you wanted to go and be a part of the study group.

JERROD: Right.

THERAPIST: That sounds very reasonable. It also could've made you feel better. I agree with you there.

JERROD: Yeah. I wish I felt more motivated. I think it might've helped to actually do something.

THERAPIST: OK, so what actually happened? **(Query-5)**

JERROD: Well, I didn't go, like I said. I stayed in and watched TV. I didn't even get dressed and I felt super-guilty about it.

THERAPIST: You wanted to go to the study group but instead you stayed at home and watched TV. That ended up making you feel guilty.

JERROD: Yeah. Exactly.

THERAPIST: So, did you get what you wanted? **(Query-6)**

JERROD: No, obviously not.

THERAPIST: It also seems like this situation can be connected with your pattern. You want to do something the right way and that interferes with doing it at all. Does that sound accurate?

JERROD: Yeah. That's what happens. I just put so much pressure on myself that it makes it impossible to accomplish. It happens a lot.

THERAPIST: So that longing to do things perfectly—no mistakes—eventually just overwhelms you and gets in the way of you doing the thing you wanted to do?

JERROD: Yes, exactly.

THERAPIST: OK, I see. Would you be willing to go over this situation and perhaps see about other ways things might've turned out? **(Query-7)**

JERROD: Sounds good. We can go over it.

THERAPIST: Well, your initial thought was, "What's the point?" Did that thought help you or hurt you in getting your desired outcome—actually going to the study group? **(Query-8)**

JERROD: It hurt me; I think.

THERAPIST: How did it hurt you?

JERROD: I felt discouraged afterwards. I was too focused on the wrong things.

THERAPIST: So, you felt discouraged because you were focused on the things you had done wrong?

JERROD: Yeah.

THERAPIST: And in this instance, what might've been a more helpful thought?

JERROD: Uh, I could've thought that I could still get something out of the group even if I'm not where I want to be with my work.

THERAPIST: Right, so you could've thought about still benefitting from the group.

JERROD: Yeah. I mean, that's the whole reason to go to the group—to get you prepared.

THERAPIST: It sounds like you didn't have to be as prepared as you thought.

JERROD: No, not exactly.

THERAPIST: How would that new thought have been more helpful?

JERROD: It would've made it more likely for me to go to the group—to notice the good parts and the reason for having group in the first place.

THERAPIST: So, you would've focused on the help that you would've gotten from the group?

JERROD: Yes, that would've been better.

THERAPIST: Great. Your second thought was people would judge you in the group, knowing that you were unprepared. Did that hurt you or help you?

JERROD: The thought definitely hurt.

THERAPIST: OK, I see. How did it hurt?

JERROD: I was focusing on all the wrong things, just like with the other thought. I didn't think about anything that I did right.

THERAPIST: Just like the first thought, huh?

JERROD: Yeah.

THERAPIST: And what is an alternative thought that might have been more helpful?

JERROD: I might've thought that my peers were also not as prepared. I'm usually more prepared than them, so I'd probably be ahead either way.

THERAPIST: Do you think you gave yourself enough credit then?

JERROD: No. Definitely not. I should definitely do that more. I also shouldn't compare myself.

THERAPIST: So, if you didn't compare yourself and had focused on the fact that you're typically more prepared, how would that have helped you actually go to the group?

JERROD: I wouldn't have felt so overwhelmed. I'd feel more reassured that I'm doing well.

THERAPIST: So, it would've been more reassuring. That makes sense. It sounds like it would also have been more accurate.

JERROD: Yeah. I really don't give myself enough credit.

THERAPIST: And your third thought was about messing up—"I really messed up." Did that help you or hurt you in getting to the study group?

JERROD: It hurt.

THERAPIST: How did that thought hurt?

JERROD: Well, it was hard to be motivated because I was beating myself up.

THERAPIST: Okay, so beating yourself up makes it hard to be motivated and do things.

JERROD: Yeah. Exactly. I really don't even notice when it happens, either.

THERAPIST: Makes sense. This is why processing it in this way can help. Sometimes we don't notice our patterns.

JERROD: I can see that.

THERAPIST: What might've been an alternative, more helpful, thought?

JERROD: Not focusing on what I did wrong. If I'd thought about doing reasonably well—I might've gone to the group and been more prepared.

THERAPIST: So, to focus on the things that you did well?

JERROD: Yeah.

THERAPIST: How would that have been more helpful?

JERROD: I wouldn't have been in my head so much. I could have focused on what I wanted.

THERAPIST: That makes sense. Now, on to your behaviors—your first behavior was that you didn't prepare for the work. Was that hurtful or helpful in making it to the study group? **(Query-9)**

JERROD: Hurtful.

THERAPIST: How would you say that it was hurtful?

JERROD: I felt sluggish because I started falling behind.

THERAPIST: So, you felt sluggish?

JERROD: Yeah.

THERAPIST: And what might've been a more helpful behavior?

JERROD: To just grab what I had or prepared to go in advance.

THERAPIST: So, you would have gotten your work together either way?

JERROD: Yes.

THERAPIST: In what way would that have been more helpful?

JERROD: I could have felt more prepared doing that. That would have been one thing that I did and recognized, instead of falling back into all-or-nothing.

THERAPIST: And it would have helped you go to have felt more prepared?

JERROD: Yeah, like I was already some of the way there.

THERAPIST: Does that sound like your pattern again?

JERROD: Yes. I don't do things at all if they don't turn out how I want them to be. I have to learn to just do my best.

THERAPIST: It sounds like you're making the connection between your very high standards and not completing the things you set out to do.

JERROD: Yes, I am getting to see that.

THERAPIST: That's good insight. Your second behavior was that you didn't get ready or dressed. Did that help or hurt in getting your desired outcome?

JERROD: It definitely hurt me because I just felt more tired and lazy.

THERAPIST: So, you felt more tired. It sounds like this also affected your mood and motivation. Did you feel those things diminish?

JERROD: (Pause) Kind of. I felt kind of defeated. I can see how it's connected.

THERAPIST: Right. And what might've been more helpful for you to do?

JERROD: Maybe picking an outfit I wanted to wear, or just getting ready.

THERAPIST: That sounds good. How would choosing an outfit you wanted to wear have helped you?

JERROD: I would've just felt more ready and actually looking forward to going out.

THERAPIST: So, it might've helped in terms of anticipation—actually looking forward to it?

JERROD: Yeah.

THERAPIST: Your third behavior was that you stayed in watching TV. Did that help or hurt you get what you wanted?

JERROD: It hurt too.

THERAPIST: How did it hurt?

JERROD: I'd given up on going to the group, so I thought I'd just watch TV and rest, but it backfired. I felt more tired after.

THERAPIST: So, you ended up feeling more tired?

JERROD: Yeah.

THERAPIST: And what might've been a more helpful behavior?

JERROD: Maybe just going for a walk or something.
THERAPIST: So, moving around and staying active?
JERROD: Yes.
THERAPIST: I agree with you there. These alternatives are excellent. Do you find these to be realistic—do you see yourself implementing these?
JERROD: Yes. I do. (Pause) They could've definitely turned things around.
THERAPIST: Alright. It also sounds like you're realizing how much of an effect these things can have instead of the all-or-nothing rule you used to uphold. Is that correct?
JERROD: Yeah. I just want to take some small steps. Even if I stayed a bit active. I think that would be helpful.
THERAPIST: I appreciate you processing this situation with me.
JERROD: Yeah, of course, thank you.

## Commentary

The behaviors Jerrod reported during the Query Sequence were all passive and involved his withdrawing from the situation. These are consistent with a mild to moderate level of depression, particularly his symptoms of lack of motivation and social isolation. It is expected that if he can use and internalize the replacement behaviors that he generated, his future PHQ-9, Mood Scale ratings, and ORS will reflect this change. Jerrod also gained insight into how his self-imposed pressure affects him. It reflects his obsessive-compulsive pattern in which he both moves against others as well as "against himself" by being self-critical and overly demanding. Toward the end of Query-9, Jerrod begins to make a case for why he should become more active as well as why he does not need to strive for perfection. His response indicates a decrease in symptoms across the duration of the session, indicated by increased motivation and the beginning of a shift toward a more adaptive pattern.

THERAPIST: Now since we have been talking about this pattern of keeping yourself from effectively completing your tasks because you are focused on not making mistakes, on a scale from 0–10, where 0 is not at all and 10 is the most, how important is it for you to change this pattern? **(Query-10-1)**
JERROD: I'd say an 8.
THERAPIST: OK, so it's quite important?
JERROD: Yes, especially now that I see how it holds me back from doing what I want.
THERAPIST: Good. Now on the same 0–10 scale, how confident would you say you are that you can change your conscientious perfectionism and pleasing pattern to a more adaptive one? **(Query-Pattern & Query-10-2)**

JERROD: Um, maybe a 6. It can be very hard and I'm not very confident in making change.
THERAPIST: That is understandable. It can be difficult to change after doing something for a while. But it is very possible. What do you think it would take to move that to a 7?
JERROD: I think if I'm able to reassure myself that I'm doing well. Focus on the positive stuff like we talked about when that comes up again.
THERAPIST: Ok, so practicing some of the thoughts and behaviors we went over here today?
JERROD: Yes, I think that will be helpful.

## Commentary

Jerrod indicates that he is motivated but hesitant to change his pattern. He reports, however, that he is not very confident he can do it. The therapist is nonjudgmental and helps Jerrod figure out strategies that can improve his confidence. Had the therapist taken a more forceful approach here, it might have triggered Jerrod's maladaptive pattern. Jerrod's importance rating was 10 in the first session, compared to 7 now. This probably reflects Jerrod's people-pleasing pattern. His ability to report the lower score in this session indicates the increasing therapeutic alliance, that is, he feels sufficiently accepted that he can risk not pleasing his therapist by giving an overly high rating.

THERAPIST: OK, now if you can just fill out the SRS form.
JERROD: OK. (Pause while Jerrod completes the SRS)
THERAPIST: It looks like you were satisfied with our session and that we covered what you wanted to talk about.
JERROD: Yes, I think it's going well. I feel a bit better now than when I came in today.
THERAPIST: Glad to hear that and I look forward to hearing about your progress next time we meet.

## Commentary

Jerrod continued to be quite engaged in the Query Sequence and most agreeable to using the agreed-upon behavioral activation activities. His active role in understanding the value of behavioral activation and planning activities is reflected in the symptom improvement that occurred during this session. It is also consistent with his need to please authority figures. Jerrod's SRS score both reflects his pattern and confirms his improvement over the session, as he states that he feels better than when the session began.

## Session 4

### Session Plan

The plan included taking the PHQ-9 and reviewing the Mood Rating Chart, the ORS, and the behavioral activation assignment. Then, a recent situation is processed in terms of Jerrod's maladaptive pattern. If another ultra-brief intervention is indicated, it is introduced. Finally, additional behavioral activation activities and continued monitoring with the mood chart are assigned.

The result of the PHQ-9 taken just prior to this session is 6, which is at the lower end of the mild depression range. Likewise, his ORS score also improved. Prior to this session, Jerrod reported that he had been able to come up with alternative thoughts and behaviors. Select sections from this transcription are presented here.

THERAPIST: Okay. Can we move on to reviewing today's ORS form?
JERROD: Sure. Let's do it.
THERAPIST: Your individual functioning rating, here—can you tell me more?
JERROD: Well, yeah—I felt frustrated a lot, but I felt like I did better managing it. I think it was pretty good.
THERAPIST: So, there were some instances that you felt frustrated. I'm glad to hear that you managed well. What were some things that helped you manage?
JERROD: Uh, exactly what we had talked about. "What's happening right now?" And then noticing that whatever was going on was not the end of the world. I was able to just chop things down into small tasks and get things done. I didn't feel as overwhelmed.
THERAPIST: So, it sounds like you were able to identify and resolve some of that perfectionistic pattern. When self-criticism surfaced, you helped yourself by chopping things down and coming up with alternatives?
JERROD: Yes, I felt really good about doing it on my own.

### Commentary

Jerrod reports that between sessions he was able to catch himself thinking and behaving in ways consistent with his maladaptive pattern. Subsequently he successfully applied alternative thoughts and behaviors on his own. This behavior indicates that Jerrod engaged in third-order change. This suggests that he can continue to respond —on his own—in adaptive ways when he has completed therapy. The therapist tied Jerrod's behavior back to his pattern. This exchange was validating for Jerrod and likely increased his level of confidence that he could and would change his maladaptive pattern.JERROD: Even though things went well at the show, I had a run in with my parents. I forgot to call them, and they were annoyed —so that brought my rating down a bit. It was the same day of the show. I called them the next day and they were upset because they had waited for me.

THERAPIST: And how did things end? Was it resolved?

JERROD: I wouldn't say it was resolved, really. We just talked about other stuff and they didn't mention it.

THERAPIST: So, there was some tension with your parents that went unaddressed. You've moved past it?

JERROD: Yeah. I think things are okay. I don't think they're going to bring it up unless it happens again.

THERAPIST: On the mood scale, how would you rate yourself?

JERROD: About a 7, I was stressed about the group project but now I'm doing better.

## Commentary

Although Jerrod briefly mentioned the incident involving his parents, the therapist decided not to pursue it at this time. Even though his family did influence his maladaptive pattern, this particular situation with his parents did not trigger Jerrod's pattern. Jerrod's ability to manage this stressful interaction with his parents reflects his move toward a more adaptive pattern. If Jerrod had been more distressed about the interaction, or if he were to bring it up again in future sessions, the therapist might consider processing it. Otherwise, it might be an unnecessary distraction from the course of therapy. Instead, Jerrod wanted to process a situation with a group project that was significantly distressing for him.

He reports being a part of a group project with three other students. He ended up doing most of the work because of lack of faith in the other students. The result was that this left no time for any relaxation or enjoyable activities. As a result, he was very stressed. His maladaptive thoughts were: "these students don't know what they're doing," and "if you want something done right, you have to do it yourself." His maladaptive behaviors were to complete portions of other group's members assignment without consulting with others and working instead of doing leisurely activities planned. His desired outcome was to "complete my work and save time to relax and have fun." The query sequence was employed to process this situation. Up to this point it included Query-1 to Query-8. The transcript picks up at this point.

THERAPIST: Okay, great. Now, on to your behaviors; your first behavior was that you took on the part that belonged to the other student. Was that helpful or hurtful? **(Query-9)**

JERROD: Um, it was hurtful. I focused on it the whole time and didn't get to relax. I was very focused on the details.

THERAPIST: I see. Do you see how that's related to your patterns again? The narrow focus?

JERROD: Yes, it crops up when I have to depend on others. Especially in terms of competence.

THERAPIST: And you find yourself being critical sometimes because of this pattern?

JERROD: Yeah. That happens sometimes.

THERAPIST: And where do things go from there? When you're critical of others?

JERROD: I focus even more on details and it makes me annoyed and frustrated. It's a cycle.

THERAPIST: So, the pattern feeds into itself, then?

JERROD: Yeah. Exactly.

THERAPIST: Right. What would've been a more helpful behavior in this instance?

JERROD: I should've just done my own part and let the rest of the group worry about their parts. I would've respected my own time and been able to relax if I'd done that.

THERAPIST: So, working on your parts and leaving the rest for the group might've been respectful of your schedule and time?

JERROD: Right. I undervalue my time sometimes. This process has helped me reprioritize.

THERAPIST: Okay. So, you're noticing that you can prioritize your time so that you take care of yourself and are respectful of yourself, and that in turn will help you. Good.

JERROD: Yeah. Thanks.

## *Commentary*

While analyzing his behaviors during the Query Sequence, Jerrod connected his perfectionistic pattern to his tendency to criticize others and recognized the self-perpetuating nature of his pattern. This is a major indicator of change for Jerrod. His shift toward a more adaptive pattern helped Jerrod become more aware of how his maladaptive pattern affected his relationships and increased his motivation to change this pattern so he could foster better relationships. Finally, Jerrod recognized some triggers of his pattern and demonstrated the ability to overcome such triggers without the assistance of the therapist. This, of course, is reflective of third-order change and will be useful in future relapse prevention planning which is covered in considerable detail in Chapter 8.

## Conclusion

This chapter reviewed the middle sessions of the case of Jerrod. Specifically, it reviewed sessions 2, 3, and 4 of this successful therapy. Specific selections from transcriptions of these three sessions were analyzed. Behavioral activation is the ultra-brief intervention that was introduced in the first session. It became a key intervention throughout these middle sessions in targeting Jerrod's presenting problem of low mood and loss of interest and pleasure. The Query Sequence was introduced in the second session with the goal of shifting the client from his maladaptive pattern to a more adaptive one. As the main therapeutic strategy in Pattern Focused Therapy, the Query Sequence effected significant change. Not surprisingly, as therapy proceeded, Jerrod becomes aware that his maladaptive pattern actually engenders his depressive symptoms. Also noteworthy in these sessions was the value of continuous monitoring with the PHQ-9, the Mood Rating Scale, the Outcomes Rating Scale, and the Session Rating Scale in order to more effectively tailor the treatment process. In addition, Jerrod began demonstrating some third-order change, ensuring that treatment gains will persist after therapy is complete. In Chapter 8 on the final sessions, third-order change is further emphasized.

# Chapter 8

# The Final Sessions

Recall that Jerrod opted for psychotherapy because he did not want to take medication when it was first proposed by his physician to treat his depression. In their first meeting, both client and therapist agreed to begin therapy and later, if indicated, to arrange for medication to be combined with therapy. Because of Jerrod's early responsiveness to therapy in the first two sessions, combined treatment with medication was not needed. This progress continued in subsequent sessions. This chapter presents the termination phase of effective Pattern Focused Therapy. These two final sessions focus on critical components of this therapeutic approach (Sperry & Sperry, 2018). In sessions 5 and 6, treatment shifts to final assessment and life after therapy. This chapter presents five guidelines for successful termination, and describes two components: relapse prevention planning and review of progress.

We return again to the case of Jerrod to illustrate how the process of Pattern Focused Therapy unfolds over the course of six sessions. As previously noted, there was a provision for additional sessions if indicated. As it turned out, no additional sessions were needed. Let's briefly review this six-session course of treatment. The first session set the initial phase for the use of Pattern Focused Therapy. Sessions 2–4 represent the middle phase of treatment. Finally, the termination phase consists of sessions 5 and 6.

## Termination

Concluding therapy with a client is an essential skill of Pattern Focused Therapy (Sperry & Binensztok, 2019a). This concluding process is commonly known as termination, and it is a process in which the relationship between client and therapist changes and the client takes on more responsibility for maintaining treatment gains. The reactions that clients have during the process of termination largely pivot on their specific patterns. Not surprisingly, difficulties and challenges in the termination process can usually be anticipated based on the client's personality dynamics and pattern, as reflected in the case conceptualization (Sperry & Carlson, 2014).

## *Preparing for Termination*

Although preparation for termination is indicated toward the final phase of therapy, some cognitive-behavioral therapy (CBT) approaches consider it important to address the task much earlier (Beck & Beck, 1995). As previously noted, the treatment formulation section of a case conceptualization functions as a guide for specifying treatment interventions and anticipating obstacles in the therapy. It can also assist the therapist in anticipating specific difficulties that the client may have with termination. Therefore, it will be no surprise to a therapist when a particular client with a history of losses or a pattern of dependent clinging experiences difficulty or begins to act out when approaching termination (Cucciare & O'Donohue, 2008).

## *Indicators of Readiness for Termination*

The criteria for determining when termination is indicated are theory-specific. On the other hand, there are general indicators that are common to various approaches. Useful indicators that the client is ready to terminate from treatment include: (1) the client's presentation is resolved and/or symptoms are diminished or relieved; (2) the client has gained insight to sufficiently comprehend both the problem and the patterns that led to the problem and treatment; (3) the client's skills for effectively coping and dealing with life circumstances are sufficient; (4) the client demonstrates increased capacity for planning and working productively (Heaton, 1998); and (5) and proactive client efforts. This is called self-therapy in CBT. The main premise is that clients begin to practice independently to be their own therapist as problems arise between sessions. This, of course, is third-order change and prepares clients to address difficulties, setbacks, or relapse following termination (Beck & Beck, 1995).

## The Five Tasks in Effective Terminations

Five main tasks comprise an effective termination: (1) discussing the client's thoughts and feelings related to the termination; (2) discussing goals that have been attained and progress achieved; (3) addressing relapse prevention and formulating a plan; (4) acknowledging client growth and how to maintain it; and (5) discussing contingencies for future contact, should future sessions prove necessary (Sperry, 2010; Sperry & Binensztok, 2019a).

## 1. Discussing Termination

In Pattern Focused Therapy, the termination process typically begins in the second last session. In reviewing therapeutic progress and the therapeutic relationship, it is essential that the therapist elicits negative as well as positive feedback from the client. These responses can vary in form and complexity. Clients can respond with pride as well as apprehension. For instance, they may feel satisfied with their therapeutic gains while apprehensive about their capacity to sustain growth or maintain achieved levels of functioning.

## 2. Review of Progress and Goals

While reviewing progress and goals, the therapist aids the client in examining past achievements by listing gains within the treatment and comparing them to the goals that the client and therapist mutually agreed upon. One by one, first- and second-order goals are addressed. The therapist can use scaling questions (e.g., 1–10 scale) to prompt the client to assess the extent to which they think they have accomplished the set goals. The client can be encouraged to continue to strive to reach even the goals that were partially accomplished within the therapy. Thereafter, the clinician can prompt the client to materialize some new goals for them to pursue on their own (Sperry, 2010).

## 3. Relapse Prevention Plan

The purpose of a relapse prevention plan is to aid the client in anticipating and reducing the probability of a return to maladaptive behaviors once treatment has ended. Relational skills, coping skills, and self-efficacy can be improved by this task (Marlatt & Gordon, 1985). Planning for relapse prevention starts by identifying potential triggers of symptoms and behaviors through a collaborative process (Marlatt & Gordon, 1985). Triggers may occur in intrapersonal, interpersonal, physical, or contextual environments (i.e., the client's immediate surroundings). The acronym HALT (Hungry, Angry, Lonely, Tired) originated in the 12-Steps tradition, and it can be useful for recognizing triggers. Strategies for avoiding, or coping with, each potential trigger must be discussed in advance, as many individuals will find one or more of these to emerge as a stressor (Sperry & Binensztok, 2019b).

Beyond trigger identification, the therapist must help the client identify warning signs of the return of previous symptoms. Additionally, it is important to provide tools for the client to anticipate when maladaptive behaviors await on the horizon. Specific strategies must be acknowledged. Encouragement is also provided for the client to maintain lifestyle changes, such as exercise and nutrition, that can help preserve treatment gains and avert relapse (Sperry, 2010).

### 4. Maintaining Treatment Gains

Therapy progress almost always consists of a combination of shifting to a more adaptive pattern, reducing symptoms, achieving more positive thinking, feeling better, and relating more effectively. However, there are no guarantees that achieved progress will be sustained in the long term. Regressions often occur in treatment. The client is challenged with applying the learned skills independently, staying the course, and continuing to practice them. These efforts are invaluable for sustaining therapeutic change. Although relapse prevention are skills that are often discussed—and adequately so—in the beginning and middle of the therapy process, so too are they important to buttress in the end, while preparing the client for termination. In particular, CBT has been effective in achieving lasting changes when clients have formulated a plan for maintaining their change through relapse prevention and when they have been motivated to sustain their growth. Given these factors, treatment effects have been likely to be maintained or even increased (Gloaguen, Cottraus, Cucharet, & Blackburn, 1998).

Sometimes, clients may want to extend personal growth beyond their original treatment goals. In these cases, the therapist does well to aid the client in setting new goals and planning for avenues through which to pursue them. This can include referrals to a support group or another therapist with a particular expertise. Or, it may include supporting clients in their own third-order change efforts.

### 5. Provisions for Future Sessions

Therapist should also discuss the possibility of scheduled future sessions, even if they are spaced at three- or six-month intervals. There are cases for which follow-on sessions are not necessary. In these cases, the therapist can collaboratively assess with the client if a follow-up session is needed. The therapist can also inform the client that returning or calling to set future appointments is welcome (Sperry, 2010).

## Session 5

### Session Plan

Jerrod's assessments (PHQ-9, ORS) continue to show increasing improvement. In the current session, the therapist and Jerrod discuss drafting a relapse prevention plan in order to prepare Jerrod to terminate therapy. Triggers for both maladaptive pattern and depression are identified for Jerrod. He also notes warning signs indicating a return of his depression and maladaptive pattern, as well as a plan to address them. Finally, the therapist assesses Jerrod's motivation to follow through with the said plan to prevent relapse. Some sections from the transcript of the session are offered below.

THERAPIST: Can you tell me how you would assess your overall functioning right now?
JERROD: I think I'm doing pretty well. Much better than at the start, that's for sure. I feel a sense of relief and my mood has changed.
THERAPIST: Your PHQ-9 score is down to 4 which is at the top of the minimal depression range. (Pause) It's so good to hear that you have noticed a favorable difference in your mood, and you feel relieved; much different from when you first came in to see me.
JERROD: Yes. A big difference. I was worried that I was going to be depressed forever.
THERAPIST: And how would you rate yourself interpersonally?
JERROD: Much better as well. I'm getting out and hanging out with friends. My parents aren't nagging me as much and our relationship has gotten better also. Things are going well in that area overall.

## Commentary

In this brief discussion, Jerrod mentions his parents for the first time. He reported an overall improvement in his mood as well as his relationship with his parents. The mitigating factor for his relationship with his parents has been his increased sense of belonging and social interest.

JERROD: Well, I'm not as irritated anymore, which I took for granted before. I never really thought about how much control I had over things that bothered me. My overall rating is good.
THERAPIST: I see. You've noticed that you have more control than you had anticipated over your mood and how you react to the people you find irritating. It also seems like you have more control over your pattern.
JERROD: Yes. People don't really consider how much they can change or how much responsibility they can take for their lives. I always thought that taking responsibility for my work was enough, but I've learned it's not. I have to keep an eye on my mood, so I don't fall back into my old ways.

## Commentary

Jerrod touches on some components that can be helpful for formulating his relapse prevention plan. He discloses a more sophisticated understanding about his triggers and pattern. His conscientiousness, which is part of his pattern, increases the likelihood that he will follow through with alternative behaviors and thoughts of his adaptive pattern, as he aspires to have increased control over his environment. Therefore, he can exercise productive and workable control over his responses to relapse triggers and signs. Jerrod's outcome measures should reflect a result of this pattern change.

THERAPIST: That's very good and important. (Pause) Now that we have reviewed some of your progress and noticed your significant changes in pattern and daily functioning, I'd like us to come up with a plan to maintain this progress. This process is called relapse prevention.

JERROD: OK, sure. I definitely don't want to relapse.

THERAPIST: OK, great. The first part of the plan is identifying some triggers. This could be a situation that you find particularly stressful. It could be a place, person, or event. Can you think of anything that could trigger your mood?

JERROD: Yes. Well, typically I start to get down on myself, being self-critical, or I'll focus too much on something that should've happened, or I should've done differently

THERAPIST: OK, so self-criticism triggers a low mood. Can you think of any other triggers?

JERROD: Yes, isolating is terrible for my mood. When I feel depressed, I try to stay away from others but it's really the worst thing I can do.

THERAPIST: I agree. (Pause) So moving away from others can be a trigger for low moods. What about factors or events that can trigger low motivation?

JERROD: Um, mostly when the perfectionism kicks in. Things seem unsurmountable. I start obsessing over little things and then things that I have no control over when it's not that big of a deal. Then, I don't get much done even if I spend a whole lot of time at it.

THERAPIST: OK, when your pattern of conscientious perfectionism and pleasing emerges, you feel overwhelmed. Then, focusing on the small details tires you out and you're not as effective at accomplishing your goals, which leads to low motivation and discouragement. Is that accurate?

JERROD: Yes. That's what right.

THERAPIST: So, what are some things that trigger that pattern of perfectionism and makes you want to focus on the small details?

JERROD: Well, being evaluated is always stressful for me. If I know I have a big paper coming up for class or a project that makes up a large percentage of my grade, I start obsessing over little things. I also struggle with working with other people because it's irritating. But I've learn how to deal with that in here.

THERAPIST: Good. It seems like evaluation and collaboration with others seem to trigger the perfectionistic pattern. Is that correct?

JERROD: Yes.

THERAPIST: OK. The next step in our relapse prevention plan is to identify some early warning signs. What are some indications that you're beginning to feel a low mood or depression?

JERROD: Um, I feel apathy or irritability. I feel like I just want to drop everything because everything gets on my nerves. I just want everyone to leave me alone.

THERAPIST: You start to notice feelings of apathy and irritation caused by most things.

JERROD: Yeah.

THERAPIST: And what are some early signs that your pattern is resurfacing?

JERROD: Oh, that's a hard one. I really start feeling frustrated or annoyed. I guess when I'm more sensitive to it because I notice it happening with smaller things.

THERAPIST: You notice that there's a decrease in your irritability threshold—how much you can take before something makes you irritable—that's when you're noticing your pattern come up?

JERROD: Yes, that sounds right.

THERAPIST: There is an acronym that's called HALT, which can help us understand our triggers. It stands for Hungry, Angry, Lonely, and Tired, which are common triggers. Have you noticed if any of those have ever triggered your maladaptive pattern?

JERROD: Huh—yes, actually. Interesting. Feeling tired, lonely, or angry have definitely triggered my pattern. My depression is triggered by loneliness. And I think my pattern comes out when I'm angry or tired.

THERAPIST: It sounds like you can see how those clearly affect you now—I'm glad you were able to identify those. Now that we've identified triggers and warning signs, what are some strategies that you can use to prevent things from escalating?

JERROD: (Pause) Well, I've been using the Query Sequence between sessions and it seems to work.

THERAPIST: You're finding the Query Sequence works between sessions. Great! (Pause) So you're replacing maladaptive thoughts and behaviors with more adaptive ones?

JERROD: Yes. I come up with alternative thoughts and behaviors. Especially with the thoughts. It has really helped me.

THERAPIST: That's wonderful! Our goal here is to help you become your own therapist, and that's what you're doing!

JERROD: Yes, it has changed the way I deal with a lot of things. I can also use affirmations, which is quick and easy.

THERAPIST: Great. Affirmations can be helpful. Can you think of anything else?

JERROD: It has been really helpful for me to exercise. It keeps my mood up. Also spending time with my friends makes me feel a lot better overall. I like being out and spending time with people.

THERAPIST: It sounds like this plan could be really helpful. And the more specific, the better. If you feel something is triggering your mood, is there something that you can do there and then?

JERROD: Um, I guess reach out to a friend or my mom.

THERAPIST: That's a really good idea. Do you have someone in mind who you would reach out to?

JERROD: My friend Jeff, probably. Or Steve. They're both very reliable people.

THERAPIST: OK, so you would reach out to Steve or Jeff if you noticed some warning signs?

JERROD: Yeah.

THERAPIST: What about if you feel that your maladaptive pattern is starting up?

JERROD: I can do some of the things we talked about—exercise or come up with alternatives. It's kind of like—I've been down that road, you know?

THERAPIST: I do, and it sounds like a great plan. It seems that both exercise and spending time with friends have been very impactful in your life, and they've helped to reduce your pattern of perfectionism.

JERROD: Yes, it's been really good.

THERAPIST: On a scale from 0–10, how important is it for you to follow through with this plan and maintain your progress? **(Query-10-1)**

JERROD: It's a 10 for sure. The work we've done together has changed my life, so I want to keep it up.

THERAPIST: OK. Good. You've put a lot of effort into this. Now, on the same scale, what is your level of confidence that you can implement the plan? **(Query-10-2)**

JERROD: Probably around an 8. I feel confident, but I know that life can still get in the way. Things tend to get hectic throughout the semester.

THERAPIST: OK, good. How do you think you could get that to 9 or a 10?

JERROD: I think my confidence will grow as I practice it and see that I can do it by myself. In a couple of weeks—if I'm able to keep it up even when I'm busy—I'll feel much more confident about it, especially knowing how it'll affect me.

THERAPIST: That's very good insight.

JERROD: I feel very hopeful about it.

THERAPIST: Great. You know, I'm happy for you (Pause) It sounds as if you can show yourself that you can maintain the lessons learned, your confidence will go up about your capacity to sustain these changes for the long term. Is that right?

JERROD: Yes. That's right.

## Commentary

Jerrod was collaboratively involved in creating his relapse prevention plan. He was agreeable to the process and identified triggers for his decreased motivation, mood, and surfacing pattern. He also identified early warning signs of his emerging pattern and depressive symptoms. Additionally, strategies to cope with warning signs and triggers were identified. The therapist made sure to prompt Jerrod for specific strategies that he could use, rather than general or vague approaches. Having a specific and carefully defined plan will increase the likelihood of follow through and can result in his sustaining his gains in treatment.

# Session 6

## Session Plan

This is the final scheduled therapy session. Jerrod's improvement is reflected by positive ratings in PHQ-9, the ORS, and the Mood Rating Scale scores. The aim of this session is to review goals and establish a concrete plan for relapse prevention. Goals are reviewed and assessed using scaling questions (i.e., 0–10). The therapist also helps Jerrod come up with new goals for future growth as well as reflecting on past goals achieved. Prior to the beginning of this session his PHQ-9 score was 2 which is in the middle of minimal depression range, which, for all practical purposes, is where most individuals score who do not consider themselves to be depressed. Segments from the transcript of the session are presented here.

THERAPIST: As we wind down our work together, I'd like to review the goals we set at the start of your treatment. Can we spend a few minutes on that?

JERROD: Sure. That's fine.

THERAPIST: OK, good. One of your main goals was to improve your mood. On a scale from 0–10, how would you rate the extent to which you've attained this goal?

JERROD: I'd say 9. I feel a lot better and I'm relieved. I felt terrible for so long and now I can really tell there's a big difference.

THERAPIST: Can you share more about that?

JERROD: Yeah. I used to wake up feeling like things were so depressing—this feeling of doom, like the day wasn't going to get any better. I was just riding waves of irritability. Just dragging along—you know? I feel much better now. Like a new person, actually.

THERAPIST: It's good to hear that. I'm happy that you were able to experience this lift in your mood and feel better now. The next goal on our list was to increase your motivation. To what extent do you feel you reached that goal, from 0–10?

JERROD: I think around a 9 also. My motivation has stayed pretty high lately. Things spiral from doing one thing to doing the next and I feel like I'm in a groove. I can handle things better and enjoy going out, which before felt like a chore.

THERAPIST: So overall things seem to be going well—you're more motivated and enjoying yourself. Your third goal was to participate in more activities and events. How would you rate yourself on achieving that goal?

JERROD: Probably 8. I'm really busy so I can't always enjoy myself. But before I felt so low that I barely went out, and even when I did go out, I didn't have fun. I'm enjoying myself much more now and have been in the past few weeks. I wasn't getting any kind of relaxation or stress relief before I came to see you.

THERAPIST: Because you weren't enjoying the things you were doing?

JERROD: Yeah, exactly. I feel relief that I was able to accomplish this because that's important to me.

THERAPIST: So you're enjoying yourself and are able to relax now. (Pause) Can you tell me about the goal of changing your pattern? Going from perfectionistic and overly focused on details to being able to let things be? On a scale from 0–10, how much have you achieved that?

JERROD: I'd say 8. I've definitely calmed down a lot and can let things go when they're not perfect. Instead, I'm focusing on the big picture. Before I was easily side-tracked by small details but now, I'm more able to let it go.

THERAPIST: I'm very happy to hear that. You've put a lot of work into making these changes for yourself and it sounds like you're reaping the benefits.

## Commentary

Jerrod gave consistently high ratings for his goal achievements. These ratings are reflective of his shift to a more adaptive pattern. Had Jerrod not shifted to a more adaptive and reasonably conscientious pattern, his ratings would have been lower due to harsh self-criticism. Still, it is likely that his ratings are lower than 10, given his attention to detail and ongoing stress from course work, which is normal and understandable.

JERROD: Thank you. I'm definitely less perfectionistic now. I wouldn't even consider some of these things before. I'm realizing that perfection is actually not achievable, and I have gotten myself upset in the past for nothing. Learning that has probably been the most impactful. I also benefitted a lot from behavioral activation. I feel very accomplished that I can maintain my moods and little things don't ruin my week.

THERAPIST: OK, so you've been using the Query Sequence and behavioral activation and you've found that you can very nicely control your moods. That's great!

JERROD: Yes, exactly. Before I came here, I'd wake up thinking "Well, I'm just going to have a terrible day." I'd just be annoyed and irritated because I didn't think I could turn things around. Instead, practicing the techniques, I've learned that I can actually change my mood.

THERAPIST: So, you've noticed that through some effort on your part, you can change both your thinking and your moods. And also, some setbacks don't cause you to give up on your whole day?

JERROD: Exactly. Yes.

THERAPIST: Of all the changes you've made, which has been the most important in regard to your daily functioning?

JERROD: Uh, definitely stopping and considering alternative thoughts and behaviors. That has been really helpful, especially if I'm feeling overwhelmed.

THERAPIST: Can you give me an example of a time when you used that technique?
JERROD: Yeah. Just the other day my friend kept texting me because he wanted to hang out. I had a lot of work to do so I started getting annoyed, thinking "he's such a slacker—doesn't he realize some of us actually do our schoolwork?" But then after I paused, I realized that it was actually nice of him to want to hang out with me and include me in his plans. I felt a lot better and I was actually able to concentrate on my work.
THERAPIST: So, you stopped and thought about the things that were going through your mind and causing some of your irritability. After that, you were able to think about an alternate thought and redirect your mood and concentration?
JERROD: Yes. Exactly.

## *Commentary*

Jerrod recalled a situation that triggered both his mood and maladaptive pattern. However, instead of blindly following through with his pattern, he was able to implement his relapse prevention plan and think of alternative thoughts. This allowed him to thwart the typical irritability he would have experienced had he followed the train of thoughts he was having, resulting in worse consequences. This instance is reflective of third-order change, as Jerrod was able to facilitate his own intervention independently. Additionally, these events help to increase his confidence that he can continue to do so and maintain the progress he had achieved.

THERAPIST: I am pleased to hear that you've managed to use the techniques and that it's had a positive impact on your life as a result. Can you tell me about some of the things you've learned throughout this process?
JERROD: Well, I had no idea how perfectionistic I was before. I also didn't realize how much of an obstacle it was to my life. I could never live up to my own standards, so I was always striving and never reaching. It caused me to be obsessed with little things.
THERAPIST: Okay, so you were able to notice your patterns and see some of the perfectionistic tendencies actually got in the way of what you were able to accomplish.
JERROD: Yes. I also noticed that I was being too critical with other people. I'm inpatient and quick to decide that people aren't doing their best. Whenever I've paused to take perspective, things have gone better for me. I don't get caught up as much in my thoughts.
THERAPIST: OK, so it seems that you've noticed that you can be critical of others and when you slow down, you can choose what to focus on by choosing alternative thoughts.
JERROD: Yeah.

THERAPIST: Have you noticed anything different in your relationships with other people because of this?

JERROD: Yes, absolutely. I feel like I'm a better person—compassionate and caring. My relationships have gotten better because I don't lose my patience as much with other people or I feel less irritated. I'm not holding everyone else to such an impossibly high standard so I'm able to enjoy myself and go out with my friends

THERAPIST: That's great. I'm delighted that you have been able to improve your relationships as well as your personal well-being. Have you thought about any changes you want to make from now on?

JERROD: Yeah, well I'd like to be freer. Spontaneous, you know? I mean, I don't want it to get to the point where I'm impulsive, but I'd just like to have a good time and do things without planning. That's kind of a struggle for me still.

THERAPIST: And what would spontaneous look like for you?

JERROD: A couple of weeks ago our professor told us about a trip to a new product design center upstate with the class. All of my classmates were going to stay in a hotel over the weekend and explore the city. I was waitlisted and when the spot opened up, I declined because it was at last minute. I felt like I didn't have enough time to prepare but now I regret it and wish I had gone. A more spontaneous me would've gone!

THERAPIST: That certainly sounds like a workable goal. Would it be possible for you to try some of the techniques we've worked on to help you with that goal?

JERROD: Yeah. I think I could. I have improved in finding alternative thoughts so I could try it for this goal.

## Commentary

The therapist and Jerrod discussed lessons learned throughout their therapy. A shift in his maladaptive pattern is reflected in his ability to discuss his perfectionistic pattern in an objective manner. Additionally, he was able to do so without triggering self-criticism or getting down on himself. He also indicated spontaneity as a new goal. This also reflects a shift in his pattern as his initial goal was to become more reasonably conscientious; his spontaneity far surpasses his initial goal, which shows an increased ability to withstand some of the discomfort that emerges as he gives up control. Finally, his goal is indicative of a desire for more social connection, as he has found it rewarding to relax and spend time with others thus far.

THERAPIST: That's great. Might we review your relapse prevention plan from last session?

JERROD: Absolutely. I'm really glad we worked on that.

THERAPIST: So, as far as your triggers, I noted that your main triggers are stressful circumstances which are likely to bring up self-criticalness, perfectionism, and isolation.

JERROD: Yes. I definitely have to stay alert so that I notice when I'm doing that stuff. If I pay attention to my mood, I'm more likely to catch it. That's what it usually depends on.

THERAPIST: Can you elaborate on that?

JERROD: Well, I used to just go with it when I was being perfectionistic and isolating. I didn't realize that it was connected to my mood or that I had any control over it. I also didn't think it was important to deal with it because I just thought that's how I was. Now, I'm noticing that if I pay attention to the triggers that affect my mood, I can do something about it.

THERAPIST: That's a great awareness. Some of the warning signs we discussed were feeling of apathy and irritability, which typically point to starting to feel depressed.

JERROD: Yes, that's true. Now I know that I can get to work on my strategies, so things don't escalate.

THERAPIST: And which specific strategies do you think you'll use?

JERROD: Behavioral activation and thought stopping, for sure. I can start there.

THERAPIST: I think those are great strategies. You also indicated that you noticed that the threshold of your irritability decreases when your pattern is triggered.

JERROD: Right. Without realizing that, I don't think I could do anything about it. Now, knowing more about it, I can change things and have better results.

THERAPIST: It seems like it has been empowering to realize that you have so much control over your mood and pattern.

JERROD: Absolutely. I feel like I'm in charge now.

THERAPIST: Great. You've made so many important changes—it's great to see you doing so well. Now that we've gone over your relapse prevention plan, I'd like to discuss follow-up sessions. In the Informed Consent form from the beginning of therapy, there are contingencies about follow-up session, but given how much you've achieved in therapy, it doesn't seem like you need follow-up sessions. Would you agree with that?

JERROD: Yes, I think so too. I was able to accomplish everything we talked about in the beginning. I didn't think I'd be able to deal with depression and stress, but I didn't realize I could change my strategy for how I was going about these issues. I also can't believe I didn't use medication.

THERAPIST: Absolutely, and without medication! It sounds like you're feeling a sense of empowerment with how much control you've noticed you have over your thoughts, behaviors, and mood. And, if later on it seems like you're getting down and the strategies aren't working, you can always get in touch with me here and schedule another session.

JERROD: (Pause) Yes, that puts me at ease. Thank you.

THERAPIST: OK, Jerrod. I am truly happy about all of the progress and changes you've made. I've appreciated our time together and seeing you work toward what's important to you.

JERROD: Thank you. I'm so thankful for all of your help. You really listened and helped me through a hard time, and I've learned a lot about myself.

THERAPIST: Thank you!

## *Commentary*

To conclude, the therapist reviewed Jerrod's relapse prevention plan once again and gaged Jerrod's readiness for termination. The possibility of future sessions was discussed and a course of action agreed upon. Jerrod terminated therapy having achieved both first- and second-order goals, and was highly motivated to maintain his gains and prevent future relapse. Here is a summary of Jerrod's goal ratings: Improvement in Mood 9; Increase in Motivation 9; Increase in Pleasure and Enjoyment 8; Shift to a More Adaptive Pattern 8.

## Conclusion

Jerrod was initially referred to psychotherapy because he was not eager to take medication for his presenting problem. Given that he responded well to therapy and was able to increase his mood with Pattern Focused Therapy, medication was not indicated. This chapter presented sections of transcripts from Jerrod's final two sessions.

The termination phase of Pattern Focused Therapy is illustrated this chapter. At the start, the therapist reviewed the progress he had made and prompted him to collaborate on a relapse prevention plan. First- and second-order goals' progress were reviewed. The therapist then helped Jerrod identify some triggers of symptoms and early warnings signs that his maladaptive pattern might resurface. Thereafter, strategies were collaboratively discussed in order to facilitate coping with triggers and symptoms after the end of therapy. The session concluded with prompts for further personal growth goals and encouragement to reach out and schedule future sessions if necessary.

## References

Beck, J. S., & Beck, A. T. (1995). *Cognitive therapy: Basics and beyond*. New York, NY: Guilford Press.

Cucciare, M., & O'Donohue, W. (2008). Clinical case conceptualization and termination of psychotherapy. In W. O'Donohue & M. Cucciare (Eds), *Terminating psychotherapy: A clinician's guide* (pp. 121–146). New York, NY: Routledge.

Gloaguen, V., Cottraux, J., Cucherat, M., & Blackburn, I. M. (1998). A meta-analysis of the effects of cognitive therapy in depressed patients. *Journal of Affective Disorders*, 49(1),59–72.

Heaton, J. A. (1998). *Building basic therapeutic skills: A practical guide for current mental health practice*. San Francisco, CA: Jossey-Bass.

Marlatt, G. A., & Gordon, J. R. (1985) *Relapse prevention: Maintenance strategies in the treatment of addictive behaviors*. New York, NY: Guilford Press.

Sperry, J., & Sperry, L. (2018). *Cognitive behavior therapy in professional counseling practice*. New York, NY: Routledge.

Sperry, L. (2010). *Highly effective therapy: Developing essential clinical competencies in counseling and psychotherapy*. New York, NY: Routledge.

Sperry, L., & Binensztok, V. (2019a). *Learning and practicing Adlerian therapy*. San Diego, CA: Cognella.

Sperry, L., & Binensztok, V. (2019b). *Ultra-brief cognitive behavioral interventions: The cutting-edge of mental health and integrated care practice*. New York, NY: Routledge.

Sperry, L., & Carlson, J. (2014). *How master therapists work: Effecting change from the first through the last session and beyond*. New York, NY: Routledge.

# Chapter 9

# Interventions for Optimizing Treatment

In my clinical experience, there are three pathways or trajectories that therapy can take: (1) go smoothly; (2) get stuck from time to time; or (3) derail and drop out. The first trajectory, "go smoothly," is nicely supported with research on clients' experience of successfully completing therapy published by Wampold and Imel (2015). They report that while some clients progress quickly through therapy, i.e., 3–6 sessions, others proceed more slowly. Still, overall, both types of clients do not use "extraordinary" amounts of therapy. The average number of sessions used by both types was 7–9 (Wampold & Imel, 2015). Should the therapist try to "nudge" the slower client along to finish sooner? So far, this matter has yet to be addressed in the psychotherapy literature.

The second trajectory, "get stuck from time to time," is common among clients who have many things that they want to talk about, and not uncommonly will veer off one from topic to another. The therapeutic corrective is to more effectively redirect the conversation back to the key focus of treatment. The first section of this chapter "Establishing and Maintaining a Treatment Focus" provides such a strategy and illustrates its application.

The third trajectory, "derail and drop out," is particularly troubling. These clients experience difficulties in treatment that unless therapists deal with them effectively, mean the clients are likely to drop out or have a premature termination. Published dropout rates suggest that up to one half of clients who begin treatment do not successfully complete it. Often quoted is a meta-analysis of 125 studies which reported a dropout rate of 47% (Wierzbicki & Pekarik, 1993). Because this study was published more than two decades ago and since there have been several changes in how psychotherapy is provided now, it is necessary to consider data from more recent studies. One of the largest meta-analyses published included 669 studies representing 83,834 adult clients. In this study, which better reflects psychotherapy practice today, Swift and Greenberg (2012) found the dropout rate was 19.7%.

Still the rate is high. While there are several reasons why clients leave therapy prematurely or derail it temporarily, many involve the ineffectual therapeutic interventions therapists use with client at risk for drop-out. Fortunately, there are a number of effective therapeutic interventions for maintaining clients in treatment (Swift & Greenberg, 2015). The second and third sections of this chapter provide some advanced therapeutic interventions for dealing with complicating situations that can derail the therapeutic process. These include transference-countertransference enactments and common therapy interfering behaviors.

## Establishing and Maintaining a Treatment Focus

An accurate case conceptualization allows a therapist to develop a treatment focus as appropriate interventions are selected (Sperry & Sperry, 2012). This process is akin to narrowing the broad scope of a floodlight which illuminates an entire worksite to a spotlight that illuminates a specific section of the project at hand (Sperry, 2010). The treatment focus functions as an action plan, or guide, toward achieving the treatment goal. As a result, focused treatment improves the probability of more successful outcomes in treatment. "There is now a convincing body of empirical evidence indicating that therapist ability to track a problem focus consistently is associated with positive treatment outcomes" (Binder, 2004, p. 23).

This section provides a discussion of a method of specifying a treatment focus as well as a discussion of the necessity of focusing treatment. Then, an illustration is provided on how the treatment focus is formed in Pattern Focused Therapy.

### Establishing a Treatment Focus

In the past, therapists were trained to provide "undivided attention" to the client's feelings, body language, words, and concerns. The field of psychotherapy espoused the view that the client's lead should be followed and that clinicians should not establish directive or evaluative environments. Therapists "should" express interest and empathic responses to what the client wants to discuss and should "never" give advice. Although this viewpoint may have been conducive to the open-ended, long-term approaches to therapy in the past, it is not conducive to the short-term, accountability-based, system of third-party payers and their demands (Sperry, 2010). Thus, therapists are increasingly expected to focus treatment. In order to accomplish this, therapists must learn the skill of selective attention. Otherwise, they risk becoming overwhelmed by following every branch of the virtually endless decision trees that surface before them. The treatment focus not only serves as a path to treatment, it also "serves as a stabilizing force in planning and practicing therapy in that it discourages a change of course with every shift in the wind" (Perry, Cooper, & Michels, 1987, p. 543).

How is a treatment focused specified? The therapist identifies the treatment focus through developing the case conceptualization. The basic theme of the case conceptualization serves to further specify the focus (Sperry & Sperry, 2018). It is no surprise that since the case conceptualization is founded on the conceptual framework of the therapist, the treatment focus is often informed by the therapist's theoretical orientation. For instance, in Solution Focused Therapy, the focus is on exploring exceptions and finding workable solutions. In Pattern Focused Therapy, the focus is established on identifying maladaptive patterns of behavior and thoughts.

Jaime is a 26-year-old third-generation Mexican American male who, until recently, was employed as a high school science teacher. He described symptoms associated with social anxiety disorder. Jaime reported feeling anxious around others, including teachers, students, and administrators at the school where he worked. He stated that his anxiety got so bad that he could not lecture even if for a short while and had difficulty instructing students during lab experiments and other assignments. In the past week, he took a medical leave from the job. His physician referred Jaime for psychotherapy because he was not able to tolerate anxiety medication.

Jaime is a single child and the only son of moderately acculturated Mexican American parents. His parents are college professors in the sciences. He reported that although his family was close, his parents were not particularly affectionate. Jaime reported an uneventful childhood. He stated that he never had a best friend because his parents often moved when either one or the other achieved a promotion. Therefore, he only had a best friend for approximately a year or so. He stated that his anxiety around others began during his elementary years. On the other hand, he excelled in science during high school and was awarded a four-year National Science Foundation college scholarship so that he could teach science. His parents were proud and thrilled about this achievement and they encouraged him to remain in the sciences, so he completed his B.Sc. degree in physics and was hired at a private high school. Jaime continued to like science but experienced a level of discomfort around students. However, given the central focus on lab experiments in his program, he was able to work largely with students on a one-on-one basis. Unfortunately, this came to an end at the beginning of the current school year as the headmaster modified the science curriculum and made lab work subservient to teacher lectures. After a few days of the school year, Jaime began to experience high anxiety levels, tightness and discomfort in his chest, and difficulty breathing.

The following case conceptualization was developed: Jaime's pattern is to move away from others as he anticipates criticism, humiliation, or rejection for making mistakes. Consistent with an avoidant pattern, he isolates from others due to fear of rejection. On the other hand, his extremely high standards set him up for the assumption that he will make mistakes. The association between making mistakes and rejection contributes to Jaime's symptoms of social anxiety and his cycles of social avoidance. In turn, the avoidance behaviors, through decreased opportunities for social engagement, prevent Jaime from learning the exaggeration and inaccuracy of his beliefs. Subsequently, Jaime has been mistakenly attributing low rates of rejection and mistake-making to his avoidance pattern.

The following maladaptive pattern, and the supporting interpretations and behaviors, are provided in the next section and identified as the *treatment focus*:

1 Avoiding situations that are likely to produce mistakes in order to reduce the risks of being rejected and increase the risks of safety.
2 Believing that others will criticize him, especially for making mistakes.
3 Believing that there is an inherent link between mistakes and rejection or abandonment.
4 Behaving in avoidant ways which serve to exacerbate or maintain the inaccuracy of such beliefs.

The treatment focus with Jaime was aimed at his avoidance pattern. Jaime came to understand that the safeguarding of isolation led to increased and overwhelming feelings of loneliness. He agreed to engaging in several behavioral experiments to increase social contact with others while minimizing the risk for making mistakes in resulting circumstances. In place of experiencing rejection or abandonment, as he had predicted, he experienced acceptance and enjoyment while engaging with others.

## Maintaining the Treatment Focus

The clinical observation that treatment outcomes are significantly improved when therapists maintain a treatment focus is beginning to be recognized in the research (Binder, 2004). Nevertheless, maintaining the treatment focus is not as uncomplicated as it may appear. Given the complex and changing lives of clients, it is expected that they will desire discussion about the events that occur in their lives between sessions. Commonly, these concerns are outside the purview of the treatment focus. The challenge for therapists is to "track" the treatment focus, "flexibly modifying the content as new information arises and digressing from the initial focus as circumstances dictate" (Binder, 2004, p. 100). This chapter will provide a brief discussion of the value of maintaining a treatment focus. Then, a case example and transcription will be provided to illustrate how a therapist can guide the client in "staying on track," especially given a client who easily shifts the focus to other issues or concerns.

The primary reason for "staying on track" is that, if the focus is lost, the treatment risks not achieving the specified treatment goals. However, maintaining this track is difficult especially as clients tend to shift the focus to less threatening or more comfortable topics, whether consciously or unconsciously. Thus, shifts from the treatment focus can slow or disrupt the therapeutic momentum and influence the success of treatment. In these cases, the therapist faces "decision points," in which they can decide to choose various appropriate responses to the client. The therapist's choices directly influence the success, or lack thereof, in maintaining the treatment focus (Sperry, 2010).

It goes without saying that maintaining a focus in treatment can be significantly challenging, especially for beginning therapists and trainees. Typically, because of limited familiarity with focusing techniques, beginning therapists and trainees tend to relate to client "shifts" with statements that convey empathy or questions to clarify. These responses can take the session in a different direction from the primary focus of the treatment. Only as therapists increase their awareness of shifts or "decision points" do they attempt to re-establish the focus of treatment.

## Case Study: Tracking the Treatment Focus

The case that follows illustrates how therapists effectively maintain the treatment focus. The transcription of the case following the overview will illustrate four "decision points" in which the therapist will weigh various options before proceeding. The therapist will endeavor to maintain or "track" the themes of the session on choice and empowerment. This presents a challenge as the themes are somewhat ironic. The goal for the therapist, on one hand, is to promote choice and empowerment whereas, on the other hand, the therapist must limit, reframe, refocus the client's attempts to shift the focus. This is a result of the limited amount of time in the session and the therapist's duty to maintain the focus. The therapist must decide whether to maintain the focus when the client shifts the conversation or follow the client's lead, even if for a short while.

Julia is a 29-year-old married female, who is seeking therapy for overwhelming feelings due to demands from her workplace, family, and personal life. She reports experiencing anxious depression, with occasional insomnia. Julia is a third-generation African American, currently working as a beautician. She also has a 10-year-old daughter. Julia is highly acculturated. The assessment revealed that her issues and proclivity for pleasing others are primarily driven by her personality and not by culture. Julia and the therapist agreed to a contract of ten sessions of individual psychotherapy. In the first session, the therapist identifies the pattern. Julia seems to meet others' expectations in a theme of "pleasing servant." That is, she pleases others and disregards her own needs. Collaborative goals were established for Julia to become more centered and empowered, to develop adaptive relationships with her husband, her parents, and her child. The treatment was to be focused on empowerment and choice. The second and third sessions were focused largely on Julia's relationship with her mother. Julia's mother had relegated child rearing to her grandmother and it was agreed, as Julia's expectations for treatment were primarily to establish a healthy relationship with her mother, that she would discuss with her mother and assert that she wanted her to have the role of a mother from there on.

At the outset of the fourth session, Julia was markedly dysphoric and stated that she had been "depressed and feeling down all week." She also reported that her sleep had been disrupted by her ruminations about future difficulties. Unable to independently control these ruminations, the therapist allotted approximately 5 minutes to the instruction and practice of breath retraining (described in detail in Chapter 4). She was able to follow along with good outcomes. Approximately halfway through the session, she stated:

CLIENT: I've just been so depressed this week. I feel like I've had such big setbacks. I'm constantly thinking about what comes next and it really gets me down.

## Decision Point I

Given the triggers, predisposing factors and maintaining factors for anxious depression, the therapist could have followed and provided an explanation of the clinical aspects of depression or maintained the treatment focus on the client's pattern (i.e., "pleasing servant"). The therapist chooses to maintain the treatment focus. The dynamic aspects of her feelings and other issues and how they are connected to the themes of self-empowerment and choice are emphasized.

THERAPIST: It sounds like you have been really struggling this week. You have been thinking about having setbacks and anticipating what comes next.
CLIENT: Yeah, and those thoughts are overwhelming.
THERAPIST: That's why some of the strategies to deal with these issues involve engaging in activities even when it's hard. Do you remember the activities we talked about last week?
CLIENT: Yes, but I don't want to do anything when I get like this. I get into a funk and everything just stops. I don't want to out, I don't want to do laundry, I don't even want to get out of bed.
THERAPIST: Okay. Do those seem like choices to you?
CLIENT: Yeah. (Chuckles) I guess I choose to do that.
THERAPIST: What do you think could be the purpose of "choosing" depression?

CLIENT: Maybe it's a way for me to not feel or have to confront the things I have to do. Maybe it's an excuse to procrastinate.
THERAPIST: So avoidance is the purpose of your depression?
CLIENT: (Smiling) I guess. That's one way to not do what I want.
THERAPIST: (Pauses)
CLIENT: It's just that it's really difficult. (Pause) I was thinking about our last conversation. I ended up getting down on myself because I was passive instead of aggressive. In the end, I end up paying for it again.
THERAPIST: I see.
CLIENT: It's hard for me to tell people how I feel. I know I don't have to be mean, but still I'm afraid. So, I've been thinking about being more assertive.
THERAPIST: So far, you've been afraid to be assertive.

## Decision Point 2

The therapist detects that Julia is starting to discuss another issue. Following her lead toward another theme could result in a derail of the treatment focus. However, assertiveness is linked to empowerment, so he thought about how to proceed. The therapist used "so far" as a therapeutic device that was initiated in the first session. This device allows the client to take some responsibility for the possibility of being more empowered in the future, which was connected to the focus on empowering her and encouraging her decisions instead of continuing the "pleasing servant" pattern. Then, there was another shift toward the primary focus.

CLIENT: So far, yes.
THERAPIST: Have you been using that qualifier in the past few days? "So far"?
CLIENT: Yeah, a couple of times. But I was focused on the negative things. You know—not doing what I wanted to do.
THERAPIST: Is it possible that you're using depression as fear and avoiding the things you want to do? Is "fear" accurate?
CLIENT: Yeah, that's accurate.
THERAPIST: Then it sounds like there are negative results: you feel guilty because you don't do anything. (Pauses) Do you think you could give yourself permission to not do anything?
CLIENT: (Fidgeting) I guess. But when I think about it, the thing that scares me the most is being assertive. I don't really know why but it's like someone would have to push me out of an airplane.
THERAPIST: I see. I just can't figure out why. It seems like that results in a lot of pain.
CLIENT: Oh, yes, it does.

THERAPIST: I also can't figure out what it is about the pain that's appealing. If you're not going to do something, why not do something else you might like? Say playing music [she is a musician] or something else. Instead of lying down on the couch, maybe go out shopping or call a friend? You know—give yourself permission to not do housework.

CLIENT: Those would be much better choices.

THERAPIST: They seem like the less depressing choices. If you're not going to do a task, what use is it to feel badly or depressed about it? Wouldn't it be more kind to give yourself permission and feel good about giving yourself a break?

CLIENT: It's that I don't feel this way when I have company or others are visiting. I feel like I'm a loner and I need to make friends. I'm just afraid.

## Decision Point 3

The focus here seems to have shifted toward her lack of friends. The therapist could have engaged with her and this topic, commiserating or finding an appropriate assignment to address friendship skills training. However, the therapist maintained the primary focus of treatment.

THERAPIST: So, if the purpose of the fear is to avoid the tasks, what would it be like to give yourself permission?

CLIENT: I don't feel depressed that often. And I'm starting to realize that it shows up because I'm avoiding things rather than facing it.

THERAPIST: I have some different ideas. It seems like making yourself miserable is something you've been good at. I just don't know if its primary cause is avoidance. I mean, you've raised a daughter, graduated from college, and you're employed full time. You also ended an abusive marriage and take care of your father and grandmother who are aging.

CLIENT: And yet I don't take care of myself. I constantly make myself miserable.

THERAPIST: What do you think is the purpose of that?

CLIENT: I really don't know. (Pause) I was kind of melancholic even as a child. I wouldn't let myself get too happy because I was afraid I would miss things that were important. I thought I'd forget to turn in a paper on time or things like that and then bad things would happen. I wouldn't allow myself to get too happy.

## Decision Point 4

The therapist has several options here: empathize with the client; ask follow-up questions about the client's childhood and issues with melancholy; or stay on track, maintaining the focus on the "pleasing servant" patterns.

THERAPIST: It seems like you have a lot of practice in taking care of others while neglecting your own needs.

CLIENT: Yeah. If I do something for me, then I won't be doing anything for someone else.

THERAPIST: I see. So, if you do something for yourself and don't do something for someone else, what would happen?

CLIENT: I think people would be disappointed.

THERAPIST: And what do you think the result of that disappointment could be?

CLIENT: I don't know. I think maybe they'd say that I was selfish or something.

THERAPIST: So what if you said something like "why don't you do that for me?"

CLIENT: Oh. (Uncomfortably) I'm not sure about that.

THERAPIST: Sounds like you'd be taking care of yourself. (Pause) Will that get you in trouble with others?

CLIENT: (Pause). There are times when I think it would be really nice if someone took care of me, but I'd feel weird. I'm terrible at accepting compliments.

THERAPIST: So, you're not very skilled at accepting compliments. So far.

CLIENT: Yeah. So far. (Smiling) I think it's corny, but I've been thinking about putting up notes—like Post-its around the house to remind myself of the things I've accomplished. I think it would be good, instead of thinking of all the negatives or all the things I haven't done.

THERAPIST: You have the choice to put up reminders of accomplishments instead of thinking about all of the failures.

CLIENT: I think I need to be really public about it at first. Maybe later I can just think about it.

THERAPIST: It sounds like you're suggesting something that could break away from your pattern. It sounds like it's definitely worth a try. What's something that you'd write on one of your Post-its?

CLIENT: "You're a great mom." Or something like that.

THERAPIST: Those kinds of reminders can really make a difference. It all comes down to choices. If you choose to think about something that went wrong, you're likely to feel bad. On the other hand, if you choose to think about something that went right, you will feel good.

CLIENT: That's what happens to me almost every day. I miss one thing and then I'm thinking about it all day and other things like it. It can really get me down. I guess I just have to take things one step at a time and make small progress.

THERAPIST: Do those seem like choices? Thinking about it all the time?

CLIENT: I guess.

THERAPIST: And do those choices help you?

CLIENT: Not at all.

THERAPIST: If what you want to do is avoid something, you don't have to stew on it. That's a choice you can make. If you avoid something and you feel bad about it, that's really two problems. You can eliminate the second problem by simply choosing to do something else. Maybe something that makes you feel better about the situation or about yourself.

CLIENT: Yeah, that makes sense. I don't have to beat myself up about it.

THERAPIST: This could be a way to break the pattern. You could think of alternative things that you could do that don't result in bad feelings or thoughts. The therapist wraps up the session. Julia is assigned to practice breath retraining at bedtime and as needed throughout the day. An appointment for a subsequent session is scheduled.

## *Commentary*

In this session, the therapist was effective in keeping the session on track with the treatment focus. Some of the client's attempts to shift the topic were borne out of avoidance and wanting not to discuss core dynamics of putting others' needs first and her pleasing disposition. She is very articulate and so it seemed that she would seamlessly shift to topics that were less uncomfortable. However, when redirected and refocused, she was able to focus on her pattern and core dynamics with ease and even suggest her own intervention.

## Transference and Countertransference

All therapeutic endeavors are based on the quality of the therapeutic alliance. On one hand, there are facilitative conditions to an effective therapeutic alliance. On the other hand, there are conditions that impede the development and maintenance of it. The focus of this section is transference and countertransference and in particular transference-countertransference enactments which have the potential to—and often do—interfere with the therapeutic alliance (Sperry, 2010). Accordingly, they can have a detrimental influence on therapeutic outcomes. The beginning of this section will cover transference and countertransference, focusing on enactments. Then, transference and countertransference will be discussed in terms of how it can be resolved. Finally, transcriptions from two cases will be presented to illustrate the enactments and their resolution.

### *Transference, Countertransference, and Enactments*

Current relationships are often affected by previous ones. Therefore, a person can meet someone in the present who reminds them of a colleague or romantic relationship from the past, whether consciously or subconsciously. However, most commonly, individuals have little to no insight into the fact that they may be "transferring" thoughts and feelings from past relationships onto their current relationships.

Additionally, conscious awareness of re-enacting unfinished business with past relationships is also uncommon. Another phenomenon which stems from past relationships and transfer to current ones is expectations. Individuals come to expect that certain individuals will behave in specific ways, due to past relationships that are unrelated. For instance, a graduate student may meet their statistics professor and react to them the same way, and have similar expectations of them, as they had of their high school algebra teacher. The student may come to be surprised if their new professor is less academically demanding and relaxed than her previous teacher. This resulting confusion stems from internal distortions that are not suited to present expectations of current roles (Good & Beitman, 2006).

## *Transference and Countertransference*

Transference is defined as an occurrence in which clients transmit feelings, thoughts, and expectations onto their current therapist that stem from past relationships (Sperry, 2010). Similar to active elements, such as trust and collaboration in current relationships, past relationships also contain active elements that clients and therapists bring to their working relationship. These active elements can be detrimental to the therapeutic relationship, of which transference is one. The distortions caused by transference can be a huge problem for the therapy process (Good & Beitman, 2006).

Transference is not exclusively negative. Instead, these forms of re-enactment of the client's common patterns of relating can also take a positive form and will typically involve *unfinished business*. Clients re-enact how they previously felt when treated in a comparable way. Most commonly, transference occurs when a client's unfinished business is triggered by an inadvertent statement from the therapist.

Similarly, when therapists transmit feelings, thoughts, and expectations onto their clients, the phenomenon is known as countertransference. These distortions can be similarly detrimental to the therapy process. Countertransference can also take positive or negative forms. Regardless of therapeutic orientation, there is growing consensus that countertransference can function as a valuable source of data about the client (Gabbard, 1999).

## *Subjective Countertransference vs. Objective Countertransference*

A distinction has been made between subjective countertransference and objective countertransference. Subjective countertransference refers to the therapist's feelings or responses to the client, based on the therapist's own personal history, issues, or sensitivities. In other words, the therapist's reaction to the client—either positive or negative—is activated by the therapist's own unresolved issues or unfinished business. In contrast, objective countertransference refers to the feelings and reactions the therapist experiences toward the client which are activated by the client's feelings and behaviors rather than the therapist's own issues (Kiesler, 2001).

Practically speaking, objective countertransference is evident when group of therapists meet in a group setting with a client and all five come away from that encounter with the same emotional reaction to the client. To demonstrate the phenomenon of objective countertransference I will ask students in a graduate course to watch ten minutes of an intake evaluation and then ask each to write down their personal reaction to the client. Typically, their responses are essentially the same, except of course, if a student's own unfinished business was activated by the client's manner. This exercise is very useful in demonstrating the difference between these two types of countertransference.

## Transference-Countertransference Enactments

Considered "separate" phenomena in the past, there is an increasing number of clinicians and researchers who maintain that the best understanding of countertransference and transference is from a relational viewpoint or model. The current emphasis is on the client and therapist interaction, whereas in the past it was solely on the client. From this perspective, the client and therapist co-create enactments and are viewed as equal participants, representing transference and countertransference configurations (Sperry, 2010). The therapist's role is to trigger and shape responses. The client's role is to respond. Therefore, transference can be understood through two factors: the client and their past, and the dynamics of the interpersonal relationship between the client and therapist. Transference involves "the here-and-now experience of the client with the therapist who has a role in eliciting and shaping the transference" (Ornstein & Ganzer, 2005, p. 567). For instance, a client who grew up in a family characterized by emotional distance and flagrant abuse may demonstrate difficulty with emotional disclosure in therapy. When prompted by the therapist, similar feelings may result in aloof, withdrawn, irritated, or angry behavior.

## Recognizing Transference and Countertransference

Transference and countertransference are common in therapy settings, although more common expressions occur in long-term therapy. This is especially likely in therapies that emphasize here-and-now feelings (Binder, 2004; Gabbard, 1999). As mentioned previously, positive or negative transference or countertransference manifestations can surface. It is crucial for the therapist to recognize indications and signs of both. These include feelings, behaviors, and fantasies.

Common feelings reflective of transference are anger, hostility, hurt, jealousy, and distrust. Some common behaviors reflective of transference are excessively criticizing the therapist, coming late for sessions, and seeking out personal information about the therapist. Some common fantasies reflective of transference are dreaming about the therapist, being in love with the therapist, becoming a colleague of the therapist, and harming the therapist. Common feelings reflective of countertransference are irritation, boredom, excessive pride in client progress, and resentment or excitement about seeing the client. Some common behaviors reflective of countertransference are extending session time, ending session early, asking the client for favors, or failure to deal with client boundary violations such as excessive phone calls. Some common fantasies reflective of countertransference are dreaming about the client, becoming a close friend of the client, having sex with the client, or harming the client (Good & Beitman, 2006).

## *Dealing with Transference-Countertransference Enactments*

In current therapy training programs, recognizing and resolving transference and countertransference issues are, unfortunately, not prioritized in the didactic portion. These topics may not surface in supervision either, unless a trainee brings it up and introduces the discussion (Sperry, 2010). This section and subsequent materials and cases are provided based upon the principle that in order for trainees to competently practice therapy, they must be able to effectively resolve issues of transference and countertransference. It is critical to address concerns of transference and countertransference straightforwardly and proactively to prevent unfortunate or detrimental interpersonal surprises.

Numerous methods have been proposed for managing transference. Gelso et al. (1999), for example, proposed five methods: (1) narrowing the focus to the immediate relationship; (2) interpretation of the meaning of the transference; (3) promoting insight into the enactment of transference using questions; (4) transference education for the client; and (5) self-disclosure from the therapist.

Likewise, variants for strategies to deal with countertransference have been suggested for therapists to avoid countertransference enactments. A research-based strategy has been proposed to aid therapists in preventing enactments of their internal reactions. These strategies include: self-insight; self-integration (i.e., possession of healthy character traits); anxiety management; empathy; and the ability to conceptualize (i.e., the therapist's ability to utilize theory to ascertain the client's dynamics in the relationship) (Gelso & Hayes, 2007). Self-insight and self-integration are particularly critical in order for therapists to have an adequate understanding of the situation in which the countertransference transpired, to include boundary issues between the therapist and client. Additionally, self-insight and self-integration are needed for the therapist's own psychological health, especially as they can manage and effectively use the therapist's internal reactions to facilitate therapeutic change.

Using countertransference therapeutically with clients depends on the therapist's level of self-integration. Clearly, optimal therapeutic assistance to clients also depends on the resolution of unfinished business on the part of the therapist. Self-reflection and supervision are two avenues that have proven helpful in processing and resolving countertransference issues; however, in terms of chronic problems with countertransference, personal therapy may also prove necessary (Gelso & Hayes, 2007).

The methods described thus far, among others, can be useful to resolve some transference and countertransference issues, after the fact. However, what methods can be employed in sessions as they arise? An increasingly *proactive*, here-and-now approach and protocols will be briefly described in the following section. This approach is presented in order to address and resolve immediate transference enactments, but also effect a corrective emotional experience. That is, the approach seeks to facilitate a client-therapist interaction that delineates the maladaptive pattern essential to the enactment (Levenson, 1995), which may serve to prevent future transference enactments.

## *Protocol for Resolving Transference Enactments*

A four-step process for recognizing transference enactments and dealing with it effectively is described below. Essentially, the therapist:

1   Identifies the origins of the transference in the client's past.
2   Assists the client in remembering and processing how the other person in the client's *past* reacted to the emotionally charged context.
3   Assists the client in relating a description of the therapist's reaction in the *present*.
4   Assists the client in examining differences and similarities between the therapist's behavior and the behavior of the past client's relationship. The therapist underlines the differences to emphasize a new corrective experience.

This protocol is illustrated in the following case example. McCullough (2005; 2015) offers a similar method.

## Illustration of Resolving Transference-Countertransference Enactments

It is fascinating that over the years, when asked, clinicians reliably indicate two types of countertransference reactions that they have had with clients. Nearly always, they indicate feelings of being exacerbated with client reactions. The second is "falling in love" with, or being sexually attracted to, their client (Sperry, 2010). The following scenario of transference enactment illustrates the first type and demonstrates how to recognize and quickly resolve it. The case is inspired by

McCullough (2005) and illustrates how it is quickly resolved with the client experiencing a corrective experience.

Cecilia is a 37-year-old single, never-married, Italian American female. She was referred by her physician, Dr. Marino, for evaluation and treatment of her anxiety and recurrent worry. She has never engaged in psychotherapy in the past and had some skepticism about its effectiveness. However, she followed up on the appointment due to her trust in her doctor, with whom she has been with for most of her life. Dr. Virginia Jones had been in practice for several years and regularly received referrals from Dr. Marino. Dr. Jones learned that Cecilia was the only child of her parents in her initial evaluation. She also learned that both of Cecilia's parents had passed away the year prior in a car accident. Cecilia disclosed that she had been a "worry wart" throughout her life, but things had deteriorated further since her parents' death. Cecilia stated that her father had been demanding and critical, regularly nitpicking and fighting with her mother. She described him as a self-effacing alcoholic. She denied any history of sexual or physical abuse, but it was apparent that she had been faced with substantial and sustained emotional and verbal abuse from her father, as well as emotional neglect from her mother. Since childhood, Cecilia worried about doing right by her father. She also worried that she could not count on her mother to protect her. However, she completed her college studies, became a nurse, and began to work at an extended care facility. Cecilia denied any substance use but disclosed that she chain-smokes in her attempt to "calm my nerves." Dr. Jones' treatment plan indicated that resolving relationship issues with Cecilia's parents had been a treatment goal that they mutually agreed upon. Additionally, Dr. Jones noted that negative transference enactments were likely to surface. At the start of the fifth session, Cecilia states:

CLIENT: Why do I keep screwing up?
THERAPIST: What do you mean?
CLIENT: Last week I missed our session because I was running very late.
THERAPIST: I see. It was unfortunate that we couldn't meet last week.
CLIENT: You're disappointed with me, huh?
THERAPIST: Why do you say that? What is disappointing?
CLIENT: That I screwed up. I overslept and was super late, missing our appointment.
THERAPIST: Well, you made a mistake. (Pause) I make mistakes all the time. So do a lot of other people.
CLIENT: I guess I'm expecting to get punished for that. I came really late and it probably messed your whole rhythm off for your day. (Client becomes tearful)The conversation suggests that transference is surfacing. Dr. Jones checks on this and begins to process it therapeutically. She prompts Cecilia to recall memories of feeling hurt by her father's anger and demanding nature.

THERAPIST: Right now, I'm wondering how your father might've reacted to this situation. What do you think he might've done if you had slept through plans with him?

CLIENT: (Pauses, sobs and breathes deeply) Oh jeez! He would've gone completely crazy! He'd start yelling and cursing at me. Then I'd just cry and run to my room. I'd stay there for hours because I'd be terrified of what he'd do.

THERAPIST: I'm betting that you're experiencing some of that pain right now. (Pause) I want to ask you another question, but I want us to maintain eye contact when you answer. Would that be okay?

CLIENT: (Blows her nose) Okay.

THERAPIST: What was my reaction to you missing your appointment last week?Dr. Jones' prompt helps Cecilia examine the differences between her father's behavior and her own behavior as they react to her mistakes and failures.

CLIENT: You said it was too bad that we couldn't meet.

THERAPIST: Yeah. Now, maintaining this engagement with me, could you describe my reaction to you missing our appointment. Make sure to point out as much detail as you can about my reactions both last week and this week—my tone, my word choice, and my facial expressions.

CLIENT: (Looking confused, she stops sobbing) I don't really know how to describe it.

THERAPIST: I think it is very important. Would you be willing to try?

CLIENT: Alright. (Pause) Last week you told me you were sorry we couldn't meet. It sounded like you meant it. Today you said that it was too bad, and you told me that both you and other people make mistakes. You didn't yell or curse at me. You didn't make me feel stupid. I don't really know—I can't tell by your reaction. I'm not used to being treated like this.

THERAPIST: Did I react at all like your dad used to?

CLIENT: Absolutely not! Not at all. (Pause) I'm not scared around you.Dr. Jones continues, now starting to facilitate a corrective emotional experience.

THERAPIST: Why aren't you scared around me, especially after making a mistake?

CLIENT: I don't know. I haven't really thought about it. I don't think that you're going to intentionally hurt me. (Pause) It's weird. I'm not used to trusting others, but I think I can trust you.

THERAPIST: I'm very happy that this is your experience with me! (Pause). What do you think this means about our relationship?

CLIENT: It means that I can be myself around you. (Smiles) I don't think I've ever been this way with anyone else.

THERAPIST: It sounds like you're entering a new phase in your life. I think it's very important to reflect on the importance of what you just shared with me and

what you learned about yourself. (Pause) In our work together going forward, I want us to build upon this experience and insight.
CLIENT: I felt really bad when I came in today but I'm feeling better now. I can't remember the last time I felt like this.
THERAPIST: Have you ever shared a moment of happiness with someone else?
CLIENT: No. I really don't think so.
THERAPIST: I think it's really important to enjoy that. I'm very happy for you as well.

### *Commentary*

In this session, Cecilia's reaction to having missed a therapy appointment was a transference enactment. This was due to unfinished business in her relationship with her father, who would behave in critical and demanding ways toward her about even the smallest of mistakes. The corrective emotional experience she shared with Dr. Jones can serve to supercharge the course of treatment. Dr. Jones' anticipation of the transference enactment enabled her to prepare and respond to it effectively. This also prevented a premature termination that could have been likely had Dr. Jones responded to Cecilia with a display of frustration or even mild rejection. Instead, not only did Dr. Jones prevent a poor outcome, but she likely facilitated healing and growth.

## Recognizing and Resolving Therapy Interfering Factors

Marsha Linehan (1993; 2015) introduced the term "treatment interfering behaviors" to describe behaviors that clients engage in within and between sessions that obstruct the therapy progress. Common examples of these behaviors are arguments that surface with the therapist, not showing up to scheduled appointments, refusing to engage in the therapy session, and overstepping the therapist's boundaries, such as by asking personal questions or attempting to go over time. This term provides a designation for the class of behaviors that can present a barrier in therapy and impede progress. However, Linehan's designation centers solely on the client. On the other hand, there are a multitude of kinds of impediments to treatment progress that can be observed in a clinical setting. Herein, the designation "therapy interfering factors" is adopted as it includes a broader scope. It includes client behaviors but also acknowledges the influence of the therapist, the therapeutic alliance, and other factors that can impede progress in treatment.

In order for treatment to succeed, therapists must identify, predict, and resolve treatment interfering factors. Skilled therapists anticipate these factors at the outset of the therapy and as early as the first meeting with the client, typically while collecting developmental and social details of the client's history. Factors that

Interventions for Optimizing Treatment 173

could impede the therapy progress as well as other challenges and obstacles must be included in the case conceptualization. Beyond that, potential strategies for facilitating these obstacles and factors must be considered before the factors surface throughout the process of treatment. This chapter lists and describes various interfering factors: the client, the therapist, the client-therapist relationship, and treatment. Subsequently, strategies for resolving these specific interfering factors are illustrated.

## *Types of Therapy Interfering Factors*

Various therapy interfering factors have been observed in clinical situations. These include the client, the therapist, the client-therapist relationship, and treatment factors (Beck, 2005; Ledley, Marx, & Heimberg, 2006). Here are some common examples. Client-based interfering factors include refusal and outright resistance, ambivalence, treatment interfering core beliefs or automatic thoughts, and using diversionary techniques. Therapist-based interfering factors include therapist errors such as an inaccurate or inadequate case conceptualization, as well as therapist inexperience, incompetence, or negligence. Interfering factors related to the client-therapist relationship include alliance strains and ruptures, and transference-countertransference enactments. Treatment factors include inadequate case conceptualization and utilizing an intervention that may be contraindicated for a particular client.

## *Protocol for Recognizing and Resolving Therapy Interfering Factors*

The first step in reducing the influence of interfering factors is recognition. The protocol provided herein covers some common therapy interfering situations.

1  Determine the operative interfering factor or factors. For example, shifting to more comfortable topics when uncomfortable, avoiding self-disclosure, and noncompliance with homework.
2  Determine the explanation or reason for the interfering factor. Among client factors that are particularly common are interfering beliefs and the unwillingness to deal with the consequences of change. Typically, this means not wanting to take responsibility for themselves and face difficult tasks that are currently avoided.
3  Continue to focus on shifting from a maladaptive pattern to an adaptive pattern while at the same time identifying skill deficits which can be addressed with one or more ultra-brief interventions.

4   Consistently indicate and point out to the client when the topic is shifted and encourage the client to identify and address the feeling and thought they find distressing.

## Strategies for Resolving Therapy Interfering Factors

Three therapy interfering factors are described in this section and a strategy is illustrated for dealing with each. Given that client interfering behaviors are most common, all three examples will involve such behaviors. The first and third cases are inspired by Beck (2005). The second case is inspired by Ledley et al. (2006).

### 1. Dealing with a Client's Interfering Beliefs and Behavior

A client's underlying core beliefs or schemas are identified as the root of the client's therapy interfering behaviors in the following example.

Julianne is a college sophomore who sought out services at her university counseling center due to difficulty in selecting a major. After completing three semesters in core classes, she was asked to declare a major, which brought up some conflict for her. She reported that her parents wanted her to obtain a degree in accounting in order to work for the family business. Her own interests lie in teaching art or being an anthropologist. However, she stated that she did not think she had the "right stuff" to be an elementary school teacher. During the initial evaluation, she disclosed that she was the second of four children. She described herself as the sickly "little runt." She described her mother as emotionally withdrawn and demanding and her father as physically abusive. The family owns a small printing company that was hardly successful. The therapist attempted to establish a treatment focus after the initial evaluation. The following was Julianne's response:

CLIENT: This is useless. I don't know how this is going to help me.
THERAPIST: What's useless right now?
CLIENT: I don't really know.
THERAPIST: What seems to be the main challenge right now?
CLIENT: I told you already! They want me to choose a major!
THERAPIST: And that's difficult for you—making decisions, and especially a decision about your career.
CLIENT: (Loudly) I just don't want to deal with it! I don't want to make any decisions! Not just career decisions!
THERAPIST: Isn't the third semester the point in time when students typically declare a major?

CLIENT: I'm not ready to do that. My advisor is crazy if she thinks she can force me to decide on being a teacher or a business major or anything else.

Julianne had completed the *Personality Belief Questionnaire* (Beck, 2005). This helped the therapist recognize Julianne's hopeless, incompetent, and vulnerable self-beliefs. It also indicated beliefs about others being demanding, rejecting, hurtful, and critical. Further prompting revealed the following assumptions and rules: "I'll be alright if I avoid difficult decisions," "I'll be safe if I blame others," and "If I let my guard down, I'll be hurt." Her overdeveloped coping strategies were rooted in these rules. These strategies were: avoiding major decisions, blaming others, and guarding against being harmed by others. This particular configuration is common in individuals with Borderline Personality Disorder. However, the therapist decided that indicating a definitive diagnosis was premature. However, he realized that Julianne's core beliefs, assumptions, and coping strategies had surfaced, and they provided an opportunity to recognize the root of her treatment interfering behaviors, mainly resisting discussion of the presenting problem.

THERAPIST: So, is there a problem that we can address right now?
CLIENT: I don't know. I feel like nothing is going to make a difference. It's hopeless.
THERAPIST: Do you think we can work on your feelings of being hopeless? Do you want to talk about your parents or school?
CLIENT: I don't know. Whatever works.
THERAPIST: Would it be possible to begin with the thoughts "Nothing will make a difference. It's hopeless"?
CLIENT: I guess.
THERAPIST: How much do you believe right now that making a decision about your major won't make a difference?
CLIENT: (Pause) A lot.
THERAPIST: I hear you. (Pause) Could you tell me what the disadvantages are if you did not choose a major?
CLIENT: I probably couldn't get into a major for another semester so I couldn't take advanced courses. It would push everything back.
THERAPIST: Anything else?
CLIENT: My parents would be all over me and my dad would probably follow through with his threat of cutting off my tuition and board this semester.
THERAPIST: And what are the advantages of choosing a major?
CLIENT: It would definitely get my parents off my back. I would keep hanging out with my friends and have classes with them. That would be cool.
THERAPIST: So, there are advantages and disadvantages. Right now, do the advantages or the disadvantages seem to be stronger?

CLIENT: I guess the advantages by a little bit. I just feel overwhelmed when I think about it.

THERAPIST: How overwhelming would it be on a scale from 1–100, 100 being extremely overwhelming.

CLIENT: I would say, like, 65.

THERAPIST: Okay, so moderately overwhelming. It doesn't sound totally hopeless, does it?

CLIENT: Yeah, I guess not. Not when you put it like that.

## Commentary

In the first session of therapy, Julianne's coping strategies were clearly operative. She demonstrated feeling hopeless, avoiding career decisions, guarding against real or perceived harm, and she blamed others about her conflicts or discomfort. These strategies also clearly accounted for Julianne's therapy interfering behavior, namely, resisting discussion about the presenting problem. Having recognized these dynamics, the therapist indirectly challenged the underlying belief of hopelessness through having her weigh advantages and disadvantages. The indirect nature of this intervention was chosen because if challenging abruptly, the therapist risked Julianne prematurely terminating treatment. Therapy interfering behaviors that are reflective of the client's coping strategies were illustrated in this case. Additionally, it provided an example of how early in the therapy these can surface. The strategies are also particularly likely to surface as the therapist endeavors to focus treatment, as this process can be laden with conflict or discomfort.

## 2. Dealing with Clients Who Use Diversionary Tactics

Seeking therapy and arriving at treatment settings do not equate to willingness to address the presenting problem for all clients. Some clients, particularly those who experience varying levels of ambivalence, engage in diversionary tactics and avoid change. Diversionary tactics are comprised of client behaviors which divert, distract, delay, or deflect attention from addressing issues or change efforts that the client seeks therapy for. For example, many clients report new and overwhelming circumstances that surface in their lives that they want to address instead of focusing on the treatment that was specified or agreed upon. They may also minimize the importance of the initial concern or the discomfort it creates in their lives. On the other hand, they may express skepticism of the chosen interventions or treatment. All of these strategies are diversionary tactics that clients may demonstrate.

The following case example demonstrates the therapist's recognition of tactics of delay due to the client's apprehension towards treatment.

Sanford is a 29-year-old male who is seeking treatment for increasing agoraphobia. He is employed as an attorney and has been struggling with agoraphobia for approximately 8 months. He reports being first diagnosed by his primary care physician and starting on medicine for a short while. Sanford stated that due to unacceptable side effects, he stopped his medication and sought therapy. He met with a psychodynamically-oriented therapist for five sessions and stated, "I didn't find it useful." As of late, he found himself homebound at an increasing rate, which began to interfere with his practice as an attorney as well as his plans for marriage. When the therapist first introduced exposure treatment in the initial session, Sanford seemed reluctant and fearful of an intervention that would make him come in contact with his current fears. However, he agreed to the protocol which was to begin in the following session.

During the second session, Sanford stated that he was extremely distraught because his partner at the law firm was mad that he did not make it to a deposition, and he wanted to discuss it. In the following session, Sanford brought up concerns that his girlfriend was threatening to call off the engagement unless he showed improvement. Noticing a pattern of diversion, the therapist anticipated that Sanford would present another crisis in the upcoming session; therefore, he devised a plan to directly deal with it. As Sanford brought up yet another crisis—his father having been in a car accident—at the start of the fourth session, the therapist asked:

THERAPIST: Have you noticed a connection between your anxiety and agoraphobia and what's been happening in your life these past few weeks?
CLIENT: Yes. I've been stressed and it's making me scared to go out.
THERAPIST: Right. That's a useful reflection. What do you think about how the relationship is going in the other direction? Could the anxiety be playing a role in the stressors you've had recently?
CLIENT: I don't really know. What do you mean?
THERAPIST: Well, consider the situation three weeks ago when Sally told you she might break off the engagement. Could anxiety have anything to do with that situation?
CLIENT: Are you joking? That's what the whole thing was about. She said she was just sick of it. I mean, I can't do anything anymore! I can't go to the gym, travel, or even go to the restaurants or movies. We used to be inseparable and now with this stuff I can't do anything.
THERAPIST: And what about the problems at your law firm recently?
CLIENT: My partner has been really frustrated with me because we were working on two cases simultaneously with very tight deadlines. Then I didn't make it

in because I was scared to drive on the highway, and he was livid. He had to drop his case to tend to that.

THERAPIST: Can you notice the direct relationship between those issues and your anxiety?

CLIENT: Yeah.

THERAPIST: Then, last week your dad was in an accident and that's what you wanted to address. For the past three weeks we've talked about all of the stressful things that have been happening in your life. (Pause) Would it be possible for there to be another way we could address your problems?

CLIENT: I don't know. When I get here, I just think about how things have gone in the week.

THERAPIST: What if there was another way to address those kinds of stressors and prevent them from happening in the following week? Would you be interested in that?

CLIENT: (Sarcastically) I wish that was possible.

THERAPIST: We could look at this more closely—if anxiety and agoraphobia are directly linked to your ongoing issues, what could happen if we address the anxiety directly?

CLIENT: So if I worked on my anxiety, Sally wouldn't have threatened me with calling off the engagement and my law partner wouldn't be furious with me. My life would just be great?

THERAPIST: There is no way to know what could have happened. What I'm saying is that maybe if we focus our work, things could improve, and you may have better outcome next time you have a relationship or work problem.

CLIENT: So, what you're saying is that I'll have an easier time dealing with things if I work on my anxiety and it gets better?

THERAPIST: Would that make sense?

CLIENT: Well, right now Sally and I don't have the best relationship—I'm not even sure she wants to spend time with me—I'm already worried about my next deadline and I can't even leave my apartment!

THERAPIST: Would you be curious to see what would happen if we stay focused on your panic for the next few sessions? See what it does for your life outside of here?

CLIENT: Are you talking about practicing those exposures out there?

THERAPIST: Yes. That's exactly what I mean.

CLIENT: I don't know if I want to do that. Are there any alternatives?

THERAPIST: We've discussed alternatives before. Exposure came up as the most feasible treatment for you. If medication didn't work out for you because of the side effects and your previous therapy experiences led to some insights but your symptoms worsened, exposure seemed like the treatment of choice when we discussed it about a month ago.

CLIENT: Yeah, I remember that, and I know that I agreed to it but I'm afraid that if it doesn't work I'll just be hopeless and stuck for ever. Then Sally will leave me for sure and—I just get really uncomfortable talking about this.

THERAPIST: (Empathically) I can see how this affects you and how difficult it is for you to discuss this. This is really difficult work. That first step may seem like the scariest of all and those who take it often become more confident that they can proceed with the rest of it. (Pauses) Thinking back, this intervention has been successful for all of the clients I've coached through it. I'm confident that it would work for you as well.

CLIENT: I know you said that, but I don't know if I believed you. I really want to believe that it would work.

The therapist in this case maintained a high level of patience with the client. The client was allowed to ventilate his concerns, which was necessary to strengthen the therapeutic alliance. The client was, in a sense, testing the therapist prior to trusting him fully and his clinical judgment. Rather than confront the anxiety and agoraphobia directly, the therapist linked these issues to the client's ongoing concerns. This became an avenue for both discussing the client's ongoing stressors and a way back toward the treatment focus, as the therapist redirected the session.

## 3. Dealing with Client Refusal

In the following example, a client's refusal will be facilitated in the case for which high reactance is the indicated therapy interfering behavior. That is, the individual has reactions to efforts to control him or her. Confrontation or coercion of the individual or withdrawal and acquiescence are two typical ways of responding to this and other forms of resistance. A third type of response is *therapeutic*. Rather than confronting the client or giving in, the therapist reflects feelings or content and rolls with the resistance (Miller & Rollnick, 2002).

Morton is a 44-year-old male who has been experiencing chronic depression (low level) for the past three years. He is employed as the chief information officer for an insurance company and prides himself on his independence. Recently, Morton began therapy at a mood disorders clinic. The clinic routinely utilizes rating scales and screeners. At the outset of the second session, which involves a structured interview for evaluation, the therapist asked:

THERAPIST: Would it be alright if we checked on your depression? Have you completed the rating scale for depression?

CLIENT: (Forcefully) No!

THERAPIST: I see. The rating scale is something I use to assess how you've been feeling since the last time we met. Would you be okay feeling it out after session today?

CLIENT: What's the point? I don't feel like filling anything out.

THERAPIST: Okay. We could try another way of assessing your mood. Can you estimate your mood on a scale from 1–10? 10 being the best and 1 the worst possible mood?

CLIENT: I don't know. (Pause) I said no. I don't like doing this, it's too simplistic.

THERAPIST: Okay. Could you tell me in your own words how you've been feeling this week as opposed to the other weeks?

CLIENT: I don't know. Rotten, I guess.

THERAPIST: I understand. (Pause) (Empathically) It sounds like it's been a really rough week.

CLIENT: Yeah, it's been hard.

THERAPIST: What was going on when you felt like that?

CLIENT: Just the whole thing was bad.

THERAPIST: I just want to make sure I understand. Could you describe what was bad about it? Was it the beginning, middle, or the end of the week?

CLIENT: I already said it was all bad.

THERAPIST: Where there any times that weren't so bad? Was there maybe something on TV that was good or interesting? Did you meet with anyone or have even a pleasant moment?

CLIENT: The Jets game was on. They were playing the Patriots. It was a good game.

THERAPIST: Awesome! You know, the reason I asked about your moods was because if we find out what was good or uplifting, then maybe you can do more of that. On the other hand, if it was bad, then maybe we can talk about changing something. (Pause) Overall, compared to two weeks ago, how would you say your mood was? Did you at least enjoy the game this past week?

CLIENT: (Pause) It really wasn't so different. I think it actually might've been worse.

THERAPIST: Okay. It's important for us to continue to check in on your mood at the start of each session. That'll help me understand if we're headed in the right direction or if we need to modify and change course. Would that be okay with you?

## Commentary

The therapist's flexibility demonstrates willingness to compromise as well as respect for the client. Statements such as, "Is that alright with you?" show respect directly by seeking permission and the client's consent to continue in the direction the therapist desires to go. In this case, the client's reactance is high. This factor continues to drive the client's refusal. Therefore, insisting that the client fill out the forms for the clinic might have strained the therapeutic alliance severely. Instead, the therapist became aware of the reactance and rolled with the resistance.

CLIENT: (Somewhat reluctantly) I guess it'd be alright.In the following session, the therapist gently probes the client for willingness to complete the rating scale.
THERAPIST: Do you think it would be okay if I asked you to rate your mood for this past week? Would that frustrate you?
CLIENT: Yes, it will.
THERAPIST: Okay, well then, I won't ask. Could I ask you what your experience is like when I ask you about your mood?
CLIENT: I just get frustrated. It's not that easy to rate my mood.
THERAPIST: Well, even if it is complicated, do you think it's important for me to understand your level of sadness or distress?
CLIENT: I guess. I just want to talk about other things.
THERAPIST: I see. What's something you want to talk about? What do you want to focus on for this session?
CLIENT: Things are pretty rocky at the office. There's a suit against the store and I have to be around for a lot of hours—way more than my boss allotted for it. I just get overwhelmed and I feel like I'm going to lose it. I feel like I'm going to freak out and start screaming so I have to leave.

## Commentary

The therapist once again demonstrated flexibility and rolled with the client's resistance. Agreeing with the client's focus and processing it over the next four weeks resulted in Morton becoming more even keeled in his mood. Eventually, Morton even thanked the therapist for his help. He also expressed willingness to utilize the rating scale, at least for some of the time. Morton's diminishing reactance was the outcome of the therapist's flexibility.

At first, the client's refusal is empathic and strong because he does not want to be told what to do. Trainees are drawn to this case because they predict that an impasse in therapy consistently equates to early termination or "treatment failure." The therapist's ability to "roll with the resistance" both encourages and surprises students and trainees as they can see the effects on the therapeutic alliance as well as treatment outcomes. If unconvinced that this "third way is the therapeutic way" prior to discussing this case, trainees are certainly convinced afterwards.

## Conclusion

Wouldn't it be nice if all clients were easy to work with and therapy always went smoothly? The reality is that some clients are not particularly easy to work with and the course of some therapies do not go smoothly. The corrective usually involves efforts to fine tune and enhance the treatment process and the therapeutic alliance. This chapter has been included to provide trainees and practicing therapists with some strategies and tactics for decreasing premature termination.

## References

Beck, J. (2005). *Cognitive therapy for challenging problems: What to do when basics don't work.* New York, NY: Guilford Press.

Binder, J. (2004). *Key competencies in brief dynamic psychotherapy: Clinical practice beyond the manual.* New York, NY: Guilford Press.

Carlson, J. (2006). *Psychotherapy over time.* Washington, DC: American Psychological Association (DVD).

Gabbard, G. (1999). An overview of countertransference: Theory and technique. In G. Gabbard (Ed.), *Countertransference issues in psychiatric treatment* (pp. 1–25). Washington, DC: American Psychiatric Press.

Gelso, C., & Hayes, J. (2007). *Countertransference and the therapist's inner experience: Perils and possibilities.* Mahwah, NJ: Lawrence Erlbaum & Associates.

Gelso, C., Hill, C., Mohr, J., Rochlen, A., & Zack, J. (1999). Describing the face of transference: Psychodynamic therapists' recollections about transference in cases of successful long-term therapy. *Journal of Counseling Psychology,* 46, 257–267.

Good, G., & Beitman, B. (2006). *Counseling and psychotherapy essentials: Integrating theories, skills, and practices.* New York, NY: Norton.

Kiesler, D. J. (2001). Therapist countertransference: In search of common themes and empirical referents. *Journal of Clinical Psychology,* 57(8), 1053–1063.

Ledley, D., Marx, B., & Heimberg, R. (2006). *Making cognitive-behavioral therapy work: Clinical process for new practitioners.* New York, NY: Guilford Press.

Levenson, H. (1995). *Time-limited dynamic psychotherapy.* New York, NY: Basic Books.

Linehan, M. (1993). *Cognitive-behavioral treatment of borderline personality disorders.* New York, NY: Guilford Press.

Linehan, M. (2015). *DBT skills training manual,* 2nd edn. New York, NY: Guilford Press.

McCullough, J. (2005). *Treating chronic depression with disciplined personal involvement.* New York, NY: Springer.

McCullough, J. (2015). *CBASP as a distinctive treatment for persistent depressive disorder: Distinctive features.* New York, NY: Routledge.

Miller, W., & Rollnick, S. (2002). *Motivational interviewing: Preparing people for change,* 2nd ed. New York, NY: Guilford Press.

Ornstein, E., & Ganzer, C. (2005). Relational social work: A model for the future. *Families in Society,* 86, 565–572.

Perry, S., Cooper, A., & Michels, R. (1987). The psychodynamic formulation: Its purpose, structure, and clinical application. *American Journal of Psychiatry*, 144, 543–551.

Sperry, J., & Sperry, L. (2018). *Cognitive behavior therapy in professional counseling practice*. New York, NY: Routledge.

Sperry, L. (2010). *Highly effective therapy: Developing essential clinical competencies in counseling and psychotherapy*. New York, NY: Routledge.

Sperry, L., & Carlson, J. (2014). *How master therapists work: Effecting change from the first through the last therapy session and beyond*. New York, NY: Routledge.

Sperry, L., & Sperry, J. (2012). *Case conceptualization: Mastering this competency with ease and confidence*. New York, NY: Routledge.

Swift, J. K., & Greenberg, R. P. (2012). Premature discontinuation in adult psychotherapy: A meta-analysis. *Journal of Consulting and Clinical Psychology*, 80(4), 547–559.

Swift, J. K., & Greenberg, R. P. (2015). *Premature termination in psychotherapy: Strategies for engaging clients and improving outcomes*. Washington, DC: American Psychological Association.

Wampold, B., & Imel, Z. (2015). *The great psychotherapy debate: The evidence for what makes psychotherapy work*, 2nd ed. New York, NY: Routledge.

Wierzbicki, M., & Pekarik, G. (1993). A meta-analysis of psychotherapy dropout. *Professional Psychology: Research and Practice*, 24(2), 190–195.

# Chapter 10

# Pattern Focused Therapy in Integrated Care Settings

What are the mental health needs of clients—called patients—in integrated care settings and what role, if any, do mental health providers have in such practice settings? These are timely questions as the delivery of health care services in America continues to change and evolve. This chapter not only addresses these questions but also sketches an exciting future for mental health providers in a new practice setting. It also describes some of the basic knowledge and tools needed to practice successfully in this setting. Because integrated care setting typically limits therapeutic encounters to sessions of 20–30 minutes' duration rather than 45–60-minute sessions in conventional psychotherapy settings, a different core therapeutic strategy and different interventions are needed. Fortunately, Pattern Focused Therapy provides that core therapeutic strategy and is easily and effectively practiced in very short time frames.

This chapter begins with data on mental health needs in primary care settings. It then identifies the different ways in which mental health services are provided in three different models of integrated care practice. Next, it describes how Pattern Focused Therapy can serve as the core therapeutic strategy for direct clinical services provided in such settings. Then, a clinical case illustrates how a therapist uses a core therapeutic strategy which incorporates ultra-brief interventions to successfully treat a medical patient with panic attacks in four sessions.

## Mental Health Needs in Primary Care Settings

Of those seeking medical care, some 70 percent present with or are diagnosed with related psychological conditions, such as generalized anxiety disorder, panic disorder, depression, bipolar disorder, and chronic pain, as well as troublesome health behaviors like sleep problems, nicotine use, sexual problems, and weight issues (Hunter, Goodie, Oordt, & Dobmeyer, 2017). Recognition and treatment of these disorders and health behaviors are important since they can trigger, exacerbate, or perpetuate medical symptoms and impaired functioning. These same problematic health behaviors are also present in those seeking conventional psychotherapy. However, until recently, most therapists simply ignored these health behaviors even though these exacerbate or otherwise complicate the client's psychological condition.

Both research-based health care policy and reimbursement sources are increasingly "disallowing" this common therapist response. A recently published national study of the 40 million Americans insured by Blue Cross Blue Shield provides very compelling evidence for the provision of integrated health care (Blue Cross Blue Shield Association, 2017). It was reported that mental health and substance use disorders significantly impact not only the physical health and well-being of Americans, but also their longevity and productivity. Collectively, depression, anxiety and mood disorders, and substance disorders have the greatest impact on Americans' health compared to any health condition, followed by hypertension, diabetes, and high cholesterol.

## Mental Health Practice in Integrated Primary Care Settings

In the standard primary care model, a primary care provider (PCP)—usually a physician, MD or DO, or an advanced practice nurse (APRN)—is supported by nurses (RNs) and medical assistants (MAs). In the new primary care model, called "integrated primary care," a health care team provides treatment. This team consists of at least one PCP, one or more RNs and MAs, as well as a therapist or other mental health clinician, usually called a behavioral health consultant or BHC.

The goal of providing integrated primary care is to achieve the *Triple Aim*, which refers to the three keys to improving health care in the USA. They are: (1) increase patients' health care experience, including quality of care and patient satisfaction; (2) improve the health of the population; and (3) reduce health care costs (Berwick, Nolan, & Whittington, 2008). Research is clear that providing mental health or behavioral health services in integrated settings definitely results in decreased cost, primarily because of reduced emergency room and hospital admissions. Because integrated care improves the identification of undiagnosed conditions and concerns, these patients are more likely to receive needed mental health services.

How might a therapist or other mental health clinician be involved in integrated case settings? It is useful to think about a continuum of integration of mental health services which range from non-integrated to fully integrated. It consists of three basic models:

- *Coordinated Model*: here the therapist is an externally employed partner who provides mental health services to a specific primary care practice.

- *Co-Located Model*: here the therapist is on-site and provides mental health services to selected patients utilizing the conventional psychotherapy model.
- *Fully Integrated Model*: here the therapist is a full-time provider who provides mental health services, within an integrated health team in a specific primary care practice.

The first two models are also known as partially integrated, in contrast to the third which is fully integrated (Sperry, 2018). Particularly in fully integrated settings, the therapist's role is to address a broad spectrum of mental health needs with the aim of early identification, quick resolution, long-term prevention, and wellbeing for primary care patients. As a core member of the primary care team, the therapist provides consultation to other team members on mental health issues related to physical health conditions as well as direct clinical care. Typically, the therapist is expected to perform 8–10 consultations, usually in 15–30 minutes time frames, each clinical day with patients, PCPs, and other team members (Sperry, 2018).

## Pattern Focused Therapy in Integrated Care Setting

We've described Pattern Focused Therapy in this book as a brief therapeutic approach for easily and effectively identifying and changing a patient's maladaptive pattern of thinking, feeling, and behaving to a healthier and more adaptive pattern. Utilizing the core therapeutic strategy of Pattern Focused Therapy, called the Query Sequence, it accomplishes this by replacing the non-productive thoughts or interpretations and behaviors that underlie the individual's maladaptive pattern with more adaptive ones (Sperry & Binensztok, 2019a). The aim is to achieve second-order change. Other interventions, particularly ultra-brief therapeutic interventions (cf. Chapter 3), such as behavioral activation, behavioral rehearsal, breath training, and stimulus control, are employed as adjunctive treatments to achieve first-order change, i.e., to reduce symptoms and impaired functioning.

Because its core therapeutic strategy is brief and easily implemented, and has very few contraindications (i.e., acute psychosis and acute cognitive impairment), Pattern Focused Therapy is a very good fit in integrated primary care settings. It is particularly well suited to integrated clinic settings where therapists are expected to perform 8–10 brief consultations in 5–30 minutes time frames. The successful use of this approach with depression, anxiety, sleep problems, chronic pain, weight problems, and diabetes is described and illustrated in the book, *Ultra-Brief Cognitive Behavioral Interventions: The Cutting-Edge of Mental Health and Integrated Care Practice* (Sperry & Binensztok, 2019b).

## Treating Anxiety Symptoms in an Integrated Care Setting

While anxiety disorders are commonplace in mental health care settings, they are also present in primary care settings and account for up to 20 percent of client complaints (Hunter, Goodie, Oordt, & Dobmeyer, 2017, p. 61). Because anxiety symptoms occur on a continuum, some medical patients might not meet the full criteria necessary for a DSM-5 anxiety disorders diagnosis. Nevertheless, these symptoms may be quite distressing and deserve effective care. Anxiety disorders have been identified as contributory factors in a number of medical problems as well. Thus, they can be treated on their own in the primary care settings or addressed as part of the treatment for other medical disorders.

### *Assessment and Screening Instruments*

Assessment of anxiety in integrated settings requires both a diagnostic and functional assessment. Interview questions should be primarily closed-ended in order to gather all necessary information quickly.

The functional assessment should include information about how anxiety affects the client on a daily basis and interferes with regular functioning. Markers of functional assessment include sleep, tension, aches and pains, difficulty concentrating, and related functions. Triggers for symptoms should also be explored as well as factors that make the symptoms better or worse. This assessment should also include the patient's related behavioral changes, worrying about future attacks, and attempts to avoid more attacks. Finally, therapists should determine if the patient uses any substances that may be contributing to symptoms, such as caffeine. It is important to note any prescribed or over-the-counter medication for anxiety taken as well as the patient's level of compliance with prescribed medications. The most common screeners used are:

- *Subjective Units of Distress (SUDS).* The Subjective Units of Distress scale is a useful, informal tool to rate a client's level of anxiety (Wolpe, 1969). Ratings on the scale range from 0–10 or from 0–100. This scale is useful for both patients and therapists to assess the intensity of symptoms and the distress and disturbance they cause. It is also a useful measure to monitor progress through therapy and after interventions.
- *The Generalized Anxiety Disorder-7 (GAD-7).* The GAD-7 is a 7-item questionnaire that corresponds to the DSM-5 criteria for Generalized Anxiety Disorder (Plummer, Manea, Trepel, McMillan, & Simpson, 2016). Each question is rated on a 4-point scale from 0–3 where 0 = not at all, 1 = several days, 2 = more than half the days, and 3 = nearly every day. Clients rate their experiences for the previous two weeks. The scoring for the GAD-7 is as follows: 0–4 =

minimal or none, 5–9 = mild, 10–14 = moderate, 15–21 = severe. The GAD-7 has been shown to be useful in screening for Generalized Anxiety Disorder, Panic Disorder, and Social Anxiety (Bardhoshi et al., 2016).

## Pattern Focused Therapy in an Integrated Care Setting: Clinical Illustration

The application of Pattern Focused Therapy in a primary care clinic is illustrated in the following case. Jenny is a 23-year-old Caucasian female referred to counseling by her PCP, William Jeffers, M.D., for symptoms of anxiety with intermittent panic attacks. Two weeks prior to referral for therapy, he had started Jenny on Klonopin, an anti-anxiety medication. Clinic policy is that therapy is the main treatment for diagnosable anxiety and depressive conditions and medication is used to support that treatment. The plan was for a short course of medication to sufficiently reduce anxiety (panic attack) symptoms so that Jenny could more effectively engage in the therapeutic process.

The clinic's policy regarding the provision of mental health treatment was discussed with Jenny: up to four therapy sessions, of 30 minutes duration, can be offered to patients with the provision that one to two additional sessions may be offered if indicated, or the patient can be referred for extended treatment outside the clinic. For patients successfully completing four sessions, one follow-up session is typically scheduled, which patients can decide to keep or cancel, depending on how well they are doing. All appointments with the therapists are scheduled as 30-minute sessions, and sessions are typically scheduled biweekly which allows time for patients to practice assigned therapeutic tasks and maximize treatment gains.

It was agreed that Jenny would be offered four sessions with the provision for a follow-up session if indicated. She would also continue with scheduled appointments with her PCP for a medication review and her therapist would be present for a discussion of discontinuing medication. After her second session with the therapist, Jenny would meet for a 15-minute medication monitoring appointment with her PCP, attended by the therapist. At that appointment Jenny reported that her symptoms had greatly improved, and she agreed to be weaned off her medication over the next two weeks. Her fourth session with the therapist was scheduled for three weeks later and she agreed to get in touch with her PCP if there were issues in weaning and stopping the medication.

Session plans and Chart Notes are provided for all sessions. Because of space limitation, transcription segments and commentaries are provided only for the following sessions: 1, 2, and 4.

## Session 1

### Session Plan

The GAD-7 will be taken just prior to the session. Then, a brief diagnostic evaluation and functional assessment with the goal of identifying the presence of DSM-5 symptom disorder(s) and personality disorder(s). Treatment goals will be set for the course of therapy. Client will be instructed in SUDS as a way of monitoring and controlling her anxiety symptoms. Psychoeducation about presenting symptoms, which the PCP's referral note suggest are panic attacks, will be provided. Presumably, the client will learn and experience how her response to her symptoms and maladaptive pattern actually exacerbate them. Her breathing pattern will be observed and if shallow and/or hyperventilative, one or more ultra-brief interventions, i.e., breath retraining will be introduced, practiced, and assigned as homework. Finally, the therapeutic strategy and process, as well as expectation for her engagement, will be discussed and homework assigned.

The following transcription segment illustrates how this breath retraining is introduced and implemented.

THERAPIST: I've been observing your breathing and it seems like you take short and shallow breaths. Diaphragmatic breathing, which is taking slower breaths from your abdomen, can help you to calm down. Clinically we call it breath retaining. Have you ever heard of it?

JENNY: I've heard it mentioned but don't know much about it.

THERAPIST: Okay, why don't we try it out? I can demonstrate. My belly will rise and fall as I'm breathing. It can help if you put your hand on your stomach. Take a couple of normal breaths and then deepen your breathing. Are you noticing any difference?

JENNY: Yes, I can feel my belly really rising as I breathe.

THERAPIST: Excellent. That can help to monitor your breath. You can also try to purse your lips as you breathe—as if you're blowing bubbles. Would you be willing to give that a try?

JENNY: Sure.

THERAPIST: Good. You're doing very well. Let's see if we can practice. Try to keep the pace and take one breath every 8–10 seconds.

JENNY: OK, I think I get it.

THERAPIST: OK, Jenny, you have done excellent work today. I'm going to provide this log so that you can keep track of your exercises. It's important to write down the date and for how long you practiced.

JENNY: OK, I'll try.

THERAPIST: Excellent. Now, on a scale from 0–10, 10 being very important, how important is it for you to practice this?

JENNY: Around a 9. I really want to improve my anxiety.

THERAPIST: Great. And on the same scale, what is your level of confidence that you can complete them?

JENNY: Probably 6. I think I can do it, but I'm worried that it won't work and it'll stress me out.

THERAPIST: I see. What do you think might bring that number up to about a 7 or 8?

JENNY: I would feel more confident if I can practice at least once a day this week.

THERAPIST: Very good. I think you can do this. I'm interested to see what your progress looks like on our next appointment.

## Commentary

Jenny responded well to the intervention and was able to learn and practice the breathing retraining exercise.

## Chart Note

Jenny presents to therapy with constant, uncontrollable worry and intermittent panic attacks. A GAD-7 score of 12 indicates moderate anxiety. She clearly presents with panic attacks—three in the last two months but did not meet full criteria for Panic Disorder. It is noteworthy that she reports SUDS scores for these attacks in the 80–90 range whereas levels of 90–100 are more typical of Panic Disorder. She met only three of the DSM-5 criteria for Dependent Personality Disorder. Nevertheless, she displays a dependent personality style with a maladaptive pattern of taking care of others while neglecting herself. The functional assessment indicated sub-clinical symptoms of anxiety and panic, consistent with her GAD-7 scores. Her symptoms interfere with her quality of life and ability to concentrate at work.

Two treatment goals were discussed and agreed upon: reduction of panic symptoms and better at meeting her own needs as well as those of others. Likely interventions, including psychoeducation, breath retraining, thought stopping, or other ultra-brief interventions, will be incorporated when appropriate. Pattern Focused Therapy will address her pattern and its role in maintaining her anxiety and panic symptoms. Progress will be monitored with SUDS and GAD-7. She states she is tolerating Klonopin and notices some reduction in symptoms. She appears to be a good candidate for four-session short-term therapy.

# Session 2

## Session Plan

Before the session Jenny will take the GAD-7. As the session begins, she will be asked to rate her anxiety in terms of SUDS. Then, her breath retraining log will be reviewed. Because she mentioned disturbing thoughts associated with her symptoms and anticipatory anxiety of having another panic attack, a thought stopping intervention will likely be introduced, practiced, and assigned.

THERAPIST: Hi, Jenny, it's nice to see you again.
JENNY: Hi. Nice to see you too.
THERAPIST: So, how has your anxiety been this week?
JENNY: A bit better, but not by much.
THERAPIST: Can you tell me more about that?
JENNY: I still feel nervous and anxious all the time.
THERAPIST: And, last time we met, you said it was getting in the way of the things you have to do on a day-to-day basis. How is that going?
JENNY: Yes. It's still hard for me to do the things I have to do, like cooking and chores, but it has been a bit better.
THERAPIST: I see. What were your SUDS rating on some of those bad days?
JENNY: Probably around 60 to 70.
THERAPIST: That's pretty uncomfortable. (Pause) But, I'm happy to hear that it has improved some. How did it go with your breathing exercises? Did you bring your log?
JENNY: It went alright. I did it for four days but only five minutes a day. I don't think that's very good.
THERAPIST: Well, you were able to do it for most days this week—I think that's a very good start.
JENNY: I guess, yeah—that's good.
THERAPIST: It really is good. I'm wondering if today we could address some of the thoughts we discussed last time. I think it would help, along with the breathing, to ease some of the anxiety and panic.
JENNY: Yeah, we could do that. Those really are annoying.
THERAPIST: I wonder if you could tell me again some of the detailed thoughts you have?
JENNY: Okay. Well, I mostly worry about people—then I start getting in my head.
THERAPIST: For example?
JENNY: Like that my mom is alone. My dad died and she's all alone. What if she chokes on her food or falls down? Nobody would be around to help her. What if someone breaks in? That's the kind of thing that comes into my mind.

THERAPIST: I can see that you care very much about her. What do you do when those thoughts enter your mind?

JENNY: I call her sometimes, but she rarely answers. She's probably asleep or busy. It usually happens when it's late. I know she's probably okay, but I can't seem to stop worrying about it.

THERAPIST: What else do you worry about?

JENNY: My brother. He drinks too much. He has an okay job and takes care of himself, but I've seen him drink a lot on a couple of occasions.

THERAPIST: And what is the nature of the thoughts you have about this?

JENNY: Kind of the same as with my mom, that he will drink and drive—crash his car. There was this one person on TV that slipped in the shower after drinking and died. I can see that happening in my mind. Very vividly! I picture him falling and really hurting himself, with no one around to help him or call someone.

THERAPIST: These very vivid thoughts seem to be very distressing for you.

JENNY: They are. And I also worry that something will happen to me and I won't be able to be there for my family. My mom would be devastated.

THERAPIST: These thoughts seem very difficult. It takes a lot of courage to deal with them.

JENNY: Yeah, I guess I deal. I just don't think I'm doing very well at it. They can stick around for hours until something else distracts me.

THERAPIST: I'm hoping that some of the tools we discuss and use here will help you to better deal with the thoughts and reduce your anxiety.

JENNY: Yes, I'd like that.

THERAPIST: Good. The first thing we'll talk about is an exercise called thought stopping. Essentially, the idea is to stop the thoughts you're having so that they don't escalate or hang around for hours as we'd discussed. Throughout the exercise, you'll find that you're more in control of your thoughts, as opposed to the other way around.

JENNY: Ok, I'm hoping it'll work out, but I'm not too sure.

THERAPIST: Some skepticism is normal and expected, especially since you've been dealing with this for a long time. We can try it out together and see how things go. Is that alright?

JENNY: Alright.

THERAPIST: One of the thoughts you mentioned was about someone breaking into your mother's house.

JENNY: Yeah, I think that's the worst one.

THERAPIST: OK, focus on that thought and I will issue the stop command. When you have the thought in your mind very vividly—someone breaking into her house—raise one finger. OK?

JENNY: Okay.

## Commentary

When Jenny concentrates on her thought and raises her finger, the therapist will loudly say, "Stop!" This will startle her and distract her from distressing thought. They will repeat this exercise approximately 20 times in a row. Then the therapist will instruct Jenny on how to practice thought stopping on her own.

THERAPIST: Stop!
JENNY: Oh my God! That really scared me. I didn't think that would be that loud.
THERAPIST: OK, how did it go?
JENNY: I'm not really thinking about it now. It's sort of a snap back to reality.
THERAPIST: Where is the thought now?
JENNY: Oh. Gone, I guess. That's interesting.
THERAPIST: OK, so we are going to repeat this exercise about 20 times. This is so that you can get used to it and begin to do it on your own.
JENNY: Alright.
THERAPIST: So, concentrate on the thought again. Make it the same thought of someone breaking in. When you have it clearly and vividly, raise one finger.

## Commentary

After completing this exercise 20 times, the therapist instructs Jenny to apply it to her own as disturbing thoughts arise.

THERAPIST: You've really done a good job today, Jenny. Some of the things I've asked you to do have been challenging, I'm proud of you for hanging in there.
JENNY: Thank you. I am feeling proud of myself too.
THERAPIST: So, do you think you can practice this when you're having those bothersome thoughts?
JENNY: Yeah, I think I can.
THERAPIST: You can do this by yourself if you just yell "Stop!" loudly in your head. You don't have to do it out loud. However, it may be best to start practicing somewhere where you can do it out loud. It also helps to picture a big stop sign when you're doing it.
JENNY: OK, I can do that.
THERAPIST: Great. Now, to go a step further, it can really help to replace the upsetting thought with a pleasant one after you give the "Stop!" command.
JENNY: Oh, OK. I could try that.

THERAPIST: Can you think of any pleasant images?

JENNY: I can think of sitting with and petting my cat. Or maybe going somewhere nice.

THERAPIST: For example?

JENNY: I could think of going to the beach or sitting at this outdoor café in Paris I really liked.

THERAPIST: That sounds great. Now, there is one more thing.

JENNY: What?

THERAPIST: It's not likely that you will stop worrying altogether. Some worry is natural and part of life, but we just don't want to be worrying all day. It can help to set up a time to worry. Maybe 20 minutes in the morning and 20 minutes at night. I suggest setting a timer so that you can stop when the time is up.

JENNY: So, you want me to worry on purpose?

THERAPIST: I want you to set aside some time to worry. Is there a good time in the morning? You want to be consistent with the times.

JENNY: Maybe 7:30. I usually get up before 7 and that's before I have to work.

THERAPIST: Ok, so let's try from 7:30 to 7:50. What about at night?

JENNY: Probably around 8 p.m.

THERAPIST: Ok, so 7:30 a.m. to 7:50 a.m. and then 8 p.m. to 8:20 p.m. Here's a log so that you can monitor your progress.

JENNY: Ok. That's kind of weird but I can try. So, this is in addition to doing the breathing exercises and stopping my thoughts?

THERAPIST: Yes.

JENNY: OK, I'll do my best.

## Commentary

After addressing Jenny's panic symptoms in the previous session, the therapist introduced two ultra-brief interventions to help Jenny deal with her anxious thoughts in this session. She was responsive to thought stopping and, although somewhat skeptical, agreed to try the worry time intervention.

THERAPIST: Good. Now, as we did before, how would you rate from 0–10 how important it is for you to complete the worry and thought stopping activity?

JENNY: Around an 8.

THERAPIST: Good. Now on that same 0–10 scale, how would you rate your confidence?

JENNY: I think a 5. I'm not sure about worrying on those specific times or that I can do it for only 20 minutes.

THERAPIST: That makes sense. What would have to happen to go from a 5 to a 6 or a 7?

JENNY: I'll probably feel more confident if I see myself stop the thoughts.
THERAPIST: You've done very well today, and it seems like you're getting the hang of it. I think these exercises can really be helpful.
JENNY: Yes. I'm really hoping it will.
THERAPIST: I look forward to discussing your progress at our next meeting.

## Chart Note

Jenny reported decreased anxiety symptoms with a GAD-7 scores of 10 and SUDS scores in the 60s or below, indicating a decrease since the last session. She was able to practice breath retraining and learn the thought stopping technique. The functional assessment indicated sub-clinical symptoms of anxiety and panic, consistent with her GAD-7 score. Treatment will continue to focus on breathing retraining and thought stopping. In subsequent sessions, Pattern Focused Therapy will be used to address the role of her maladaptive pattern in maintaining her anxiety and panic symptoms.

## Session 3

### Session Plan

The GAD-7 will be taken just prior to the session. First, her experience with weaning and discontinuing her medication will be discussed. Because Dr. Jeffers' chart note from earlier this week indicates that Jenny had very little discomfort with the weaning process, the focus here will be on her anxiety and SUDS levels as her Klonopin was weaned and discontinued. Next, her experience and logs with breath retraining, thought stopping, and worry time will be reviewed and discussed. She will be introduced to the Query Sequence by processing a recent situation. Finally, brief mention will be made that her next session involves termination and a review of her overall progress.

### Chart Note

Jenny's GAD-7 score of 8 is now at the top of mild range. This indicates that she has experienced considerable improvement from the last session. Her SUDS levels during the medication weaning process ranged from 60 down to 30, and 30 appears to be her baseline. She responded well to the Query Sequence. She agreed to continue logs on breath retraining and thought stopping. She appears ready for termination which will be the focus of session 4.

## Session 4

### *Session Plan: Termination Session*

The GAD-7 will be completed prior to the session. She had now been weaned off her medication completely for more than a week, presumably without withdrawal or other side effects. Her weaning experience will be processed along with SUDS ratings. Next, a problematic situation will be processed with the Query Sequence with a focus on the influence of her dependent pattern. If indicated, another ultra-brief intervention will be employed. Next, termination is discussed, beginning with a review of gains made on the treatment goals set in session. Finally, third-order change efforts will be discussed along with scheduling of a follow-up session in three weeks which she could cancel if her improvement continued and she did not consider it necessary.

THERAPIST: Hi, Jenny, I'm happy to see you. I see a lot of improvement in your GAD-7 scores.
JENNY: Yes, I've been feeling a lot better. Especially since last time.
THERAPIST: It's good to hear that. On the Anxiety Scale from 0–10, how would you rate your anxiety since we met last?
JENNY: Most days it's about a 6, but I have had some 7s.

### Commentary

Now that Jenny's symptoms have improved and she has no issues with her medication, the Query Sequence will be used again to shift Jenny's maladaptive caretaking pattern to a more adaptive one. Because her anxiety is largely related to interactions with her family, in which she is overly concerned with others while ignoring her own needs, the query sequence will be tailored to process such situations.

THERAPIST: I'm very happy to hear that. That's a definite improvement. Do you recall that we discussed your maladaptive pattern as taking care of others' needs while ignoring your own needs? (**Query-Pattern**)
JENNY: Yeah. I remember.
THERAPIST: Would you be willing to discuss that in our session today?
JENNY: Sure. That sounds okay.
THERAPIST: Ok, can you think of a situation recently when this pattern surfaced? (**Query-1**)
JENNY: Um, yes. The other day at my mom's house.
THERAPIST: OK, can you tell me what happened, beginning to end?

JENNY: Well, I was over at my mom's house and walked into the kitchen and saw her standing on a chair and reaching into a cabinet! She could've asked me to get it and I would have! I freaked out and my heart skipped a beat.

THERAPIST: OK, what happened after that?

JENNY: I started yelling at her—asking her what she was doing. She brushed it off and acted like it was no biggie. Then we got into a huge argument because I was serious, and she finally realized it. She said I needed to grow up. It made me so mad.

THERAPIST: Was that the entire event?

JENNY: Yes.

THERAPIST: Okay, so I want to make sure I've heard you correctly. You were at your mother's house and when walked into the kitchen, you saw her standing on a chair and reaching into the cabinets. You were scared that she was going to hurt herself and told her not to do that. Then, instead of listening, she laughed it off and you two got into an argument. Is that accurate?

JENNY: Yes.

THERAPIST: OK, can you tell me what was going through your mind at the time? What kind of thoughts did you have? **(Query-2)**

JENNY: I thought she was going to fall and die!

THERAPIST: So that she might fall. Any other thoughts?

JENNY: I wondered what other dangerous things she does when I'm not around. More for me to worry about!

THERAPIST: Okay, so you thought about other things that she might do to cause herself harm.

JENNY: Right.

THERAPIST: Anything else?

JENNY: Honestly, I thought that she didn't care about how I felt about this kind of thing—that it was inconsiderate of her, you know?

THERAPIST: And what did you do during that situation? **(Query-3)**

JENNY: I yelled at her, "Are you serious?! Why are you doing that?!"

THERAPIST: So you started yelling. What else?

JENNY: I told her that she was a crazy old lady. I'm not proud of it.

THERAPIST: Alright. Anything else you remember doing?

JENNY: Yeah, when she got down, I slammed the chair against the table.

THERAPIST: Okay. Sounds like you were very frustrated. What were you hoping to accomplish in this situation? **(Query-4)**

JENNY: I wanted her to stop putting herself in dangerous situations.

THERAPIST: Is that something that you have control over?

JENNY: Not really. I can't control her.

THERAPIST: Right. Can you think of an outcome that could have been in your control?

JENNY: It would've been nice if she at least listened to me.

THERAPIST: So, a good outcome would have been to express your concerns more effectively?

JENNY: Yeah.

THERAPIST: And what actually ended up happening? **(Query-5)**

JENNY: Like I said, we started arguing. It was awful.

THERAPIST: So, did you get what you wanted in that situation? **(Query-6)**

JENNY: Not at all.

THERAPIST: OK, would you be willing to discuss some alternate ways it could have turned out differently? **(Query-7)**

JENNY: Sure.

THERAPIST: Great. So, your first thought was, "She's going to fall and die." Do you think that thought was helpful or hurtful in getting what you wanted—effectively expressing your concerns? **(Query-8)**

JENNY: It wasn't helpful because that's when I started getting anxious. I couldn't think straight after that.

THERAPIST: So it hurt the outcome because it triggered your anxiety. What do you think would be an alternate thought? One that would not trigger your anxiety.

JENNY: Um, I guess she looked okay on the chair. Maybe that she wasn't going to fall.

THERAPIST: So, instead thinking, "She looks stable on the chair." And how would that be helpful?

JENNY: I wouldn't start in with all the worry.

THERAPIST: OK, and your second thought was, "I wonder what other things she does when I'm not around." Did that thought help you or hurt you get your desired outcome?

JENNY: It hurt because then I was angry on top of being worried.

THERAPIST: So it was upsetting. What is a substitute thought?

JENNY: If I stopped thinking about it. Or instead that she can take care of herself.

THERAPIST: So, she can take care of herself. How would that have helped?

JENNY: Well, she's an adult. I would just stop worrying about her.

THERAPIST: OK, good. And the third thought was that she doesn't care about how you feel. Did that thought help or hurt in getting what you wanted?

JENNY: It hurt. I know she's not like that.

THERAPIST: So, what would be a more helpful thought?

JENNY: That it's not about me. She was just doing something she needed to do and it's not about me.

THERAPIST: OK, so that you were completely unrelated to what she was doing. How is thinking that helpful?

JENNY: I would've just let things be.

THERAPIST: Yes, that makes sense. Now, your first behavior was yelling at her. You yelled something like, "Seriously?" Do you think that helped you or hurt you to successfully communicate your concerns? (**Query-9**)

JENNY: It wasn't helpful because she hates when I yell. That's actually what started the argument.

THERAPIST: Alright. Then what would be a more helpful behavior?

JENNY: I could've tried offering to help instead.

THERAPIST: So, you could've offered?

JENNY: Yeah, definitely more helpful than starting a yelling match.

THERAPIST: Good. And then the second thing you did was call her a crazy old lady. Do you think that helped or hurt you get your desired outcome of communicating your concerns?

JENNY: No, it definitely hurt. I'm not really communicating effectively if I'm calling her names.

THERAPIST: Then what would have been more helpful behavior?

JENNY: Just keep my cool and not call her names.

THERAPIST: Okay, and finally you slammed the chair against the table. Was that helpful or hurtful in getting what you wanted?

JENNY: Hurtful. That's when she lost her cool.

THERAPIST: OK, so it's hard to communicate when neither of you keeps their cool?

JENNY: Yeah, for sure.

THERAPIST: So, what is a different behavior that could have helped you get what you wanted?

JENNY: I could have kept my cool and spoken calmly. I could've said something like, "Mom, I'm worried about this. Can we talk?"

THERAPIST: So you would be asking to talk to her instead of expressing your anger through slamming the chair?

JENNY: Yeah.

THERAPIST: I think some of your alternative thoughts and behaviors could definitely lead to effective communication. Do you see yourself implementing these?

JENNY: Yes, I think I can.

THERAPIST: Good. So, on a scale from 0–10, where 10 is very important, how would you rate how important it is for you to change the pattern of taking care of others while neglecting yourself? (**Query-10-1**)

JENNY: I would say 10. Extremely important. I want to be able to deal with situations that make me upset and anxious.

THERAPIST: Excellent. It sounds very important to you. Now on the same 0–10 scale, how would you rate your confidence that you can change that pattern? (**Query 10-2**)

JENNY: Oh, probably around 7.

THERAPIST: What would need to happen to get to an 8?

JENNY: I just worry that I won't actually be able to do it in the moment.

THERAPIST: I see. It can be difficult to do things differently in the moment, especially when we're not used to it. That's why it can be very important to practice and see what it is like to do it. Would you be willing to try that with me?

## Commentary

Engaging in behavioral rehearsal will not only give Jenny a chance to practice her new skills and alternative behaviors, but also confidence in her ability to change her pattern to a more adaptive one. The form that behavioral rehearsal takes here is role-playing which focuses on Jenny's primary area of concern: her caretaking behavior and associated worries.

JENNY: Yeah, we can do that.

THERAPIST: OK, can you think of any scenarios in the near future in which you might be able to use the skills we discussed?

JENNY: Actually, yes. I'm supposed to go to dinner with my mom and brother. It's nice but also stressful.

THERAPIST: What do you find stressful about it? Can you tell me more?

JENNY: Well, I worry about his drinking. Whenever I say something, it ends up in an argument. Also, my mother is hell-bent on driving herself, which leads to an argument between us. I always get worked up and worried about it.

THERAPIST: OK, so things typically end up in an argument. What are the events that lead up to that?

JENNY: Well, I offer to drive my mom, but she refuses. Then I tell her she's too old and she gets offended. Then I start yelling at her about how hard-headed she is.

THERAPIST: I wonder if we can do a role-play of this. Imagine that I am your mom. Think about some of the alternatives we just discussed. What would be the first thing you say to me?

JENNY: OK. Mom, can I pick you up to go to dinner?

THERAPIST: No, thanks. I want to drive.

JENNY: Um, you sure? It would be more convenient.

THERAPIST: No. I want to drive myself.

JENNY: OK. Well, I just want to say that I worry about you and want to make sure you're safe.

THERAPIST: I can see that, and I appreciate it. I just think you could stand to give me some credit. I can take care of myself.

JENNY: OK. Well, can you please feel free to ask me if you ever do need anything?

THERAPIST: Yeah, I can do that. (The role-play ends) How did that go for you, Jenny? You did really well and kept your cool nicely.

JENNY: Yes, it felt different, but good.

THERAPIST: And what do you think about using this strategy with your mom when you speak to her?

JENNY: I think I can do it. I think it's really important for me to stay calm and remember that she's stronger and more capable than I give her credit for sometimes. And, I really just want to be there for her.

THERAPIST: Wonderful! (Pause) Since this is our termination session, it is important that we review our progress. You may recall that we set some goals for treatment the first time we met. Shall we review those?

JENNY: Sure. Let's do it.

THERAPIST: There were two goals we discussed and agreed upon. The first was to reduce and hopefully eliminate your panic symptoms. How did we do on that one?

JENNY: We definitely met that one. I haven't had a panic for over a week now. And, I can deal so much better when I'm stressed and anxious. Overall, I think I'm as good as I've ever been, and maybe even better.

THERAPIST: That's great. Congratulations! (Pause) The second goal was for you to be better at meeting your own needs along with meeting the needs of others. To what extent did you meet that one?

JENNY: (Pause) I am taking better care of myself. I am different. And, yes, my pattern now seems a lot healthier. (Pause) I don't think I would have ever imagined that would have happened in such a short period of time.

THERAPIST: Well, the more adaptive it is, that is, the more you take care of yourself while you're taking care of others—instead of just taking care of others—the better it will be for you and for others too.

JENNY: I can see that. Wow!

THERAPIST: You've done remarkably well and I'm proud of your progress and our work together!

JENNY: Me too! (Pause)

THERAPIST: (Pause) As we discussed at our first session, we would meet for four sessions and then review progress. If sufficient, we would stop our meetings with the proviso that a follow-up session would be scheduled which you could decide to keep or cancel.

JENNY: Yes, I recall. (Pause) Sure, I'm ready to set the follow-up appointment, although at this point, I don't think I'll need it.

THERAPIST: Well, it has been very encouraging to watch you become more your own therapist lately. That's what we call third-order change. You've not only effectively used the interventions you learned here on your own, but you're also beginning to care of yourself as you take care of others. That basic shift in your pattern helps all the way around, including undercutting your symptoms.

The remaining 3 minutes were spent finalizing termination, scheduling the follow-up in three weeks, and extending well wishes for the future.

## Commentary

Processing the role-play continued. The remainder of the session focused on assessing progress toward the treatment goals mutually established in the first session. She agreed that she had met both her treatment goals and was feeling much better and is more confident.

## Chart Note

Jenny reports no appreciable anxiety symptoms since our last session. Her GAD-7 score of 4—the minimal level of anxiety—suggests she is ready for termination. The session focused on her dependent pattern using the Query Sequence to therapeutically process a recent problematic situation. She was also introduced to and practiced behavioral rehearsal. Treatment gains were discussed, and she agreed that she had met her treatment goals and stated: "I think I'm as good as I've ever been and maybe even better."

She also agreed to continue breath retraining and thought stopping on her own as needed. Also discussed was scheduling a subsequent session in three weeks which she could cancel if her improvement continued and she did not consider the session was needed. She is already relying on her own resources to deal more effectively which is indicative of third-order change and readiness for termination.

## Conclusion

Pattern Focused Therapy is well suited for clinical practice in integrated primary care settings. A case example illustrated the process of assessment, interventions, a focus on first-, second-, and third-order change, and progress monitoring that is characteristic of Pattern Focused Therapy. This very brief treatment included both the Query Sequence and three ultra-brief interventions implemented over the course of four short-term therapy sessions.

# References

Bardhoshi, G., Erford, B. T., Duncan, K., Dummett, B., Falco, M., Deferio, K., & Kraft, J. (2016). Choosing assessment instruments for posttraumatic stress disorder screening and outcome research. *Journal of Counseling and Development*, 94(2), 184–194.

Berwick, M., Nolan, A., & Whittington, J. (2008). The triple aim: Care, health and cost. *Health Affairs*, 27, 759–769.

Blue Cross Blue Shield Association (2017). Blue Cross Blue Shield Association report finds link between a population's health and a growing economy, higher incomes and lower unemployment (March 29). Retrieved from www.bcbs.com/news/press-releases/blue-cross-blue-shield-association-report-finds-link-between-populations-health

Hunter, C. L., Goodie, J. L., Oordt, M. S., & Dobmeyer, A. C. (2017). *Integrated behavioral health in primary care: Step-by-step guidance for assessment and intervention*, 2nd ed. Washington, DC: American Psychological Association.

Plummer, F., Manea, L., Trepel, D., McMillan, D., & Simpson, A. (2016). Screening for anxiety disorders with the GAD-7 and GAD-2: A systematic review and diagnostic meta-analysis. *General Hospital Psychiatry*, 39, 24–31.

Sperry, L. (2018). You're needed on the team! Your role in practicing mental health counseling in integrated care settings. *Advocate Magazine*, 41(3–4), 20–22.

Sperry, L., & Binensztok, V. (2019a). *Learning and practicing Adlerian therapy*. San Diego, CA: Cognella.

Sperry, L., & Binensztok, V. (2019b). *Ultra-brief cognitive behavioral interventions: The cutting-edge of mental health and integrated care practice*. New York, NY: Routledge.

Wolpe, J. (1969). *The practice of behavior therapy*. New York, NY: Pergamon Press.

# Index

Locators in **bold** refer to figures and tables.

adaptive patterns: case conceptualization 36, 37, 38–39; case illustrations 54–55, 61; final sessions 150, 152; middle sessions 138; pattern 17–18, 30–31; pattern focused therapy premises 45; pattern identification 19–20; pattern recognition 21

anxiety: assertive communication 65; case illustrations 158–159, 170, 188–202; diagnostic screening **22**; exposure 11; Generalized Anxiety Disorder-7 (GAD-7) 87, 187–188, 195–196, 202; integrated care settings 187–188; mindfulness 72–73; scale measure 88; Subjective Units of Distress (SUDS) 87, 187, 191; thought stopping 75; treatment goals 33

Anxiety Scale 88

assertive communication 54, 64–65

assessment: case conceptualization and 37; cultural 28; diagnostic 21, **22–23**, 101, 109; duration of 27; first session 98–99, 100–101; functional 23–25, 101, 187; goals 26; implications for treatment planning 27; integrated care settings 187; outcomes 26–27; pattern and 16; purpose and use 18, 28–29; risk and protective factors assessment 25

awareness *see* client awareness

Beck, A. 69
behavioral activation 65–66, 117, 122
behavioral rehearsal 67
Binensztok, V. 77
biological vulnerabilities 31
breath retraining 67–68, 190, 191, 202
brief case conceptualizations 41–42
Brief Patient Update form 85

brief therapeutic interventions 48, 63; *see also* ultra-brief therapeutic interventions

care settings *see* integrated care settings
case conceptualization: case illustration 52–53, 104–105; clinical formulation 31; clinically useful 37–41; core therapeutic strategies 34; cultural formulation 32–33; definition of 29; diagnostic formulation 30; explanatory and predictive power 36–37; first session 101; pattern and 16, 30–31, 92; pattern focused therapy practice 46–47; perpetuants 32; precipitant 30, 37–38; predisposition 31–32; presentation 30, 37–38; purpose and use 29–30; treatment challenges **40–41**; treatment focus 34, 158; treatment formulation 33; treatment goals 33; treatment interventions 35; treatment obstacles and outcomes 36; very brief conceptualizations 41–42

case of Eliana 52–61
case of Jaime 158–159
case of Jerrod 104–118, 120–129, 130–136, 137–139, 144–154
case of Jenny 188–202
case of Julia 160–169
Choice Therapy 11
client awareness 90–91
client logs 27
client motivation: Motivational Interviewing 45, 90; positive expectations 90
client refusal 179–182
client-therapist bond: fostering a bond 99; permission seeking 106; transference-countertransference 165–172; *see also* therapeutic alliance

clinical formulation 31
clinical outcomes monitoring 8–9
clinically useful case conceptualization 37–41
Cognitive Behavioral Analysis System of Psychotherapy (CBASP): in pattern focused therapy 12, 13, 44–45; Query Sequence 47–48; replacement 11
cognitive defusion 11, 68–69
cognitive disputation 10, 69–70
cognitive restructuring 10
cognitive-behavioral therapy (CBT) 12, 34, 44, 142, 144
Columbia Suicide Severity Rating Scale (C-SSRS) 86
concluding therapy *see* final sessions, pattern focused therapy
consent *see* informed consent
coping skills 73–74, 176
core beliefs 174–176
core therapeutic strategies: case conceptualization 34; common strategies 9–12; integrated care settings 186
corrective experiences 91
countertransference 165–172
cultural assessment 28
cultural formulation 32–33
culturally sensitive treatment 35–36
Current Opioid Misuse Measure (COMM) 89
Current Procedural Terminology (CPT) 4–5, 12

depression: assertive communication 65; behavioral activation 65–66; case illustrations 52–61, 104–118, 135, 141, 144–149, 161–163; client refusal 179–180; Cognitive Behavioral Analysis System of Psychotherapy 47; common measures 85–86, 101; diagnostic screening **22**
diagnostic assessment 21, **22–23**, 101, 109
diagnostic formulation 30
diagnostic impression 104
distancing 11, 68–69
diversionary tactics 176–179
dropout (from therapy) 156–157
Drug Abuse Screening Test (DAST) 88
duration of assessment 27
duration of sessions 4–5, **5**, 12, 63, 184; *see also* ultra-brief therapeutic interventions

Ellis, A. 69
ethics, evidence-based approaches 7–8
etiological factors 31–32
evidence-based approaches 6–8, 51–52
evidence-based practice 2, 6–8, 51–52, 80
experience, of psychotherapists 3–4, 91–92, 93–94
expertise of therapist 94
explanatory power 36
exposure 11, 178–179
Eysenck, Hans 93

family, social vulnerabilities 31–32
feedback: clinical outcomes monitoring 8–9; developing expertise 94; outcomes assessment 81–83; pattern focused therapy practice 48–49; psychotherapist quality 3; *see also* progress monitoring
final sessions, pattern focused therapy 141; case illustration 144–154; termination 141–142; termination tasks 142–144; *see also* dropout (from therapy)
first session, pattern focused therapy 98; case illustration 104–118; essential tasks 98–104, 118–119
first-order changes 92
first-order goals 102, 105, 114
focus treatment 91–92
functional assessment 23–25, 101, 187

Generalized Anxiety Disorder-7 (GAD-7) 87, 187–188, 195–196, 202
goals: assessment 26; review of progress 143, 150; of treatment 28, 33, 102

habit reversal 70–71
HALT (Hungry, Angry, Lonely, Tired) 143
health issues, predicted trends in psychotherapy 5–6
Health Maintenance Organization (HMO) 6
homework: assertive communication 65; case illustration 54, 55, 61; cognitive disputation 70; first session 103–104; mindfulness 73; treatment focus 34; typical session 51

informed consent 98, 100, 114
initial change 103
initial session *see* first session, pattern focused therapy
Insomnia Severity Index (ISI) 88
integrated care settings: case illustration 188–202; mental health needs 184–185; mental health practice 185–186; pattern

focused therapy 186, 202; predicted trends 5–6; treating anxiety 187–188
interfering factors 172–182
interpersonal functioning 31, 33, 53; *see also* personality
interpersonal strategies 38; *see also* client-therapist bond
interpretation, psychotherapy 10–11
intervention *see* brief therapeutic interventions; treatment; ultra-brief therapeutic interventions

last session *see* final sessions, pattern focused therapy
length of sessions 4–5, **5**, 12, 63, 184
limit setting 71–72

maintaining factors (perpetuants) **18**, 32
maladaptive patterns: case conceptualization 36, 37, 38–39; focus treatment 91–92; middle sessions 136, 137, 138; pattern 17–18, 30–31; pattern focused therapy premises 45; pattern identification 19; pattern recognition 21
medical assistants (MAs) 185
mental health providers *see* integrated care settings
middle sessions, pattern focused therapy 139–140; purpose of 120; session 2 plan and case illustration 120–129; session 3 plan and case illustration 130–136; session 4 plan and case illustration 137–139
mindfulness 72–73
modification of behavior 11
Mood Scale 86, 121
motivation *see* client motivation
Motivational Interviewing (MI) 45, 90
movement types 38

Norcross, J. C. 1–2
nurses 185

objective countertransference 166–167
obsessive-compulsive personality style 41, 104–105, 112, 118, 135
optimization *see* treatment optimization
OQ-45 83, 85
outcomes assessment 26–27; common measures 26–27, 48–49; definition 80–82; indicators of success 80, 89–94; measures and screeners 83–89; *see also* treatment outcomes

Outcomes Rating Scale (ORS) 83, 84, 137
outcomes research 45

Partners for Change Outcome Management System 83
Patient Health Questionnaire-9 (PHQ-9) 85–86, 101, 104, 118, 120
Patient Intake form 85
Patient Uptake form 85
pattern **18**; assessment 16; case conceptualization 16, 30–31, 92; first session 101–102; key terms **18**; middle sessions 136; in pattern focused therapy 16–18
pattern focused therapy: components 45–49; contemporary trends 12–13; origins 44–45; pattern in 16–18; premises 45; third-wave CBT approaches 12
pattern focused therapy practice 44, 49–50; case illustration 52–61; evidence-based practices 51–52; process and sequence summary 50; typical session 50–51; *see also* final sessions, pattern focused therapy; first session, pattern focused therapy; middle sessions, pattern focused therapy
pattern identification 18–20, **20**, 46, 91–92
pattern recognition 19–21
pattern shifting 47
PCL PTSD Checklist 87–88
PEG Pain Scale 88–89
perpetuants **18**, 32
personality: cultural formulation 32–33; treatment challenges 39, **40–41**; vulnerabilities 31–32; *see also* interpersonal functioning
Pfund, R. A. 1–2
Polaris MH 84–85
practice *see* pattern focused therapy practice; psychotherapy practice
practice-based evidence 4, 80
precipitant **18**, 30, 37–38
predictive power 36–37
predisposition **18**, 31–32
presentation **18**, 30, 37–38
primary care providers (PCPs) 185
Prochaska, J. O. 1–2
professional prognostication 1–3
professional training *see* training
progress monitoring: case illustrations 54–55; clinical value 82–83; common measures 48–49, 86–88; definition 80–82; practice-based evidence 4, 80; purpose of 26–27; *see also* feedback

protective factors assessment 25
psychological vulnerabilities 31
psychotherapist quality 3–4
psychotherapist training *see* training
psychotherapy practice: contemporary changes 1; outcomes research 45; pattern focused therapy contemporary trends 12–13; predicted trends 4–12, **13**; professional prognostication 1–3; research questions 3–4; *see also* pattern focused therapy practice
psychotherapy research 3–4
PTSD screening 87–88
quality of psychotherapy 3–4, 93–94

Query Sequence 47–48, **49**; case illustrations 56–60, 117, 123–124, 129, 138–139, 147, 196–199; integrated care settings 186; middle sessions 124–129, 135, 136, 139; typical session 51; ultra-brief therapeutic interventions 63

rapport 99, 106
Reality Therapy 11
relapse prevention 73–74
relapse prevention plans 143, 145–146, 148, 151, 154
relationships *see* client-therapist bond; interpersonal functioning
replacement 11
risk factors assessment 25
routine outcome monitoring 80–82, 83

Sackett, D. 7
schemas 174–176
screening: diagnostic assessment 21, **22–23**; integrated care settings 187
screening instruments 26, 98, 187
second-order changes 92–93
second-order goals 102–103, 105
selective attention 157–158
self-efficacy 73–74
self-insight 168–169
self-integration 168–169
self-therapy 142
Session Rating Scale (SRS) 51, 83, 84, 100, 118, 136
sessions *see* final sessions, pattern focused therapy; first session, pattern focused therapy; middle sessions, pattern focused therapy
sexual attraction, client-therapist 169–170

short-term therapy practice 4–5, **5**, 28–29
Silverman, W. H. 2
skills training (for individuals experiencing psychological disturbance) 11; *see also* training
social context of therapy 99–100, 102
social isolation case 52–61
social vulnerabilities 31–32
Sperry, L. 44, 77
stimulus control 74–75
strengths 25, 50, 53
subjective countertransference 166–167
Subjective Units of Distress (SUDS) 87, 187, 191
success indicators 80, 89–94; *see also* outcomes assessment
suicide, Columbia Suicide Severity Rating Scale (C-SSRS) 86

termination 141–144; *see also* dropout (from therapy); final sessions, pattern focused therapy
therapeutic alliance 89–90, 99–100, 165, 179
therapeutic orientation 34, 51; *see also* core therapeutic strategies
therapist effect 94
therapy interfering factors 172–182
therapy pathways 156
third-order changes 92–93
third-order goals 103
third-wave CBT approaches 12, 34, 44
Thomason, T. C. 2
thought stopping 75–76
training: developing expertise 94; evidence-based approaches 6–8; skills training (for individuals experiencing psychological disturbance) 11
transference-countertransference 165–172
treatment: case conceptualization and 37; challenges 39, **40–41**
treatment focus 157–160; case conceptualization 34, 158; case illustration 158–159, 160–169; treatment optimization 157–160
treatment formulation 33, 142
treatment goals: assessment 28; case conceptualization 33
treatment interventions 35
treatment obstacles and outcomes 36
treatment optimization: case illustration of focus 160–169; interfering factors 172–182; therapy pathways 156;

transference-countertransference 165–172; treatment focus 157–160
treatment outcomes: assessment 26–27; clinical outcomes monitoring 8–9; definition 80–82; goals 28; indicators of success 80, 89–94; maintaining gains 144; outcomes research 45; psychotherapist quality 3–4
treatment planning 27, 85; *see also* core therapeutic strategies
triggers 143
triple aim (of health care) 6, 185

ultra-brief therapeutic interventions: assertive communication 64–65; behavioral activation 65–66; behavioral rehearsal 67; breath retraining 67–68; cognitive defusion 68–69; cognitive disputation 69–70; definition 63; habit reversal 70–71; homework 103–104; limit setting 71–72; middle sessions 130; mindfulness 72–73; protocols **64**, 64; relapse prevention 73–74; stimulus control 74–75; thought stopping 75–76; use of 76–77; *see also* brief therapeutic interventions

very brief therapeutic interventions *see* brief therapeutic interventions; ultra-brief therapeutic interventions